PRz75.M63
CON

QM Library

23

D1757610

MAIN LIBRARY
QUEEN MARY, UNIVERSITY OF LONDO
Mile End Road, London E1 4NS
DATE DUE FOR RETURN

1 4 NOV 2003

WITHDRAWN
FROM STOCK
QMUL LIBRARY

Consuming Narratives

GENDER AND MONSTROUS APPETITE IN THE MIDDLE AGES AND THE RENAISSANCE

edited by

LIZ HERBERT MCAVOY and TERESA WALTERS

UNIVERSITY OF WALES PRESS
CARDIFF
2002

© The Contributors, 2002

British Library Cataloguing-in-Publication Data.
A catalogue record for this book is available from the British Library.

ISBN 0–7083–1743–X hardback
    0–7083–1742–1 paperback

All rights reserved. No part of this book may be reproduced, stored in a retrieval system, or transmitted, in any form or by any means, electronic, mechanical, photocopying, recording or otherwise, without clearance from the University of Wales Press, 10 Columbus Walk, Brigantine Place, Cardiff, CF10 4UP.
www.wales.ac.uk/press

Typeset at University of Wales Press
Printed in Great Britain by Dinefwr Press, Llandybïe

Contents

જી

List of Illustrations

❧

Foreword and Acknowledgements

❧

The subtitle of this book, 'Gender and Monstrous Appetite', was adopted by the editors from the main focus of an interdisciplinary conference convened at Gregynog Hall, the conference centre of the University of Wales, in April 2000. Thanks are owed to all who took part and contributed to the success of the conference. The papers collected in this volume are but a small selection of the many and varied interpretations of its theme and we are only sorry that we are unable to include more.

We would like to extend our particular thanks to Diane Watt for her constant support and invaluable advice from the onset of this project through to its conclusion; Lyn Pykett for departmental support for the venture; Joan Crawford and June Baxter for their efficient secretarial back-up; Becky Moss for her administrative assistance; and finally to the helpful and co-operative staff at Gregynog Hall. In addition, thanks are offered for the generous financial support provided by the Gregynog Staff Colloquia Fund and the British Academy grant, without which neither the conference nor this volume would have been possible. Thanks also to Duncan Campbell of the University of Wales Press for his enthusiastic backing for the publication of this volume and for his unlimited patience during its production. Finally, to all our contributors, whose efficiency and painstaking efforts to meet deadlines have made the editing of this volume a pleasurable and painless activity.

Parts of Chapter 13, 'Monstrous Tyrannical Appetites' by Margaret Healy have previously appeared in Margaret Healy, *Fictions of Disease in Early Modern England* (Palgrave, 2001). The publishers would like to thank Palgrave for permission to reproduce this material.

Editors and Contributors

∾

Liz Herbert McAvoy teaches at the University of Wales, Aberystwyth. She is currently working on a book which examines representations and reconstructions of the female body in the writing of Margery Kempe and Julian of Norwich, and her research interests include anchoritism, women's writing, monstrosity, mysticism and issues of gender.

Teresa Walters has recently completed a Ph.D. thesis entitled 'Discourses of discovery and the writing of empire, 1580–1630' at the University of Wales, Aberystwyth. She now works with a community organization aimed at developing a sustainable rural economy in the Dyfi Valley, in mid Wales.

Bettina Bildhauer has recently obtained a Ph.D. at Pembroke College, Cambridge, focusing on blood in thirteenth-century German literature. Current research interests include medieval German literature, feminism and body studies.

Kimberly Anne Coles is a Visiting Professor teaching at Bowdoin College. Her doctoral thesis examines women as reformers, writers and subjects in the early English Reformation.

Isabel Davis has recently completed doctoral research at the Centre for Medieval Studies, University of York, in which she examines representations of the working man in fourteenth-century literature.

Ruth Evans is Senior Lecturer in the Department of English at the University of Wales, Cardiff. Her main areas of research are

Middle English cycle drama, medieval translation, the politics of the vernacular in late medieval England and Scotland and feminist theory, on all of which she has published widely.

Andrew Hadfield is a Professor in Renaissance literature at the University of Wales, Aberystwyth. As well as a wide range of journal articles, he has edited and co-edited several volumes of essays and has produced a series of monographs, the most recent of which is *The English Renaissance, 1500–1620* (Blackwell, 2001).

Margaret Healy is a lecturer in English at the University of Sussex. She is the author of *Fictions of Disease in Early Modern England: Bodies, Plagues and Politics* (Palgrave, 2001) and *Richard II* (Northcote House, 1998).

Margo Hendricks is an Associate Professor of Literature at the University of California, Santa Cruz. She has published widely on the subjects of race and Renaissance literature and is currently finishing a book on Aphra Behn.

Marion D. Hollings is Associate Professor of English at Middle Tennessee State University. Her teaching and research interests include questions of gender in medieval and Renaissance literature, and early modern discourses of Orientalism.

Sujata Iyengar is Assistant Professor of English Literature at the University of Georgia. Her writings include essays on third-wave feminism, *Othello*'s stage history, fictionalized early modern women healers, Shakespeare's reluctant Adonis and an article on Margaret Cavendish's science and fiction.

Claire Jowitt is a lecturer in Renaissance Literature at the University of Wales, Aberystwyth. Her main research interests include women's writing, Jewish–Christian relations, gender and travel literature. She has just finished a book on travel writing entitled *Gender Politics and Travel Drama 1589–1642*.

Sue Niebrzydowski teaches at the University of Warwick. Her research interests lie primarily in the representation of race and women in the later Middle Ages and she has an article on the representation of black women in England before the early modern period forthcoming in *Women's History Review*.

Emma L. E. Rees is Senior Lecturer in English at Chester College. Her main research has been on the exilic writings of Margaret Cavendish, duchess of Newcastle, on whom she has produced several articles and a monograph. Other research interests include issues of gender and representation, especially in the visual arts.

Kirstie Gulick Rosenfield is Assistant Professor of Theatre at Utah State University. Her research interests are divided between Shakespearian texts in their own time and Shakespearian production in the present. She also continues to direct Shakespeare and contemporary plays for the professional stage.

Nicholas Watson is Chair of Medieval English at Harvard University and is the author of *Richard Rolle and the Invention of Authority* (1991). He has also published numerous articles on the history of religious writing in Middle English, the topic of his book in progress being entitled *Balaam's Ass: Vernacular Theology in England, 1200–1500*.

Diane Watt is Senior Lecturer at the University of Wales, Aberystwyth. Her main research interests are medieval literature, gender studies and the history of sexualities, on all of which she has published widely. Currently, she is working on a study of masculinity and confessional discourse in the works of John Gower.

1

Introduction

ॐ

LIZ HERBERT McAVOY and TERESA WALTERS

Any volume which claims as its focus an examination of gender practices must acknowledge its debt to the enormous developments which have taken place within Women's Studies in recent decades. An intensely feminist gaze and an imperative to demystify patriarchal (as opposed to masculinist) practices have, however, since the early 1990s given way to a much broader and more critical examination of *gender* issues which encompasses both femininities and masculinities. This, in turn, has impacted radically upon the way in which research and teaching in Medieval and Renaissance Studies are now undertaken, and it has become clear that issues of gender – and gender as a type of 'moveable feast' – must now be considered a core factor within the formative ideologies as well as the material productions of the Middle Ages and the Renaissance.

As early as 1993, Allen J. Franzen stressed the crucial importance of examining performances of femininity in the Middle Ages alongside the multifarious performances of masculinity in order to gauge more effectively how such performances of gender affected each other. In the course of his discussion on the demystifying potential of gender – as opposed to feminist – theory, Frantzen concludes:

> Gender theory unmasks various constructions of identity that have been confused with the natural reality: to talk about gender is to talk about how identity has been shaped by custom and institutionalized social possibilities that exclude certain forms of behaviour. The benefit of discussing gender is not only that gender constructions are

examined, but that their basis in nature, the ground on which 'natural' sexual identities rest, is also scrutinized. One cannot, of course, dispute the existence of 'male' and 'female' bodies, but one can debate – and revise – the cultural interpretations those bodies have been made to bear and the social possibilities that contain them.[1]

In more recent times, too, in the context of the shift towards Gender Studies as a more sophisticated means of analysis, Clare Lees has reminded scholars: 'the focus on men . . . is . . . not a return to traditional subjects that implies a neglect of feminist issues, but a calculated contribution to them, which can be formulated as a dialectic'.[2] It is such a dialectical approach to issues of gender and its interaction with concepts of monstrosity and appetite during the periods in question, which underpins this present volume.

However, theories pertaining to the very notion of gender have also been subject to intense scrutiny, particularly during the last decade or so. Most significantly, the work of Judith Butler has led to a reappraisal of the term itself in her examination of the effects of gender upon discourse and discourse upon gender. In her groundbreaking work, *Gender Trouble: Feminism and the Subversion of Identity*, Butler points towards inherent instabilities within the very terms 'sex' and 'gender', suggesting that, rather than being fixed or 'essential' entities, in fact these terms are both constitutive of and constituted by the *effects* of hegemonic discourse.[3]

Such has been the influence of Butler's work on gender, it is hardly surprising that the majority of essays in a volume which takes as its overriding theme narrative consumption should be either implicitly or explicitly dependent upon Butler's theoretical paradigm of gender performativity and its interaction with hegemonic discourse. Revised notions of the gendered body are therefore paramount in many of these essays. In the same way as our contributors have drawn upon Butler's reassessment of the validity of fixed gender categories, so many of them have adopted and extended the scope of her arguments concerning the body as developed in her later volume, *Bodies that Matter: On the Discursive Limits of 'Sex'*.[4] Here, Butler identifies the body as 'a kind of materialization governed by regulatory norms in order to ascertain the working of heterosexual hegemony'.[5] She concludes that 'materialization of the norm in bodily formation produce[s] a domain of abjected bodies, a field of deformation, which, in failing to qualify as the fully human, fortifies those regulatory norms'.[6] Responding to the body as a type of 'cultural project' in the service of normativity, many of these essays reveal it to be a site of continuous construction that is actively, as well as passively, participated in, taken on or subverted. Moreover, within these paradigms, both male and female writers during the period in question and/or the characters within their texts can be read as actively engaging in gender performances, often 'disguising' themselves in order to become productive of, resistant to and sometimes transformative of dominant discourses on the gendered body. And not only those on the gendered body: when the body is conceived of as a cultural locus of meaning, discourses of race, class, sexuality, motherhood, spirituality and the nation may also be mapped onto this body as a function of its appetites, as illustrated most coherently in the essays in the final section of this collection.

Using as their starting point the radical dismantling of gender as a transhistorical and transcultural 'given' then, the majority of essays in this volume provide a contemporary response to Franzen's and Lees's call for change. They proceed to articulate the complex interaction between concepts of gender and appetite – and the processes through which they were, and continue to be, defined, constructed and regulated by each other.

But how exactly do we define the notions of appetite and monstrosity as conceived of in the Middle Ages and the Renaissance? To begin to answer this, we might draw upon the opening lines of Canto 9 in Book 2 of Spenser's *The Faerie Queene*. Here Spenser provides us with a firm correlation between bodily appetite and the condition of the human soul, using the perfect – and male – body as his paradigm:

> Of all Gods workes, which do this world adorne
> There is no one more faire and excellent,
> Then is mans body both for powre and forme
> Whiles it is kept in sober government;
> But none then it, more fowle and indecent,
> Distempred through misrule and passions bace:
> It growes a Monster, and incontinent
> Doth loose his dignitie and native grace.[7]

In this representation of the male body as a reified form of essential, classical perfection, Spenser links aesthetics with an ethical code which is entirely dependent upon masculine self-governance for its perfect expression. Like the nation which it also represents, this body must be kept under 'sober government' or else its all-consuming appetites will cause it to turn 'Monster' and lead it to devour its own 'dignitie and native grace'. Implicit in this description too is the need for a temperance that must come from within for best effect, and yet the notions of 'government' and 'misrule' are explicitly *external* forms of control and hegemony which are bound up with notions of class and gender. Thus, the formulation of the (gentleman) subject's notion of 'self' is effected by the imposition of civilizing government (law) from without, and by its consumption in the form of narrative (like this one of Spenser's), until it is wholly devoured and assimilated. While government, then, is internalized by the subject, ideally becoming *self*-governance, so his own destructive appetites are simultaneously externalized, projected and reified as a threatening monstrous 'other'. Such monstrosities – 'incontinent' and 'distempred' – as in parallel discourses of gender, are always lurking in the shadows, at the border of selfhood and perpetually threatening to render the 'faire and excellent' subject a 'fowle and indecent . . . Monster'.

Such a reading of monstrous appetite in terms of the inscription of the undesirable 'self' upon the 'other' is supported by a recent study by David Williams, *Deformed Discourse: The Function of the Monster in Mediaeval Thought and Literature*, in which he examines the role played by the monstrous in medieval imagination and literature.[8] According to Williams, the Middle Ages cast the monstrous as a paradigmatically apophatic 'other' which functioned to represent what ultimately 'is-not' or 'should-not-be' as a means of expressing the full human potential of what *is*.[9] In other words, by representing the impossible in a process which externalized the internally realized, it rendered it possible, and in so doing cast into relief the normative and desirable 'self' within a community of other normative and desirable 'selves'. This is, of course, just what we have seen happening in Spenser's representation of the gentleman subject who is fashioned in the mode of other gentlemen subjects by means of the reification and projection of his own monstrous appetites. It is just such a self-fashioning which

Nicholas Watson discusses in his response to the essays in the first section of this volume and in his examination of the multivalent image of the 'Trusty Servant'. By effectively putting on a dualistic display of 'what-is-not' alongside 'what-is', and then conflating the two, the strategic representation of monstrosity paradoxically casts into relief what is *not* monstrous and thus serves as a template for the limits of what it is to be a 'normative' human being. Monstrosity thus entails the simultaneous externalization of the internal and its re-ingestion in the assimilation or consumption of cultural narratives. Like the discourses which they embody, both narratives and texts are pressed into the service of monstrous appetite and its control and therefore into the formation of the speaking subject. Like the well-governed nation of Spenser's poem, narration assimilates the body into itself in order to reconfigure it in its own image. But while the reified monstrous appetites of body, state and narrative are held at the margins of identity, they constantly threaten the body politic from both without and within. Cultural narratives can thus be seen as simultaneously consumed and consuming. The overarching theme of this volume, then, is consuming narratives, both in the active and the passive sense, and the ways in which they can be put to work in shoring up the ostensibly hegemonic systems of gender, class, race and nation.

To date, work on the subject of appetite and consumptive practices in the Middle Ages and the early modern period has been patchy, leaving a vacuum which it is hoped this present collection will help to fill. In Medieval Studies, for example, what has been undertaken has tended to focus on the emotive area of Christ's body and consumptive practices connected with the Eucharist and women's bodies. The most important contribution in this area has been by Caroline Bynum, whose study of the symbolism of food and appetite within female religious practices in the Middle Ages has transformed our readings of female piety and potential routes to female empowerment during the period.[10] Although subject to some criticism in recent years (and challenged again by Isabel Davis in this volume), the growing number of critiques of her work nevertheless reflects the huge influence it has had upon all areas of Medieval Studies. Her ambitious study, *Holy Feast and Holy Fast: The Religious Significance of Food to Medieval Women*, has, for example, had a major impact upon how medieval scholars view female religiosity and female responses to cultural practices in the Middle Ages.[11] Similarly, Miri Rubin (*Corpus Christi: The Eucharist in Late Medieval Culture*) and Sarah Beckwith (*Christ's Body: Identity, Culture and Society in Late Medieval Writings*) have examined the complex interactions of gender and symbol as inscribed upon the body of Christ during the later Middle Ages.[12] In spite of their paucity, however, studies of appetite and consumption in the Middle Ages (informed as many of them have been by the theoretical appraisal of the 'abject' by Julia Kristeva,[13] and by the work undertaken on the polluted and taboo by Mary Douglas[14]) have nevertheless suggested that food and its significance as symbolic of the external world has long provided a motif for the assimilation or rejection of the 'other'. Food, therefore, becomes a primary means by which the external world is ingested – and controlled. If it is not controlled, the food itself becomes the controlling factor by means of this same internalization, whether in the ingestion of the host in medieval times or in the overindulgent banqueting represented in the Stuart court masque in the early modern period. Such an ingestion of the external becomes synonymous with empowerment and, like the externalizing and reinternalizing of the dangerous monstrous appetites examined earlier, is crucial to the formation of an individuated but social 'self'. Such a formation can therefore be recognized as dependent upon the externalizing of an appetitive interiority, as well as upon an internalizing of a socially desirable exteriority. Both processes, like those of monstrosity, are thoroughly imbricated in notions of appetite and consumption.

Gastronomic appetites have, of course, long been inter-changeable with sexual ones – at least rhetorically – and many of the papers in this volume examine the ways in which this inter-changeability of inner and outer 'selves' has contributed to the creation of the monstrous 'other' in discourses on sex and gender. This is particularly pertinent in the case of representations of woman as the demonic (m)other, as, for example, in the depiction of the Sowdanesse in Chaucer's *Man of Law's Tale*, who plots to murder her own son during the course of a feast; or, indeed, Spenser's duplicitous and deformed hag, Duessa, whose 'neather partes misshapen, monstruous', bear the inscription of her own monstrous appetites (*Faerie Queene*, 1. 2. 41). Again like the gentleman subject of Spenser's poem, woman's excess threatens to metamorphose into monstrosity if not kept firmly regulated by the imposition of patriarchal narratives on the one hand, and her consumption and self-disciplinary assimilation of these narratives on the other.

In the context of woman as the monstrous '(m)other', recent early modern studies too have tended to focus on what has been (erroneously) classified as a *newly* emerging discourse of the monstrous body which 'epitomizes the shift of the traditional discourse of monstrosity to the realm of gendered relations' – in particular, the unregulated sexual behaviour of women.[15] Susanne Scholz, for example, in a full-length examination of the ways in which narratives of the body contributed to self-fashioning in early modern times, 'discovers' (as if for the first time) that 'in times of increasingly capitalist economic structures a woman's virginity was becoming of value on the marriage market', which led to a 'new' need to control her bodily orifices.[16] Indeed, Scholz proceeds to assert that the unity and wholeness of the female body 'was increasingly imagined as enforced by rigid boundaries' and suggests that depictions of this body as enclosed garden or as fortress under siege reinforced the paradigm.[17] These analyses reflect perfectly what Lee Patterson has famously identified as the 'othering' of the medieval period by many of those who work in the Renaissance field, who fail to recognize its continuity with both past and present and who consign it to a dark age of history.[18] However, as many of the essays in this volume attest, the status of the seemingly unregulated and therefore monstrous body (and the monstrous female body in particular) was as much a cause for deep anxiety within the medieval period as it was in early modern times. Indeed (and again in keeping with a Butlerian view of the body), far from seeing the body as a hypostatized object, or even a product of simple biological mechanisms, the essays in this collection reveal it to be a related and relational concept, consumed by and consumer of cultural narratives and codes, throughout the entire period under scrutiny.

Thus, throughout the Middle Ages and the Renaissance the (monstrous) body constituted and was constitutive of a complex, multivalent system of sexual, psychic, religious, corporeal and spiritual dialogues and discourses. These were encoded and decoded in varying ways in varying historical and social contexts and for a variety of purposes, both consciously and unconsciously. Although, as Michael Schoenfeldt reminds us, '[b]odies have changed little through history . . . we all are born, we eat, we defecate, we desire, and we die',[19] the cultural meanings inscribed upon and performed by those seemingly 'unchanged' bodies are, nevertheless, highly fluid. It is, therefore, the complex interplay of consumed and consuming narratives and their impact upon the gendered representation of bodies and their appetites from the late Middle Ages through to the 'end' of the Renaissance which this volume unravels for the first time.

The essays included in this volume all address issues of narrative consumption and monstrous appetite – real or imagined – as agents of particular hegemonies or as subversive of them. They serve to identify a conceptual framework within the Middle Ages and the Renaissance in which an excess of appetite – for food, sex, money, power or piety – was frequently regarded as monstrous within familial, social, religious or nationalistic contexts. Hence, they lie at the cutting edge of developing interests among scholars in consumptive practices and how those practices intersect with cultural narratives of gender, race, sexuality and monstrosity. This collection is thus the first to focus on the cross-overs, clashes and dis/continuities within these narratives from medieval through to early modern times, and we have chosen deliberately to divide it thematically rather than temporally. To counter the potential charge of ahistoricism, however, we have found that local and provisional contextualization is actually *more* historically productive than adherence to epistemic shifts. Moreover, the reading of narratives as *competing for* rather than achieving historical preeminence provides a more nuanced conceptual framework than do the grander (and sometimes teleological) paradigms of Marxism or the 'single drama' of Foucault's genealogy.[20]

Each of the three sections is headed with a response from a leading scholar. The group of essays comprising the first section, 'Sexual/Textual Consumption', interrogates the ways in which bodies – whether human or textual – are implicated in the process of consuming discourses connected with sex, and how one type of body exerts influence upon the representation and production of other types of bodies. They are thus concerned with the notion of *relationship* within consumptive practices, as Nicholas Watson perceptively suggests in his response to this group of essays. Watson identifies how, in their concern with the conceptualization of the relationships between the self and 'other', the medieval and early modern texts examined in these essays reveal appetite to be as much a matter of power as it is of desire, taste or need.

In our second section, 'Monstrous Bodies', the essays develop this theme to examine the ways in which the body – and the 'female' body in particular – is rendered monstrous through its association with excessive appetite. They examine, in addition, the process through which this monstrous body was produced discursively as a measure of what it was to be the normative 'male' within medieval and early modern culture. However, whereas in recent times Jeffrey Jerome Cohen (*Of Giants: Sex, Monsters, and the Middle Ages*[21]) has strongly identified the monstrous as representative of the non-elite *masculine*, the majority of the essays in this section adhere to a more Bahktinian view of the body's grotesque openness, and the paradigmatically open female body in particular. [22] These essays, therefore, discover the *female* body as a primary site for the repressive projection of masculine activities and appetites during the period under examination and as a principal locus for the cultural inscription of monstrosity. On the other hand, the variety of counter-discourses extracted from between and beyond the lines of the text in these essays would suggest that the charge of monstrosity could be, and *was*, appropriated and subverted, often by literary women in possession of such monstrous bodies.

The final group of essays, 'Consuming Genders, Races, Nations' widens these arguments, and in particular those introduced by Margaret Healy's examination of the monstrous (male) political body at the end of the previous section, to examine how discourses of monstrosity and appetite are transformed into issues of nationhood and racial purity when applied to the body of the state. As Andrew Hadfield points out in his response to these essays, the 'nation', rather than being a single, unified body, is always constituted by multiple and complex socio-political alliances, each competing for the right to speak for others and each intent on subsuming the narratives of rival groups. These essays therefore illustrate the ways in which narratives of race, gender and nationhood seek to contest and consume one another in attempts to achieve their own hegemonic expression.

Thus, the volume taken as a whole yields a wide and varied examination of the myriad ways in which discourses concerning sex, gender, appetite, consumption and monstrosity during the late

Middle Ages and the Renaissance contributed to the construction of various cultural narratives and of the bodies on which these narratives had their inscription.[23] It provides a rich source of analysis of what constituted the normative and the monstrous during these periods and ultimately reveals how, as a result of the tension between these two apparent polarities, many medieval and early modern identities were not just assumed, but also passively or even actively 'performed'.

Notes

[1] Allen J. Frantzen, 'When women aren't enough', *Speculum* (1993), 445–71 (452).

[2] Clare Lees (ed.), *Medieval Masculinities: Regarding Men in the Middle Ages* (Minneapolis and London, 1994), introduction, p. xv.

[3] Judith Butler, *Gender Trouble: Feminism and the Subversion of Identity* (New York and London, 1990).

[4] Judith Butler, *Bodies that Matter: On the Discursive Limits of 'Sex'* (New York, 1993).

[5] Ibid., p. 16.

[6] Ibid.

[7] A. C. Hamilton (ed.), *Spenser: The Faerie Queene*, ed. A. C. Hamilton (London, 1977), 2. 9. 1.

[8] David Williams, *Deformed Discourse: The Function of the Monster in Mediaeval Thought and Literature* (Exeter, 1996).

[9] Ibid., p. 4, for example.

[10] Caroline Walker Bynum, *Fragmentation and Redemption: Essays on Gender and the Human Body in Medieval Religion* (New York, 1991).

[11] The most vociferous of Bynum's critics in recent years have been Kathleen Biddick, 'Genders, bodies, borders: technologies of the visible', *Speculum* 68 (1993), 389–418; and David Aers, 'The humanity of Christ: reflections on orthodox later medieval representations', in David Aers and Lynn Staley (eds), *Powers of the Holy: Religion, Politics, and Gender in Late Medieval English Culture* (Pennsylvania, 1996), pp. 16–42.

[12] Caroline Walker Bynum, *Holy Feast and Holy Fast: The Religious Significance of Food to Medieval Women* (Berkeley, Los Angeles and London, 1987); Miri Rubin, *Corpus Christi: The Eucharist in Late Medieval Culture* (Cambridge, 1991); Sarah Beckwith, *Christ's Body: Identity, Culture and Society in Late Medieval Writings* (London, 1993).

[13] Julia Kristeva, *The Powers of Horror: An Essay on Abjection*, trans. Leon Roudiez (New York, 1982).

[14] Mary Douglas, *Pollution and Danger* (London, Boston and Henley, 1969).

[15] See Barbara M. Benedict, 'Making a monster: socializing sexuality and the monster of 1790', in Helen Deutsch and Felicity Nussbaum (eds), *'Defects': Engendering the Modern Body* (Ann Arbor, 2000), pp. 127–53 (127).

[16] Susanne Scholz, *Body Narratives: Writing the Nation and Fashioning the Subject in Early Modern England* (London and New York, 2000), p. 83.

[17] Ibid., p. 83.

[18] Lee Patterson, 'On the margin: postmodernism, ironic history, and medieval studies', *Speculum* 65 (1990), 87–108.

[19] Michael Schoenfeldt, *Bodies and Selves in Early Modern England: Physiology and Inwardness in Spenser, Shakespeare, Herbert and Milton* (Cambridge, 1999), p. 6.

[20] Michel Foucault, 'Nietzsche, genealogy, history', in *Language, Counter-Memory, Practice: Selected Essays and Interviews by Michel Foucault*, trans. Donald F. Bouchard and Sherry Simon, ed. Donald F. Bouchard (Ithaca, NY, 1977), p. 150.

[21] Jeffrey Jerome Cohen, *Of Giants: Sex, Monsters, and the Middle Ages* (Minneapolis and London, 1999).

[22] On Bahktin's theory of the grotesque body see Mikhail Bahktin, *Rabelais and his World*, trans. Hélène Iswolsky (Cambridge, MA, 1968), pp. 303–67.

[23] See Michel Foucault, *Discipline and Punish: The Birth of the Prison*, trans. Alan Sheridan (New York, 1979), in which he discusses various ways in which discourses are inscribed upon bodies, making them docile and useful. Judith Butler, however, emphasizes the impossibility of a pre-discursive body in *Gender Trouble*, p. 130.

I

Sexual/Textual Consumption

2

The Monstrosity of the Moral Pig and Other Unnatural Ruminations

∾

NICHOLAS WATSON

For hundreds of years the fellows, scholars, and quiristers of a venerable English educational institution, Winchester College, have walked several times a day past a freakish emblematic painting, strategically hung next to the kitchens, at the foot of the stairs to the dining hall. The painting, which was last updated during the reign of George III, depicts a pig, trimly dressed in the costume of an upper household servant. Adorned with ass's ears, stag's hooves and various other allegorical appurtenances, the pig stands in an empty landscape, wearing a profoundly moral but still somehow inscrutably porcine expression (as though it were contemplating its own roasting with philosophic calm), its always subdued colours now further darkened by time. On either side of the painting are panels containing doggerel verses in Latin and English that explain its import:

> A trusty servants portrait would you see
> This emblematic figure well survey.
> The porkers snout not nice [fussy] in diet shows,
> The padlock shut, no secret he'll disclose,
> Patient the ass his masters wrath will hear,
> Swiftness in errand the staggs feet declare,
> Loaded his left hand apt to labour saith,
> The vest his neatness, open hand his faith.
> Girt with his sword upon his arm
> Himself and master he'll protect from harm.[1]

The Trusty Servant, reproduced by kind permission of the Warden and Scholars of Winchester School.

The trusty servant reflects back a didactic image of the schoolboy viewer, showing him the shape he must make it his business to assume: the shape of an official, his life, his appetites, the very form of his body organized around the uses for which he is being fashioned. Lacking a human brain or the capacity to speak, the trusty servant is ill-suited for public command, living only to serve, protect and suffer his master. Lacking leisure time, or any open orifice, he is equally ill-suited for private intimacies: he is too sexless to be chaste, too indiscriminate to consume with appetite, too unaware of pleasures to deny himself. Lacking sexual organs in particular, and existing in an exclusively masculine environment, he cannot even procreate; the school itself must replicate him, seemingly unassisted by normal heterosexual process. An image of a tenacious English version of professional male subordination, the trusty servant bridges the gap between the late Middle Ages (when the school was founded) and the present, a reminder of the continuities that keep our Western political and social institutions in being. At the same time, however, this emblem of one powerful form of normative masculinity is, of course, monstrous: an inhuman (not to mention unporcine) hybrid whose complacent acceptance of his lot, whose lack of selfhood, is the stuff of adolescent nightmare. Laugh at him as they will, Wykehamists must also fear him, for his capacity to inscribe himself in their bodies, to straiten them into the social straight men it has always been the school's genius to produce. The trusty servant proclaims, with the unnerving candour so often associated with the in-struction of children, the cost of the privileges to which a career at one of England's public schools can lead, the price of becoming a living emblem of bourgeois masculine virtue.

I begin with this monstrous moral pig because I think it provides a helpful viewing station from which to survey the ground covered by this book in general, and this first part of the book in particular. These essays exist to bring to bear a very contemporary fascination with the monstrous, the perverse, the unnatural on various bodies of medieval and early modern thought and imagining about gender and appetite. The essays (like their prospective readers) are products of an intellectual culture that is more richly permeated by sexuality, more preoccupied with the intersections not just of gender, race and class but of pain and pleasure, dominance and submission, and all the permutations of the queer, than any has been since the late Victorian period. As mouthpieces of that culture, the contributors to this volume have a sophisticated appreciation of all the slippages that destabilize relationships between empowered and powerless, normative and unnatural, but also an equally contemporary, sometimes anxious determination not to allow this appreciation to undermine the political incisiveness to which current work in the humanities aspires. The natty pig, forever damned with the faint praise of the epithet 'trusty', serves to remind us that earlier periods were as aware as ours of the pressures, the concessions to the monstrous, involved in the forging of institutional power and virtue, and of the narrowness of the divide that separates power and virtue, once forged, from their seeming opposites, weakness and deviance. An Elizabethan gloss on Winchester's medieval motto – 'Manners makyth man' – the trusty pig proclaims the political message that *this* is the form the normative shall take for those men whose lot it is to be the privileged servants of masters. But if we listen carefully we can hear another note, painfully oinked through its poor padlocked mouth: the suggestion that the normative might itself be only a form of deviance, that the rightful rule of male civil servants and their masters over the mass of the poor, women, slaves and animals might be, at best, only the government of the monstrous by the monstrous. The trusty servant inducts its schoolboy viewers into a postlapsarian, almost Hobbesian world, in which the natural is hardly a conceivable category and virtue is maintained under the emblem not of innocence but of strain.

All five essays in this first part are about texts or topoi in which consumption figures prominently, sometimes as itself (consumption of food), sometimes as a figure for sexual consumption, and in one case as a figure for martyrdom by fire; consumption, in these essays, is also sometimes 'monstrous', that is, inappropriate, excessive or unregulated (John Gower's good word is 'wild'). The essays are appropriately diverse and concerned with their own topics, but they do cohere, it seems to me, not only around the topic of consumption but still more around the theme of *relationship* consumption always seems to imply. Indeed, these essays can most helpfully be read as concerning some of the ways in which medieval and early modern texts conceptualized relationships between the self or a certain gender, class or culture, and an 'other'. As their use of the figure of consumption suggests, such conceptualizations all have in common a concern with power; appetite is a matter of power at least as much as it is a matter of desire, taste or need – which is why the trusty servant must be presented as 'not nice in diet', as without particular appetite. Yet this concern works itself out in opposing directions. Whereas in some essays the destruction of the other is threatened through its consumption, in others it is being consumed, not consuming, that confers power, and corporeal consumption is a gesture of anxiety, futility or despair. Taken as a whole, the essays thus provide a rich resource for thinking through the complex ways some of our cultural and/or biological ancestors imagined and reasoned towards and away from a normative sense of what constitutes ethical relationships, what precipitates a lapse into the monstrous, and how a difference between normative and monstrous can be maintained when appetite – the desire to consume – is in play.

Three of the five essays – Diane Watt's discussion of the Apollonius of Tyre story from Gower's *Confessio Amantis*, Teresa Walters's of Fletcher's and Massinger's *The Sea Voyage*, and Claire Jowitt's of Brome's *The Antipodes* – deal with self-consciously fictional texts (one poem and two plays), which cultivate, or at least fail to exclude, a polyvalence that renders any attempt to understand them as simple statements of normative values problematic. If all three texts have didactic aspirations (most obvious in *Confessio Amantis*), their complexity as narratives of sexual desire and confusion also tend to pull them in the direction of expressing a more dubiously appetitive attitude towards the unregulated desires they concern. This is not simply because of their common use of variations on the romance plot. Neither the early modern play nor the secular vernacular poem of the late Middle Ages occupied a comfortable niche in its respective literary hierarchy, and this discomfort is very much part of the thematic load works in these genres carry, a discomfort characteristically pushed outwards to implicate the audience or reader through satire or the cultivation of moral ambiguity. This is, indeed, the purpose for which these genres may be claimed to have existed: to use their lack of established authority to explore, rather than resolve, the issues they raise. Middle English court poetry and Jacobean theatre were, no doubt, much concerned with establishing their own status within the literary canon, as many modern scholars have tried to show, but we do well not to underestimate the extent to which both also understood and accepted their function as dangerous games whose role was to court the very charge of monstrosity their apologists were most anxious to avoid.

To think of any work by 'moral Gower' as a 'dangerous game' may seem strange, given the weight of scholarship that consigns the whole of his trilingual corpus of poetry to the category of the didactic, but in fact this is precisely the aspect of Gower Diane Watt's current work is teaching us to see and that her essay in this volume illuminates. Watt discusses the last and longest of the poem's many exemplary narratives, the story of Apollonius of Tyre and his peregrinations around the Mediterranean after his unfortunate success in solving the riddle set by the incestuous king Antiochus for anyone foolhardy enough to become a suitor for the hand of his daughter:

With felonie I am upbore,	Scelere vehor,
I ete and have it noght forbore	materna carne vescor,
Mi modres fleissh, whos housebonde	quaero patrem meum
Mi fader forto seche I fonde,	matris meae virum
Which is the Sone eke of my wife.	uxoris mee filium[2]

Building on recent Freudian/Lacanian readings of this famously difficult rhyme (far more complex than the version, for example, found in Shakespeare's *Pericles*), Watt shows how Antiochus' incest with his daughter is doubled both by Apollonius' ambiguously 'kindely' relationship with his own daughter, Thaise, and by the elderly narrator's relationship with his youthful beloved – a relationship Venus herself eventually defines, delicately but firmly, as itself outside or against 'kinde' (VIII. 1705–8, 2321–76). Watt searches out the Oedipal resonances that unite Antiochus and Apollonius into a composite portrait of masculine rule whose potential for monstrosity is ever-present, and touches on the manifestations of female desire, as well as self-control, also present in the narrative.

From my own perspective here, a reading of the riddle along the lines she proposes focuses its most revealing attention on the gender confusion and refusal of relationship inherent in the riddle and its narrative situation. The easiest way to interpret the riddle is as about a son's incestuous relationship with his mother: 'Crime defines me, I have not resisted eating my mother, whose husband –

also my wife's son, me – I became, in search of my father'. The sexual puns on 'upbore' as 'gives me an erection', 'ete' as 'have sex with', and 'fonde' as 'attempt, seduce, attack' and possibly 'sodomize' (also 'found' and 'became'), as well as the intricate web of implied motivations given by the riddle, are particular to its vernacular version. Only here do we learn that the son sins partly because it excites him, that his search for his father undergirds all his other searches (Gower's Latin gloss has 'patrem', 'virum' and 'filium' in paratactic relation to one another, as objects of 'quero', but the English uses hypotaxis), and that this search is as much about the father's destruction as about the anxiety of his absence. Yet the riddle's narrative situation suggests that all the gender relations in this reading may be backwards, and that the speaker in the riddle is voicing Antiochus' daughter seeking her lost mother through eating the flesh of her father – in other words, that it is as much about the speaker Antiochus' inability to accept that he is distinct from his daughter as about his attempt to give perverse finality to his patriarchal authority. An absolutist in a sense even Gower's king, Richard II, never imagined, Antiochus' desires and anxieties are such that he must incorporate everything, male and female, into himself, and refuse all possibility that there is any 'other'. No wonder Apollonius flees when Antiochus calls him 'mi Sone' (VIII. 432), spending the rest of the romance almost failing to establish his own network of family relationships in the face of attempted murder, storms at sea, and his own lack of a centred identity. (Apollonius is far from a satisfactory alternative to his would-be father-in-law and killer.) You would think that patriarchal authority would be feeling chipper about itself in the world of this tale, since it remains intact no matter what crimes or negligences its representatives perpetrate; Apollonius has his own trusty servants to cover his absences from his kingdom, even if he does cower before Antiochus' supercharged masculinity. Yet the threat of slippage into feminization, of decline from the separateness that defines power, is everywhere in this tale, even corrupting the quest for power itself, when it loses the principle of restraint Watt associates with the mother. At the end of *Confessio Amantis*, the narrator preserves his own masculine integrity only by being persuaded that he is too old to play the game of sex, a game whose riskiness yet also necessity is everywhere in this long poem. Living in the world, like writing in the vernacular, is as much a matter of

'lust' as of 'lore' (Prologue 26), and incest can stand in as a representative of the many forms of misbegotten appetite such lusty
living entails.

Apollonius' many travels never take him into truly foreign
territory; his tale is less about the threat of the other than about the
dangerous possibility that, in the patriarchal imaginary, the other
may disappear. On the face of it, the same can not so easily be said
for the journeys dramatized in *The Antipodes* and *The Sea Voyage*,
both written in response to the astonishment of the new world,
with its burden not only of cultures whose otherness could at first
be comprehended only through contempt, but also of opportunities for Europeans, as novice settlers, to realize the
weakness of their own moorings in a secure sense of social self. Yet
according to Claire Jowitt and Teresa Walters, both plays are
actually so exuberantly committed to setting those moorings adrift
– sending up the attitude of cultural superiority and the sentiment-
ality about the noble savage endemic to European travel literature
since ancient times – that neither the otherness of the rest of the
world, nor the possibility of relationship with it, ever fully arises.
In *The Antipodes*, Brome's comically named protagonist, Peregrine
(from *peregrinus*, a pilgrim), has gone mad with longing for an
Antipodean world he cannot visit (since it is mere invention), and
so seems to have *forgotten* to consummate his relationship with his
sex-starved wife, Martha. Cured by the childish device of making
him believe he has found the country of his longing, where he is
easily persuaded to behave with due manliness towards Martha in
her disguise as an Antipodean queen, the world of normal relations
he and Martha now join is, Jowitt argues, thoroughly com-
promised by the deviant sexual histories of all the play's other
characters, including the doctor who cures Peregrine. The play is
thus a demonstration of 'the pointlessness of travel', at least for the
denizens of a society with so perverse a relation to its own customs
and ethical norms as Brome's Londoners. The dramatic travelogue
cooked up by Lord Letoy on Peregrine's behalf is meant to convince him that the Antipodes is literally a society upside down,
where everything is monstrous because everything is backwards. By
looking in the face of the other, Peregrine is to be brought to a
sense of himself. In practice, however, Letoy's version of the
Antipodes is no more than a projection of his own upside-down
living, and Peregrine's cure no more than an induction into the

deviance of Letoy's world, a world in which 'relationship' evidently means the same as 'appetite'. A famous scene in Mandeville's *Travels*, a text still very much alive in mid-seventeenth-century England through its publication in the first edition of Hakluyt's *Voyages*, has the Sultan of Egypt rendering a scathingly critical verdict on European morals, making Sir John blush for the hypocrisy of the one society in the world to boast the advantages of the true faith; thanks to its ethical and geographical proximity to Europe (not to mention its brilliant spy network), Islam, Christianity's other, is well equipped to expose Christendom's unnaturalness. If Brome's Antipodes in one sense function like Mandeville's Egypt in providing a vantage point for satire, they also, in another sense, parody Mandevillean idealism about the ethical potential of the travelogue in a society whose loss of all sense of the normative is such that satire itself no longer has corrective authority.

The Sea Voyage works rather differently, for behind this play there does lie a real New World (the Virginia colony and its Algonquin neighbours), besides the long European literary tradition of geographical writing that gives rise to the play's central literary trope: the Amazon kingdom, which a group of Portuguese women – discovered on a neighbouring island by the shipwrecked French pirate, Captain Albert, seeking food for his captive, Aminta – are attempting to revive. Focusing attention on the ambiguous category of the 'trinket', Walters analyses the play's depiction of the collapse of the pirates' commodity culture after their shipwreck: their fight over the gold they discover, rendered pointless by the fact that they have nothing to eat; their quarrel over the body of Aminta, originally valued for the beauty and virginity that make her marriageable but looking ever more edible as the pirates's last meal becomes a distant memory. Faced with the demands and the confusion of the New World, European systems of exchange are revealed as arbitrary, very much as European gender hierarchies are reversed by the neo-Amazons, who first want to procreate with the French pirates, then nearly execute them, before the play's last-minute resolution. With a careful attention to the play's historical moment, Walters reads the Amazons as a multiple allusion to the Virginian colonists, the Algonquins on whom they were so heavily dependent, and the women sent out to Virginia *en masse* three years before the play's production in 1622 to marry with the men of the colony and so ensure its stability. Such a plethora of associations in itself suggests the level of confusion about society, gender and profit that structured the first audience's experience of the play, as a direct result of the Virginia colony's encounter with a culture and set of circumstances for which it was so poorly prepared. Yet although *The Sea Voyage* does to this extent recognize the other, and uses it to throw new light on European society, it is interesting how far the anxieties that give the play its tension and humour are seen through the lens of ancient mythology, not early modern anthropology. Just a hint of the cultural other (the New World shrunk to a desert island) is enough to destabilize the civilized order of things, revealing the bestiality and feebleness of the play's society of men (pirates, after all), and bringing back to life that ancient threat to patriarchal order, Amazonia, not as an invading outsider but in the form of a practical adaptation to circumstance from within (the women's old men are gone, and for most of the play they see no need to tie themselves to new ones). The New World throws European society back on a vision of itself as still as close to dissolution into the unnatural spectres of cannibalism, female independence and the rest, as Gower's Mediterranean.

The other essays in this part – Isabel Davis's analysis of late medieval depictions of the working man, and Kimberly Anne Coles's of the strange absence of Anne Askew's body in the *Examinations* – deal with different kinds of text, whose primary concern is not with the depiction of 'monstrous appetites' but with a type of monstrous distortion of the body employed in the service of fortifying 'normative' behaviour and attitudes. In both cases, though, these are attitudes maintained under duress, whether the ubiquitous duress of peasant labour or the singular duress of martyrdom. Depictions of the medieval working man, which Davis shows to be organized around his corporeality, his role as food provider, and the physical damage he sustains in fulfilling this role, bear an obvious resemblance to the Elizabethan image of the trusty servant with which I began. Here again are bodies that exist to serve, distort themselves for the sake of others, find their proper (their socially determined) form through damage and suffering. Yet there are real differences. First, the trusty servant is an image more conscious of its own potential perversity than, say, the suffering servant of Julian of Norwich's *A Revelation of Love*, because the trusty servant is intended to be seen by those it represents, while the suffering servant is a metaphor for human living whose audience of well-born literates can only appropriate it from without, as pastoral stereotype. Where the pig is monstrous, Julian's servant is pathetic, seen with sympathy, but always imaginatively from the point of view of the lord, who represents both God and the higher part of the human soul (since Julian's vision is born at the point of junction between God and this 'substantial' soul). Second, it follows from this that the trusty servant is a less compliant image than the suffering servant, containing the germs of dissent, or at least of horror at its own condition, that the suffering servant lacks. This is because Julian is so good at making the sufferings of her servant meaningful, caused as they are by his zeal in trying to serve his lord, necessary both to his service and to the lord's worship – the lord needs the servant as much as the servant the lord – and resulting, eventually, in a surpassing heavenly reward. The lord and the servant are in a relationship of mutual love, only apparently interrupted by the servant's fall, which in the larger scheme of things proves a labour of love, a necessary step towards perfection. The trusty servant is offered no such promise of reward. Davis makes cogent points about the social mobility and ambition of the English rural workforce after the Black Death, although I do wonder if the divide between literary stereotype and social reality was always as wide as she suggests. Medieval peasants knew how they were supposed to think of themselves through sermons, plays, and other narratives, and presumably internalized some of what they heard, even if they turned it towards their own ends; if Julian of Norwich reached only a small audience, we know that *Piers Plowman* had a powerful effect on one, partly peasant-driven movement, the rebellion of 1381. But it is surely true, as Davis argues, that the feudal allegory of *A Revelation*, with its denial of the very possibility of the monstrous – its vision of a universe where all appetite is a form of holy desire – works best when all connection with social reality has been lost.

Davis ends her essay with a call to scholars to pay as much attention to representations of the working man's body as we have learned to pay to the bodies of medieval and early modern women, long recognized as sites of special meaning and, perhaps, empowerment. As Coles suggests, however, one of the most distinctive things about Anne Askew's account of her trial and torture, the *Examinations*, is precisely its *lack* of emphasis on

Askew's body. Noting that Askew is equally taciturn when it comes to defining her heretical beliefs before her examiners, on the grounds that scripture does not allow women to preach, Coles reads the *Examinations* as a defence of private, local faith – as an oddly reticent act of defiance – rather than as the explicit expression of Protestant heroism it becomes in Foxe's *Acts and Monuments*. Coles contrasts Askew's attitude to the body and the heresy trial to the glorification of the body consumed by fire as a 'candle', a testament of faith, found in the records of other Reformation martyrs. I wonder, too, if Askew is not conducting her defence in a tradition of evasiveness that derives from the Lollard heresy trials of the fifteenth and early sixteenth centuries, rather than from the more theatrical and confrontational examinations that became the norm after the Reformation; Lollards generally tried quite hard to survive, rather than to testify.[3] As a Protestant woman, one of Askew's principal targets in the *Examinations* is likely to be a literary one, the *passiones* of the virgin martyrs such as Katherine, Margaret and Cecilia, which were enormously popular in Catholic England and which are full of bodies racked, boiled in oil, torn by hooks and sometimes swallowed by dragons. Seeking to avoid the seductive dichotomies of these narratives – and writing, not as a virgin, but as a married woman who had come to London seeking a divorce – Askew created an interestingly anti-heroic martyrdom narrative, in which death itself has no particularly spectacular function, but is simply the only workable response to worldly power when that power seeks to eat up the space in which the soul sits free to contemplate and put into action the law of God. (Whatever that law may be: a fascinating aspect of the *Examinations* is Askew's apparent perception of the scriptures as a fluid entity, from which God may speak in quite different ways at different times. No wonder that Foxe, seeking to institutionalize Askew into the new order, provided the *Examinations* with the accounts of her body's torment it lacked.) The trusty servant bends his body into inhuman shapes in order to be part of the structure of secular power, to reflect the infinite variety and voracity of its needs. Askew ignores her body, then submits it to be burned, in order to evade, to evade even answering to, the servants of that power. Bodies, especially bodies sublimated in texts, can never cease to signify, suggest analogies, define themselves in terms of other bodies or bodily norms. Askew's appetite, however, is apparently to be the nearest thing to a blank slate, a *tabula rasa* on which only her immediate responsiveness to God's immediate demands need be written. 'A trusty servants portrait would you see?' Not, apparently, here.

Notes

[1] See Figure 1. The most recent study of the trusty servant is Mark Thornton Burnett, 'The "trusty servant": a sixteenth-century English emblem', *Emblematica: An Interdisciplinary Journal of Emblem Studies* 6 (1992), 237–53, from which the verses above are quoted. Burnett shows that the painting and Latin verses were produced in 1579, although the doggerel English translation probably dates from the first years of the nineteenth century. My reading of the emblem has points in common with Burnett's, but pushes in a different direction.

[2] Quoted from *The English Works of John Gower*, VIII. 405–9, ed. G. C. Macaulay, EETS es (Oxford, 1979), pp. 81, 82.

[3] Evasion, rather than confrontation, is certainly the strategy practised by the majority of suspected Lollards discussed, for example, in John A. F. Thomson, *The Later Lollards, 1414–1520* (Oxford, 1965).

3

Consuming Passions in Book VIII of John Gower's Confessio Amantis

DIANE WATT

According to Michel Foucault, in the Graeco-Roman world, power was inextricably linked to ethics, politics, knowledge and liberty. Power was not itself perceived negatively; it was the abuse of power which was threatening.

> In the abuse of power, one goes beyond what is legitimately the exercise of power, and one imposes on others one's whims, one's appetites, one's desires. There we see the image of the tyrant or simply the powerful and wealthy man who takes advantage of power and his wealth to misuse others, to impose on them undue power. But one sees – at least this is what the Greek philosophers say – that this man is in reality a slave to his appetites. And the good ruler is precisely the one who exercises his power correctly, that is by exercising at the same time his power on himself. And it is the power over self which will regulate the power over others.[1]

A concern with the relationship between power, ethics and selfhood connects the philosophy of the classical period with contemporary thinking, and is also demonstrated in the writing of the Middle Ages. It is certainly central to the *Confessio Amantis*, a late fourteenth-century work by the English poet, John Gower.[2] In this essay, I focus on Gower's Tale of Apollonius, which takes up the most part of the final book of *Confessio*. In this narrative, Gower demonstrates a preoccupation with power and its abuse which is similar to that of Foucault,[3] and like Foucault, Gower draws on metaphors of appetite in this context to discuss human desire. However, whereas (as the passage just quoted demonstrates) Foucault appears to be blind to the issue of gender, Gower is not. Masculinity and chastity (or controlled sexuality) are associated in Gower's text with government of appetite and are opposed to effeminate and feminine desires, and to sexual licentiousness, which are figured in terms of unrestrained or monstrous appetites. Gower's narrative of Apollonius of Tyre is at one level concerned with the satisfaction of 'legitimate' male appetites and destruction or frustration of appetites judged to be illegitimate, although, as I will argue, the simple opposition of legitimate and illegitimate, masculine and effeminate/feminine is ultimately undermined. In the analysis I offer here, I will draw on the insights of psychoanalysis in order to examine the extent to which Gower's tale is revealing about gendered and sexual identity.[4]

One compelling reason for drawing upon psychoanalysis here is that the popular medieval story of Apollonius – a tale of murder, incest and self-destruction – seems to be related to that of Oedipus, which since Freud has been so influential in our understanding of gender and sex, but which does not itself seem to have been very well known in the Middle Ages.[5] Clear similarities exist between the plots of Sophocles' *Oedipus* and Gower's main source, the medieval Latin *Historia Apollonii*.[6] In addition to the focus on incest and its ruinous consequences, in both texts the solving of a riddle by the hero either before or near the beginning of the narrative precipitates later developments.[7] Gower's version of the tale of Apollonius is typical in that it begins with the story of King Antiochus, who after the death of his wife rapes his only child. In order to keep his daughter for his own use, Antiochus devises a riddle for her suitors to solve and then executes those who are unable to provide the correct answer. On Apollonius' arrival in Antiochus' court, the king explains the terms of the agreement, and repeats the riddle:

> With felonie I am upbore,
> I ete and have it noght forbore
> Mi modres fleissh, whos housebonde
> Mi fader forto seche I fonde,
> Which is the Sone eke of my wife.
> (VIII. 405–9)

Inconsistencies in punctuation in the manuscripts of the text, or its complete omission, render any attempt at translating such

grammatically ambiguous verses at best only provisional. Gower's
inclusion at this point in the narrative of a Latin gloss may initially
seem to help with the rendering into modern English. The gloss
reads 'Scelere vehor, materna carne vescor, quaero patrem meum,
matris meae virum, uxoris mee filium' (I am carried along by my
crime, I feed on my mother's flesh, I seek my father, my mother's
husband, my wife's son: at VIII. 405). However, the careful reader
of Gower's text will be suspicious of looking for a close cor-
respondence between the English verses and the Latin verses and
prose summaries. As previous critics have illustrated, Gower's
Latin rarely clarifies the meaning of the English verses, and sometimes undermines or contradicts it.[8] In fact the Latin gloss does
little to clarify the meaning of the English text in this instance.
Although, at this juncture in the narrative, the reader has every
reason to expect Apollonius to explain the riddle's meaning, and
thus to identify the speaking persona (or personification), he fails
to do so. His answer is curiously unspecific. Apollonius goes no
further than suggesting that the solution lies in the relationship
between father and daughter, and hinting darkly that the answer to
the riddle is secret and of a sexual nature (VIII. 423–7).

  Unsurprisingly, the meaning of this riddle has vexed critics for
the last hundred years and more. Yet it clearly makes some sense in
its narrative context. The reference to 'felonie' or crime points
towards Antiochus' rape of his daughter (incest is of course a crime
as well as a sin). The reference to monstrous appetite would seem
to be metaphorical and directs us to the same event. It has already
been anticipated twice in the text: first when Antiochus' assault on
his daughter is described in the following terms: 'The wylde fader
thus devoureth / His oghne fleissh' (VIII. 309–10); and, again, a
couple of lines later in a reference to 'this unkind fare' (VIII. 312),
where *unkinde* of course means unnatural and *fare* may mean
'feasting' as well as 'business'.[9]

  In an important recent essay on Gower entitled 'The riddle of
incest', Larry Scanlon follows Georgiana Donavin in arguing that
the riddle lends itself to Freudian interpretations.[10] Certainly,
psychoanalysis can explain the figuring of incest as monstrous
appetite in Antiochus' riddle, and in the account of his rape of his
daughter. According to Freud's theory of the Oedipus Complex,
the child's first love is its mother, who feeds and nurtures it. Freud
emphasizes the link between food and sex: a connection made

manifest in what he calls the oral phase of infant sexuality. Antiochus' riddle with its references to the devouring of the mother's flesh expresses the speaker's repressed desire to devour or to sleep with his own mother. The riddle also points directly to father–daughter incest, in which, according to psychoanalysis, the adult male's Oedipus Complex has not been adequately resolved and the repressed infantile desire for the mother re-emerges in the desire for the daughter. Antiochus resembles Sophocles' Oedipus in that his desire for his mother/daughter results in both his own destruction and hers. Gower emphasizes that both father and daughter suffer the same fate: killed by a bolt of lightning (VIII. 999–1002). The *Historia Apollonii* actually has them struck down while they are in bed together.[11]

But psychoanalysis can only take us so far in solving Antiochus' riddle, because in Gower's version of the story at least, the role of the mother appears to be more far-reaching than this Oedipal interpretation would suggest. The *Historia Apollonii* is littered with absent and often nameless women. The events at the beginning of Gower's version of the tale are precipitated by the loss of Antiochus' wife. Her death is not related in order to explain the events which follow (although the king's isolation, and the proximity as well as beauty of his daughter are stressed), but rather to draw the reader's attention to the vulnerability of the daughter. We are told that she is particularly defenceless because her serving women are absent, including the nurse, who has looked after her since her childhood. When she is later told about the rape, the nurse, who has in a sense taken the place of the young girl's mother, offers no protection but only empty words of consolation (VIII. 336–40). In effect, the nurse, in remaining silent, colludes with the king.

Later in the text, the suffering of Antiochus' daughter is doubled in that of Apollonius' daughter, Thaise. Although Apollonius' wife does not die, she falls into a death-like state giving birth on board ship during a storm, and is placed in a coffin and thrown overboard. Apollonius then leaves his daughter in the care of foster-parents. Initially, this does not seem an unfortunate act of entrustment – although the sheer length of Apollonius' absence (at least fourteen years) might imply a degree of paternal neglect. But the cancerous jealousy of Thaise's foster-mother (who is concerned that Thaise casts shade on her natural daughter) makes her situation a dangerous one. The parallel between Thaise's situation and that of Antiochus' daughter is made explicit when we are told of the death of Thaise's nurse. In contrast to the nurse of Antiochus' daughter, this retainer is described as a 'trewe' servant (VIII. 1350), but even she cannot protect her ward beyond the grave.[12] Once again, the absence and, in this case, also the cruelty of the maternal figures, combined with the incontinence, or as here the neglect of the father, imperils the daughter's chastity, and Apollonius' child finds herself captured by pirates and sold to the keeper of a brothel. Thaise's own mother does not reappear in the narrative until after her daughter's marriage.

In the *Historia Apollonii*, the daughters of Antiochus and Apollonius are further doubled in the unnamed figure of Apollonius' wife (in other words Thaise's mother): the daughter of the king of Pentapolis. Like the other two, this princess is her father's heir. One significant change Gower makes to his sources is to give the king of Pentapolis a wife. Although this queen does not figure largely in the narrative, she is mentioned three times at VIII. 659, VIII. 721 and VIII. 930–7. It is the third mention which is the most significant because it reveals some of the importance of the figure of the queen as wife and mother. The king of Pentapolis consults his wife, seeking her approval for their daughter's marriage. The crucial point to note here is that this princess is the one daughter whose mother is present and she is the one daughter in the narrative who is not vulnerable to assault.

The importance of the mother figure may also be linked to the metaphors of monstrous appetite discussed already. Incest is likened elsewhere in Gower's text to poisoned food. In the frame narrative of *Confessio*, the priest Genius warns the lover Amans against such love, which he compares to the fruit known as the bittersweet (VIII. 190–6). Incest may be sweet to the taste, but its after-effects are unpleasant, and seemingly even deadly. Even though Genius does not make the connection, the first three examples he gives of incest – Caligula, Amnon and Lot – are all linked to feasting and drinking. In Suetonius, Caligula seats his sisters below him at a banquet. In 2 Samuel 13, Amnon has Tamar prepare his food with her own hand and instructs her to feed it to him. In Genesis 19, Lot's daughters intoxicate him with wine before sleeping with him.[13] It is something of a commonplace to remark on the close association of women and food in the Middle

Ages, although, as Isabel Davis suggests in the following essay, its symbolism was not necessarily restricted to the feminine. Nonetheless it remains the case that food was an important, and sometimes scarce, commodity, and, within the household, women, as wives and mothers, tended to be responsible for providing safe and nutritious sustenance.[14] Indeed, such women are sometimes depicted as offering both figuratively and literally their own bodies to supply the needs and wants of their husbands and children. In Gower's Tale of Constance, the heroine is represented as the perfect, self-sacrificing mother who forces herself to provide her infant child with sustenance, even when (cut adrift in a rudderless boat) she feels overwhelmed by despair (II. 1068–83). Women are likewise responsible for controlling the intake of tempting but potentially illness-inducing foodstuffs. The message of the Tale of Apollonius seems to be that without their wives to check their unhealthy desires, men are irresistibly drawn to such comestibles. Like Antiochus, who indirectly confesses his desire to cannibalize his own mother and who seeks to satisfy his lust in his daughter, such men indulge their 'likinge and concupiscence' (VIII. 293).

Yet, women who pervert the maternal role, who kill rather than nurture, are also represented as monsters with uncontrollable appetites. Thaise's wicked foster-mother takes the part of the archetypal anti-mother and false-nurturer, the wicked stepmother from fairy tale. Her role in the Tale of Apollonius bears a close relationship to the parts played by the Sultan's mother and Domilde in the Tale of Constance (II. 587–1612), Chaucer's retelling of which is examined by Sue Niebrzydowski later in this volume: both evil mothers-in-law plot the overthrow of their sons' wives, and the Sultan's mother even plans a feast (II. 677–92) at which she can slay her son and his advisers. The murder of the child is itself, metaphorically, an incestuous act, as the mother devours her offspring, rather than offers it sustenance. The eventual punishment of the foster-parents at the end of the Tale of Apollonius parallels the earlier divine retribution to which Antiochus and his daughter fell victim.

In Gower's tale, then, the role of women as wives and mothers is crucial to the proper functioning of the household. But if mothers are important, fathers are more so, if sometimes for reasons we might not anticipate. Returning to Antiochus' riddle, it should be noted that Gower's version is derived from a corruption of the medieval Latin prose romance. In the *Historia Apollonii* the riddle reads 'Scelere vehor, maternam carnem vescor, quaero fratrem meum, meae matris virum, uxoris meae filium: non invenio' (I am borne on crime; I eat my mother's flesh; I seek my brother, my mother's husband, my wife's son; I do not find him).[15] Gower's Latin and English versions, and the version of the text which Gower used as his source, have made two transformations to the original: *fratrem* has become replaced by *patrem*/father, and *non invenio* has been dropped. With these corruptions in the Latin, and thus the English, the whole meaning of the riddle has changed. I would like to argue that these corruptions could be read as examples of parapraxes (so-called Freudian slips). That is, they have a meaning beyond that intended by the speaker/translator.[16] In these corrupt lines, repressed material forces its way to the surface of the reader's consciousness. The parapraxes in Gower's version of the riddle stress the significance of the mother's husband, the father, as the object of desire, and draw our attention to the equivalence of these terms to the wife's son. The parapraxes also suggest that this Oedipal quest is not fruitless, that the husband, father and son are in fact found.

In this context, it is significant to note that, according to the theory of the Oedipus Complex, the child not only forms a primary bond with the mother, but also becomes possessive and sexually jealous of the father. The child seeks to usurp the father's place *vis-à-vis* the mother. The male child's fear of castration however means that he learns instead to obey and to imitate the father, to become like him, and to renounce his desire for his mother, displacing it on to other women. In Lacanian terms, it is the Name of the Father, rather than the father himself, which disrupts the primary bond with the mother. In Scanlon's analysis, it is this, the Name of the Father, not the actual father, that Antiochus is lacking, and that he simultaneously fears and desires.[17] Scanlon develops his argument by suggesting that Antiochus is doubled in the figure of Apollonius. Apollonius is embroiled in the sins of Antiochus in that, in attempting to replace and to succeed Antiochus, he too seeks to acquire paternal and patriarchal authority. Furthermore, incestuous elements are present in the reconciliation between Apollonius and his daughter.[18]

Rather than contest this line of argument, I would like to develop it in a slightly different direction by suggesting that Antiochus' riddle also reveals that he is suffering from a father-fixation.[19] For Antiochus, as an abusive patriarch, who has defied the paternal prohibitions on incest, and whose Oedipus Complex has been repressed rather than destroyed, the obsession with the father is critical. However, just as the infantile desire for the mother is transferred on to the daughter, so the fixation on the father re-emerges in a search for a son or son-in-law. Because, in desiring his mother, he has tried to take his father's place, the quest for the father is in turn redirected into the narcissistic pursuit of his would-be son-in-law and narrative double, Apollonius. This search may itself have a sexual dimension. If we accept this to be the case then latent homoerotic desire is another manifestation of Antiochus' monstrous appetite. What is more, further similarities can be detected between Antiochus and Apollonius. Apollonius' behaviour is rather erratic, since he keeps on fleeing after Antiochus has stopped pursuing him. One interpretation of this behaviour is that Apollonius suffers from a persecution complex. Apollonius' fear is tied in with what Freud calls ruler taboos. According to Freud 'When a paranoiac names a person of his acquaintance as his "persecutor", he thereby elevates him to the paternal succession and brings him under conditions which enable him to make him responsible for all the misfortune which he experiences.'[20] Freud sees the persecution complex as a form of megalomania, which, like incest, is the result of a narcissistic magnification of the ego.[21] He also notes that the imagined persecutor is usually the same sex as the person suffering from the complex and concludes that a persecution complex is a symptom of repressed homosexuality. Like Antiochus, then, Apollonius has his own monstrous appetites in that he too appears to be suffering from a father-fixation, which may have a homosexual dimension.

Teresa de Lauretis argues that the appearance of the Sphinx in the story of Oedipus draws attention to the elusive nature of female desire in the narrative.[22] As de Lauretis notes, the Sphinx, like the Medusa and other monsters inscribed in hero narratives, is recognizably female.[23] The Sphinx is not only monstrous but destructive as well: she kills men and then devours them. Michel Zink suggests that the riddle in the *Historia Apollonii* is actually derived from the Sphinx's riddle in the legend of Oedipus.[24] If we accept this, then Antiochus' daughter takes the role of the Sphinx herself. In the Latin prose narrative, the king sets the riddle, and the princess remains silent, as is appropriate in a patriarchal state.

Antiochus and his daughter with Apollonius. *Confessio Amantis*, Pierpont Morgan MS M126, fo. 187ᵛ. Reproduced by permission of the Pierpont Morgan Library.

This is also the case in Gower's narrative. However, the association between the riddle and the princess is preserved in the one surviving manuscript illustration to the story which is found in the elaborately decorated Pierpont Morgan MS M126 (one of only two manuscripts of *Confessio Amantis* to include a whole series of miniatures).[25] This illustration shows Antiochus and his daughter face-to-face with Apollonius, who is offering his answer to the riddle. Patricia Eberle, in her analysis of this miniature, draws our attention to Apollonius' horrified expression and to the exchange of glances between Antiochus and his daughter.[26] These, she suggests, reveal that the couple share a terrible secret. Eberle also comments on the barren landscape in the foreground, which may reflect the unnatural, unfruitful, savage and ultimately self-consuming passion of the king. But what I find most striking about the image is the depiction of the two decapitated suitors, who are lying at the princess's feet, their limbs and bodies entangled behind her skirts, and their heads rolling ominously in Apollonius' direction. The artist here deviates from the attendant narrative in that the decapitated heads are left in the mud, rather than, as Gower has it (VIII. 369), placed on the gate of the city (visible in the background). The woman's role in the drama is placed in the foreground; her guilt is exposed; and she is represented as monstrous as well as cruel (the hero cannot meet her gaze). This association between the riddle and the princess rather than her father is found in other versions of the Apollonius story: there exists an Anglo-Saxon version of the riddle in which the speaker changes halfway through, and in Shakespeare's *Pericles* the speaker is Antiochus' daughter throughout.[27]

In Freud's analysis of Sophocles, and in his theory of the Oedipus Complex, the focus is inevitably on men, and female desire is associated with the riddle of the Sphinx and represented as a mystery, and by implication, as dangerous and potentially monstrous.[28] As de Lauretis points out, we do not know the Sphinx's story: why, like Oedipus' mother Jocasta, does she kill herself?[29] Gower, however, uses the Apollonius story to examine and to attempt to unravel female desire. In other words, at least to some extent, Gower allows the Sphinx to tell her own story. If, according to Vladimir Propp, the Sphinx is an assimilation of the princess and the dragon of traditional folklore,[30] then Antiochus' daughter is an assimilation of the Sphinx and Jocasta of

Sophocles' play, and like them, she has to die. Remarkably, however, at the very start of the tale, Gower does depict the rape from
the victim's as well as the aggressor's point of view, and thus gives a
voice to her suffering. Yet, thereafter, Antiochus' daughter is
dropped from the narrative, and only mentioned again in the brief
report of her death, which is represented as just punishment for her
albeit unwilled sinfulness.

But soon after he has finished describing the events surrounding
the rape of Antiochus' daughter, Gower returns to the question of
female sexuality. Just as Apollonius has journeyed from his own
kingdom of Tyre to Antioch and placed himself amongst the
potential suitors of the king's daughter, so he travels from Tyre to
Pentapolis and finds himself in competition with the suitors of the
princess there. Once again he encounters a king who expresses his
power through the handing over of his anonymous daughter's
'privete' to Apollonius. Antiochus simultaneously hides and exposes
his crime through the riddle; the king of Pentapolis reveals his
daughter's 'secret' desire for Apollonius through a private letter. Yet
despite the fact that Antiochus' daughter and Apollonius' wife and
daughter find themselves in similar situations and are all to a greater
or lesser extent represented as chattels, there are marked differences
between them. Most obviously, whereas Antiochus' daughter
expresses no desire, and can only lament the loss of her virginity
(VIII. 327–31), the princess of Pentapolis feels the full force of
overwhelming passion for Apollonius. She is able to express to her
father her wishes in the strongest possible terms. Yet she still has to
live by the rules of the patriarchal society of which she is a member:
she is concerned for her good name and fears for her womanly
reputation (VIII. 855–6), and she realizes that she cannot pursue
Apollonius without her father's approval and connivance. Indeed,
Apollonius' wife cannot really be seen as a desiring female subject,
because, as de Lauretis would have it, the narrative is governed by an
Oedipal logic in which her desire can only be congruent with that of
the hero.[31] Even as she appears to be expressing her own desires, she
is consenting to those of Apollonius, and enabling *him* to fulfil *his*
destiny. So even when Gower appears to be representing female
sexuality sympathetically – even when he seems to be suggesting that
it is not necessarily monstrous – he represents it as something which
has to be restrained by the rules of traditional courtship and
marriage which keep men in the position of power.

In conclusion then, within Gower's narrative of Apollonius of Tyre we encounter many and various manifestations of monstrous appetite, from the consuming narcissistic passion of incest to the devouring cruelty of the anti-mother, from the cravings of latent homosexuality to the 'unnatural' hunger of female sexuality. The message of Gower's text appears to be that proper manly behaviour requires the controlling of the appetites: the hero, Apollonius, learns self-government and is rewarded with a wife, daughter and son-in-law (and heir). But the *Confessio Amantis* is not simply a conduct book for men. It has a wider political context: part of it at least is advice to princes aimed, in the first instance, at that dissolute young monarch, Richard II. If Gower had his own sovereign in mind when he translated the Apollonius story, it is probably the king of Pentapolis rather than Apollonius who is intended as a model of kingship.[32] After all, the king of Pentapolis is the one male character exempted from the taints of incest, narcissism and homosexuality. Furthermore he has a wife, who, while always remaining in the background, offers him counsel and support. The tale might then be read as an implied celebration of the queenly counsel of Anne of Bohemia (who died in 1394, four years after Gower had completed the first version of *Confessio*).[33] So far, so conservative. But in the frame narrative of *Confessio*, it is the figure of the lover Amans who is often interpreted as a double for Richard II.[34] Although Amans repeatedly insists that his priest's tales of incest are irrelevant to his own situation, at the end of Book VIII we discover that he too has been indulging his own monstrous appetite because he is too old for the role he has been playing. As an aged lover, Amans has also taken his love 'unkindely' – like incest and other forms of 'unnatural' love, his love has been misdirected. And this is where the more radical elements of Gower's text creep in – in the form of female resistance. Unlike Apollonius, Amans cannot and does not win his beloved. Amans's absent lover never consents to his desire, and consequently in some senses narrative closure is impossible. Figuratively speaking, Amans never solves his riddle. The Sphinx does not kill herself, and the Oedipal quest remains unfulfilled. Although unlike Antiochus in Book VIII, Amans is not actually punished for his monstrous appetite, in the conclusion of Gower's *Confessio*, the protagonist's own consuming passion remains unsatisfied.

Notes

[1] Michel Foucault, 'The ethic of care for the self as a practice of freedom: an interview with Michel Foucault on January 20, 1984', in *The Final Foucault*, ed. J. Bernauer and D. Rasmussen (Cambridge, MA, 1994), p. 8.

[2] All references to *Confessio Amantis* are to *The English Works of John Gower*, ed. G. C. Macaulay, EETS ES (Oxford, 1979), pp. 81, 82.

[3] Claire Fanger, 'Magic and the metaphysics of gender in Gower's "Tale of Circe and Ulysses"', in R. F. Yeager (ed.), *Re-Visioning Gower* (Asheville, NC, 1998), p. 204 n. 3.

[4] I develop this analysis more fully in relation to the poem's political message in my article, 'Oedipus, Apollonius, and Richard II', *Studies in the Age of Chaucer* (forthcoming, 2002); and in the final chapter of my monograph, *Amoral Gower: Language, Sex and Politics in* Confessio Amantis (Minneapolis: Minnesota University Press, forthcoming).

[5] See, for example, Lowell Edmunds, 'Oedipus in the Middle Ages', *Antike and Abendland* 22 (1976), 140–55; and Elizabeth Archibald, 'Sex and power in Thebes and Babylon: Oedipus and Semiramis in classical and medieval texts', in Gernot Wieland (ed.), *Classical Antiquity and the Middle Ages* (Kalamazoo, MI, forthcoming).

[6] Elizabeth Archibald (ed. and trans.), *Apollonius of Tyre: Medieval and Renaissance Themes and Variations* (Cambridge, 1992), pp. 112–79.

[7] Ibid., p. 29.

[8] See, for example, Siân Echard, 'With Carmen's help: Latin authorities in *Confessio Amantis*', *Studies in Philology* 95 (1998), 1–40.

[9] *MED* s.v. *fare* 8a and 4.

[10] Larry Scanlon, 'The riddle of incest: John Gower and the problem of medieval sexuality', in Yeager (ed.), *Re-Visioning Gower*, pp. 93–127; Georgiana Donavin, *Incest Narratives and the Structure of John Gower's* Confessio Amantis (Victoria, BC, 1993), pp. 71–2.

[11] Archibald (ed. and trans.), *Apollonius of Tyre*, pp. 136 and 137.

[12] Gower significantly reduces the role of Thaise's nurse, thus making the parallel more explicit: ibid., pp. 142–5.

[13] J. C. Rolfe (ed. and trans.), *Suetonius* (London, 1914), II, pp. 440 and 441; 2 Samuel 13: 5–14; Genesis 19: 32–6.

[14] See, for example, Diane Purkiss, *The Witch in History: Early Modern and Twentieth-Century Representations* (London, 1996), pp. 277–81.

[15] Archibald (ed. and trans.), *Apollonius of Tyre*, pp. 114 and 115.

[16] Sigmund Freud, 'Parapraxes', in *Introductory Lectures in Psychoanalysis*, trans. James Strachey (London, 1991), pp. 96–9.

[17] Scanlon, 'Riddle of incest', p. 125.

[18] See María Bullón-Fernández, *Fathers and Daughters in Gower's* Confessio Amantis: *Authority, Family, State, and Writing* (Cambridge, 2000), p. 97.

[19] Freud argues that father-fixations are usually caused by the displacement of feelings for the mother: see 'A seventeenth-century demonological neurosis', in *Art and Literature*, trans. James Strachey (London, 1990), p. 406.

[20] Sigmund Freud, *Totem and Taboo*, trans. A. A. Brill (Harmondsworth, 1938), p. 77.

[21] Sigmund Freud, 'The libido theory and narcissism', in *Introductory Lectures*, trans. Strachey, p. 471; see also 'A seventeenth-century demonological neurosis'.

[22] Teresa de Lauretis, 'Desire in narrative', in *Alice Doesn't: Feminism, Semiotics, Cinema* (London, 1984), pp. 103–57.

[23] Ibid., p. 109.

[24] Michel Zink (ed.), *Le roman d'Apollonius de Tyr* (Paris, 1982), pp. 25–6.

[25] New York, Pierpont Morgan, MS M126 fo. 187^v.

[26] Patricia Eberle, 'Miniatures as evidence of reading in a manuscript of the *Confessio Amantis*', in R. F. Yeager (ed.), *John Gower: Recent Readings* (Kalamazoo, MI, 1989), pp. 340–1.

[27] P. Goolden, 'Antiochus's riddle in Gower and Shakespeare', *Review of English Studies*, NS 6 (1955), 245 and 247 n. 3.

[28] Sigmund Freud, 'Femininity', in *New Introductory Lectures on Psychoanalysis*, trans. James Strachey (London, 1991), p. 146.

[29] De Lauretis, 'Desire in narrative', p. 110.

[30] Vladimir Propp, 'Oedipus in the light of folklore', in Lowell Edmunds (ed.), *Oedipus: A Folklore Casebook* (New York and London, 1983), p. 109.

[31] De Lauretis, 'Desire in narrative', esp. pp. 136–55.

[32] Bullón-Fernández takes the view that Apollonius is a model of kingship: *Fathers and Daughters*, p. 63.

[33] On Anne of Bohemia, see David Wallace, *Chaucerian Polity: Absolute Lineages and Associational Forms in England and Italy* (Stanford, CA, 1997), pp. 295–8 and 363–4.

[34] See Elizabeth Porter, 'Gower's ethical microcosm and political macrocosm', in A. J. Minnis (ed.), *Gower's Confessio Amantis: Responses and Reassessments* (Cambridge, 1983), p. 146.

4

Consuming the Body of the Working Man in the Later Middle Ages[1]

୧

ISABEL DAVIS

Usage of labour is a greet thyng, for it maketh, as seith Seint Bernard, the labourer to have stronge armes and harde synwes; and slouthe maketh hem feble and tendre.[2]

In this didactic description from Chaucer's 'Parson's Tale', the male working body reflects the work it undertakes. The industrious man is rewarded with physical strength while his indolent brother is consigned to a delicate and effeminate form. But the muscles which flex in the Parson's pleasing portrayal are absent from other depictions of exemplary labouring men, where the stress is often upon physical damage. The trope of the honest workman produced pathos by accentuating his industry and resulting bodily injury. This essay will look at the discursive construction of the ideal workman in order to readdress the seminal and inspiring work of Caroline Walker Bynum on the female body in the Middle Ages. Her influential studies of female religious have encouraged some uncritical readings of somatic representations of men in the Middle Ages.[3] Representations of extraordinary male bodies have been unproblematically described as effeminate rather than being analysed in terms of masculine modalities.

Bynum has described a special relationship between women and the body in religious practice. Her project often privileges a dualist perspective by focusing both on the misogynist clerics who consigned women to the unspiritual body and the lives of female religious who rehabilitated the female body, making it spiritually significant:

Another aspect of medieval theological views of woman has also been deplored by modern scholars, and there is reason to think that this notion did influence medieval women. This is the notion that, allegorically speaking, 'woman is to man as matter is to spirit.' Thus *woman* or *the feminine* symbolizes the physical, lustful, material, appetitive part of human nature, whereas *man* symbolizes the spiritual, or rational, or mental.[4]

From Hildegard of Bingen and Elizabeth of Schönau to Catherine of Siena and Julian of Norwich, women theologians in the later Middle Ages saw woman as the symbol of humanity, where humanity was understood as physicality.[5]

This close association between woman and the body manifested itself in two interrelated ways. First, there was an emphasis upon the female body as a site of suffering; secondly, women were identified with food and food production on account of their maternal and domestic roles.[6] These correlations made it apposite that religious women, often damaged by penitential asceticism, were compared with the humanized Christ, sacrificed to feed the world; '[f]or it seems likely', Bynum writes, '. . . that women were drawn to identify with Christ's suffering and feeding flesh because both men and women saw the female body as food and the female nature as fleshly'.[7] She describes this as an empowering phenomenon giving women a means to be like God, offering a vehicle by which they could turn dualist discourses to their own purposes, becoming positively, as opposed to negatively, bodily.[8]

Bynum's project passes incidentally over the problems of the male body and the relationships between different groups of men. She ignores issues of class, race or age and conceives men as an unproblematic standard against which women are measured. She has been challenged by Kathleen Biddick on the grounds that her inquiry avoids the issue of the ethnic body.[9] This essay will show that she also overlooks the physicality of the man who worked with his hands. The working man could be a very fleshly construction. The working man, too, had a special relationship with food and, by extension, Eucharistic devotion. However, my conclusion is not that this gave workmen any greater control or agency. Rather, this discourse often reinforced, whether consciously or unconsciously, the prevailing late medieval social hierarchies.

The image of the honest workman was ubiquitous in estates literature which classified men into three orders: those who fought, those who prayed and those who worked.[10] Humble and poor, the workman fulfilled his social duty when he produced food for the rest of the community. Disseminated via the pulpit, the triadic estates model percolated into the popular consciousness, permeating a range of sources including the self-consciously literary productions of *The Canterbury Tales* and more especially *Piers Plowman*, which enhanced the workman's iconic status.[11] This schema offered a model for those who aspired to eternal life; it operated in the interests of the community's spiritual health. Piers's ploughing of the half-acre in Langland's text is a spiritual pilgrimage, and the fruit of his labour, the symbol of eternal life, is the prize that Christ secures in his joust with the devil.[12] A political vision of the proper structure and condition of earthly society was an epiphenomenon of that spiritual doctrine. The estates model was revived in England in reaction to the labour problems of the late fourteenth century, themselves a corollary of the prevailing demographic shifts.[13] Prior to the Black Death in 1348–9 and the subsequent population fall, much of the English landscape was characterized by intensive arable farming.[14] Land of indifferent fertility was worked by a labour force which was cheap because it was large. Peasant labourers, 'the class potentially most exploitable by the lords, great or small', were compelled to multiply their efforts to achieve subsistence.[15] The poem 'The Song of the Husbandman', first recorded around 1340, describes the exploitation of the peasant agriculturalist through taxation. Continued sequestration of profits and assets lead him to despair that work is futile.[16] Need is not satisfied by work ('Nede in swot and in swynk swynde mot swo'); one might as well die as work so hard ('Ase god is swynden anon as so forte swynke').[17] Thus the husbandman-narrator reveals the abjection of even the highest echelons of the peasantry.[18]

   The rise of labour costs and the plummeting price of land in the decades following the Black Death improved workers' standards of living. Some peasant agriculturalists acquired or added to their land holdings, increasing their workload but also their output. Others found that they could buy leisure time by working fewer hours for the same living.[19] Workers could also migrate in search of a better wage.[20] This seller's labour market rendered workers more powerful than they had been before; these men and women were far from stuck in the rut or furrow, as they had previously been.[21] The Ordinance and Statute of Labourers, in 1349 and 1351 respectively, were attempts to control the labour market artificially and to reposition the labouring population in its traditional place.[22]

The labour legislation of the latter half of the fourteenth century reveals how anxious law-makers were that agricultural workmen should not abandon their occupation which was clearly considered to be crucial, not only to food production processes but also to larger economic and social systems of which agriculture was an integral part. Both literary and legal representations of ploughmen exhorted them to stay at their labour. A statute of 1388 ordained that:

> he or she, which use to labour at the Plough and Cart, or other Labour or Service of Husbandry, till they be of the Age of Twelve Years, that from thenceforth they shall abide at the same Labour, without being put to any Mystery or Handicraft.[23]

The unisex focus of this legislation undermines Bynum's assertion that:

> women had many ways of manipulating and controlling self and environment through food-related behaviour, for food formed the context and shape of women's world – of their responsibilities and privileges – more fundamentally than it did the world of men.[24]

The men under consideration in this essay, however, were crucial to the food production process and their identities were formed, in part, by the work that they did to feed themselves and others.[25] The didactic paradigm of the working man was much more regularly invoked than any positive model of female industry; the historiographical treatments of the centrality of women's labour to the post-plague economy reveal this to be a telling oversight.[26] The search for a healthy body politic was linked to the notion of the industrious but impaired male body; the gathering strength of the workforce was synecdochically signed by pampered and inordinate male bodies. For example, Langland represents a precocious workforce as one overfed on luxury foods; Wastour and his friends duplicitously tuck healthy legs under idle bodies to simulate disability and excuse themselves from work.[27]

While the ploughman literature, energized by current labour concerns, seems at first glance to be socially radical in its sympathy for the put-upon labourer, it is not possible to identify the 'authentic voice' of medieval labour within this group of texts.[28] For example, 'Pierce the Ploughman's Crede', an anti-fraternal satire of about 1394, has been admired for its supposed empathetic portrait of the poor, ragged ploughman and his destitute family. This is the harrowing and much quoted description of his wife:

> His wijf walked him with a longe gode,
> In a cutted cote cutted full heyghe,
> Wrapped in a wynwe schete to weren hire fro weders,
> Barfote on the bare ijs that the blod folwede.[29]

The compelling contrasts of colour and temperature envisioned in this pool of blood leaking on to ice has singled this passage out for special critical attention.[30] Yet elsewhere in the same text the anonymous poet laments the improving educational opportunities for cobblers' sons and beggars' brats.[31] The poem invokes the penurious ploughman in order to embarrass a slothful and luxurious clerical class who are unable to educate the narrator in the *Credo* as Pierce can; there is no commitment, in this text, to the economic and social betterment of the peasantry.

The female mystic, Julian of Norwich, had a vision of a lord and labourer in 1373 which she wrote up in an account of her mystical experience, *A Revelation of Love*.[32] This parable reflects contemporary social and economic concerns and contributes to the cultural discourse which constructed the workman as a bodily figure. The agricultural worker, in her vision, is depicted as a man in pain. The servant falls while running to do the lord's will: 'in which wo he suffrid vii grete peynes. The first was the sore brosyng that he toke in hys fallyng, which was to hym felable peyne'.[33] The hurt the man receives is, she stresses, 'felable' and so corporeal. The figure of the lord recognizes the pain that his servant sustains in his employ:

> Than seith this curtes lord in his menyng: 'Lo, lo, my lovid servant. What harme and disese he hath takeyn in my service for my love, ya, and for his good will! Is it not skyl that I award hym his afray and his drede, his hurt and his maime and al his wo?'[34]

The eager servant is somatically scarred. It is this which gives him a right to his reward.

In these passages work becomes synonymous with physical pain. Indeed, elsewhere the Middle English word 'werk' is glossed by modern editors as 'suffering'.[35] The somatic torment of the ploughman was an eschewing of bodily comforts which rendered the sufferer more spiritually healthy. Paradoxically, however, this emphasized rather than denied the flesh. Moreover, work was somatically signed in innumerable texts at this time by the bodily fluid, sweat.[36] The conventional phrase 'swinke and swete' picked up God's injunction to Adam to work in Genesis 3: 19: 'In the sweat of thy face shalt thou eat bread, till thou return unto the ground'. The phrase, 'to swink and sweat', is alliteratively convenient but also indicates that work and sweat were seen as indivisible phenomena. Julian of Norwich uses the idiom when she describes the workman, whom she recognizes as a representative of the fallen Adam: 'And than I understode that he shuld don the gretest labor and herdest travel that is – he shuld ben a gardiner; delvyn and dykyn, swinkin and swetyn, and turne the earth upsodowne, and sekyn the depnes and wattir the plants in tyme.'[37] Sweat marks the clothing of the servant which is described as 'sengil, old and al defacid, died with the swete of his body'.[38]

Bynum notes, and Joan Cadden's recent work confirms, that it was commonly held in the Middle Ages that bodily fluids were interchangeable.[39] Breast milk flowed directly into the blood of Christ and the wine of the Eucharist: 'all human exudings – menstruation, sweating, lactation, emission of semen and so on – were seen as bleedings; and all bleedings – lactation, menstruation, nosebleeds, haemorrhoidal bleeding and so on – were taken to be analogous.'[40] 'Sweat' was a Middle English synonym for blood; this linguistic coincidence marks a perception that the two were different manifestations of the same substance.[41] Given the homogeneity of bodily fluids, the sweating workman was not substantially different from the lactating mother or, for that matter, the bleeding Christ. Indeed, Julian of Norwich insisted that the bruised and industrious worker was not only Adam but also the humanized Christ. Christ's fall into manhood mimics Adam's fall into the body in Genesis:

> Adam fell fro lif to deth into the slade of this wretchid world and after that into hell. Gods Son fell with Adam into the slade of the mayden

wombe, which was the fairest dauter of Adam, and therfor to exuse
Adam from blame in hevyn and in erth; and mytyly he fetchid him out
of hell.[42]

Anne Laskaya has described the Christlike masculine ideal as one
which insisted on a renunciation of the body and a 'devotion to an
inner world'.[43] But Julian and Langland before her represent the
workman as visually similar to the suffering Christ:

> I fel eftsoones aslepe – and sodeynly me mette
> That Piers the Plowman was peynted al blody,
> And com in with a cros bifore the comune peple,
> And right lik in alle lymes to Oure Lord Jesu.[44]

Working men do not resemble Christ because of any claim to be
'spirit' but because of the condition of their bodies. These authors
were anxious to ascribe the locus of non-fleshly divinity elsewhere:
in Langland's case to Christ himself, in Julian's to the allegorical
figure of the Lord. The workman's bodily denial becomes so great
and he exudes so much sweat that he becomes, in Langland's
words, 'like in alle lymbes' to the crucified Christ.[45] The workman's body and his sweat come to symbolize the flesh and blood of
Christ – the bread and wine of the Eucharist.[46]

The relationship between the workman, food and feeding
further amalgamated his sweating body with that of the bleeding
Christ. The literary and religious representations of exemplary
labouring frequently stressed its twin products: food and the
workman's physical distress. The boundaries between the work
done, the effect on the body and the fruit of that labour were not
clear-cut. Contemporaries used the image of the edible labourer to
castigate feeding idlers, recognizing a social dimension to the
religious motif. The late fourteenth-century *Fasciculus Morum*,
with reference to Habukkuk 3: 14, complained that the idle did not
just waste the food of those who worked but that they actually
devoured the poor:

> In this way the slothful person lives off other people's labour, and what
> others have gained by hard and painful work, he eats up in idleness; the
> Psalmist says: 'They devour the poor man in secret,' that is, the
> sustenance on which the poor should live.[47]

Just as the seed of the tree of life germinates in the mouth and nostrils of the dying Adam in the Middle English *Life of Adam and Eve*, crops seem to grow directly out of the body of the industrious ploughman.[48] The verdancy of the plant he tends is commensurate with the dilapidation of his physical form as he sacrifices his body for the nourishment and salvation of others.

Julian of Norwich, of course, displays a much greater commitment to the notion of the motherhood of God than she does to her depiction of Christ as a workman: her feminine theology is radical and assured. However, she does offer a paradigm of the male body which cannot be described simply as feminized. Recent criticism has pointed to the maternal countenance of the lord figure in the parable of the lord and servant, revealing the absence of a dualist theology in this text.[49] Instead of a gender binary, Julian sees the social dichotomy of lord and labourer as a suitable parallel for the differences between God and man which she is keen to establish as antitheses. While the vision is first shown to her in an eidetic 'bodily' form, she comes in time to understand it as an 'inward gostly shewing'. In her spiritually meaningful interpretation of the vision she identifies the lord with God, heaven and Christ-the-divine, while the agricultural worker is coterminous with Adam, humanity, earth and the humanized Christ.

Julian's conservative dichotomy in the lord and servant parable reinforces class inequality, and the orthodoxy of hegemonic rule goes unquestioned: a social hierarchy is seen as an appropriate and simple rationalization of the relationship between God and man. Her account is poised between strata of visual description and layers of interpretation. She receives and interprets her visions in three phases which directly correspond to Augustine's hierarchy of visionary experience, as noted by Sixten Ringbom:

> Saint Augustine divided visions in three categories: corporeal, spiritual and intellectual; the first being the lowest form and the third the highest, infallible one (*De Gen. ad Litt.* XII. 4ff). Corporeal sight is that of the eyes, when the object is present at the moment of perception. Spiritual vision is that of the spirit, and consists of the recollection of objects earlier seen, or else the imagining of things given in a verbal description. Intellectual vision is connected with the intellect of *mens . . .* and deals with matters intelligible, things that do not have images.[50]

Each time she reaches a new level of interpretation in her revelation she represents her sequential translation up the mystical scale in a way which echoes the hierarchical arrangement of servant and master. In her quest for self-authorization she, understandably, does not stop to champion the causes of the working man.[51] Instead he is chosen as a typical image of inferiority and his body is left as she found it as the traditional and 'natural' location of abject suffering.

In conclusion, therefore, the way in which cultural, legal and religious productions constructed the body in the late medieval period was complex and inspired by disparate motivations. While Bynum's work has successfully analysed discourses of the female body, men's bodies need a more nuanced reading than they have so far received. Toril Moi has called for more polysemic understandings of the body and, in her revival of Simone de Beauvoir's notion of the body as 'situation', recommends that the body is defined in relation to its unique contexts:

> the body is our perspective on the world, and at the same time that body is engaged in a dialectical interaction with its surroundings, that is to say with all the other situations in which the body is placed. The way we experience – live – our bodies is shaped by this interaction. The body is a historical sedimentation of our way of living in the world, and of the world's way of living with us.[52]

In this context, I propose that the bodies of men, not just of workmen but of all kinds of men, idle or occupied, need to be subjected to more protean modes of enquiry.

Notes

[1] I am indebted to Jeremy Goldberg, Lara McClure and Felicity Riddy for their incisive comments on drafts of this article. This essay is derived from my MA thesis which was funded by the British Academy.

[2] Geoffrey Chaucer, *The Riverside Chaucer*, ed. L. D. Benson, 2nd edn (Oxford, 1987), l. 689. All quotations will be from this edn.

[3] See, for example, Robert S. Sturges, *Chaucer's Pardoner and Gender Theory: Bodies of Discourse* (New York, 2000), pp. 13, 28 and 45.

[4] Caroline Walker Bynum, *Holy Feast and Holy Fast: The Religious Significance of Food to Medieval Women* (Berkeley, Los Angeles and London, 1987), pp. 261–2.

[5] Caroline Walker Bynum, *Fragmentation and Redemption: Essays on Gender and the Human Body in Medieval Religion* (New York, 1991), p. 171.

[6] Bynum, *Holy Feast*, p. 208.

[7] Ibid., p. 260.

[8] Bynum, *Fragmentation and Redemption*, p. 149.

[9] Kathleen Biddick, 'Genders, bodies and borders: technologies of the visible', *Speculum* 68 (1993), 389–418 (*passim*).

[10] Ruth Mohl, *The Three Estates in Medieval and Renaissance Literature* (New York, 1933); George Duby, *The Three Orders: Feudal Society Imagined* (Chicago, 1980) and Stephen Knight, 'The voice of labour in fourteenth-century English literature', in J. Bothwell, P. J. P. Goldberg and W. M. Ormrod (eds), *The Problem of Labour in Fourteenth-Century England* (Woodbridge, 2000), pp. 101–22 (pp. 105–6).

[11] Gerald R. Owst, *Literature and Pulpit in Medieval England*, 2nd edn (Oxford, 1961), p. 549. Chaucer, *The Canterbury Tales*, General Prologue, ll. 529–41, and William Langland, *The Vision of Piers Plowman: A Critical Edition of the B-text*, ed. A. V. C. Schmidt, 2nd edn (London, 1987), esp. Passus VI. All quotations will be from this edn.

[12] Langland, *Piers Plowman*, Passus XVIII, ll. 19–20.

[13] Mohl, *The Three Estates*, pp. 140–2, and Rodney Hilton, *Class Conflict and the Crisis of Feudalism* (London, 1985), p. 117.

[14] See James L. Bolton, *The Medieval English Economy 1150–1500* (London, 1980), pp. 36, 59 and 82.

[15] Bolton, *Medieval English Economy*, p. 109.

[16] 'Song of the Husbandman', in J. M. Dean (ed.), *Medieval English Political Writings* (Kalamazoo, 1996), pp. 251–3.

[17] 'Song of the Husbandman', ll. 20 and 72.

[18] Christopher Dyer, 'Piers Plowman and plowmen: a historical perspective', *Yearbook of Langland Studies* 8 (1994), 155–76 (162). The term husbandman denotes 'a substantial peasant, without carrying any stigma of servile status'.

[19] James L. Bolton, ' "The world upside down": plague as an agent of economic and social change', in W. M. Ormrod and P. G. Lindley (eds), *The Black Death in England* (Stamford, 1996), pp. 17–78 (47) and Christopher Dyer, 'Work ethics in the fourteenth century', in Bothwell et al. (eds), *The Problem of Labour*, pp. 21–41 (35).

[20] Bolton, ' "The world upside down" ', p. 47 and Simon A. C. Penn and Christopher Dyer, 'Wages and earnings in late medieval England: evidence from the enforcement of the labour laws', *Economic History Review*, 2nd ser. 43 (1990), 356–76 (362–5).

[21] Christopher Dyer, *Standards of Living In the Later Middle Ages: Social Change in England, c.1200–1520* (Cambridge, 1989), p. 145.

[22] Bolton, *Medieval English Economy*, p. 209; Maurice Keen, *English Society in the Later Middle Ages, 1348–1500* (London, 1990), p. 39 and Christopher Given-Wilson, 'Service, serfdom and English labour legislation, 1350–1500', in A. Curry and E. Matthew (eds), *Concepts and Patterns of Service in the Later Middle Ages* (Woodbridge, 2000), pp. 21–37 (*passim*).

[23] 12 Richard II, c. 5, *Statutes of the Realm*, vol. II, p. 57.

[24] Bynum, *Holy Feast*, p. 208.

[25] David Aers, 'The humanity of Christ: reflections on orthodox late medieval representations', in David Aers and Lynn Staley (eds) *Powers of the Holy: Religion, Politics and Gender in Late Medieval English Culture* (Pennsylvania, 1996), pp. 15–42 (30).

[26] P. Jeremy P. Goldberg, *Women, Work, and Life Cycle in a Medieval Economy: Women in York and Yorkshire, c.1300–1520* (Oxford, 1992), p. 83; Barbara A. Hanawalt (ed.), *Women and Work in Pre-Industrial Europe* (Bloomington, 1986), pp. xv–xvi and Simon A. C. Penn, 'Female wage earners', *Agricultural History Review* 35 (1987), 1–14 (5).

[27] Langland, *Piers Plowman*, esp. Passus VI, ll. 121–8. See also the chroniclers' accounts of the peasant rebellion in 1381. See, for example, Barrie Dobson, *The Peasants' Revolt of 1381*, 2nd edn (London, 1983), p. 368.

[28] Miri Rubin, *Corpus Christi,* cited in Biddick, 'Gender, bodies, borders', p. 415, criticizes Bynum for describing her female subjects as representing the authentic voice of women. Knight, 'The voice of labour', *passim*, also addresses the problems of uncovering 'voices' from the past.

[29] 'Pierce the Ploughman's Crede', in Helen Barr (ed.), *The Piers Plowman Tradition* (London, 1993), ll. 433–5.

[30] For example, Margaret Drabble (ed.), *The Oxford Companion to English Literature*, 5th edn (Oxford, 1985), p. 764 describes this passage as 'the most effective piece of social criticism in Middle English'.

[31] 'Pierce the Ploughman's Crede', ll. 744–5.

[32] Julian of Norwich, *A Revelation of Love*, ed. Marion Glasscoe (Exeter, 1976).

[33] Ibid., p. 72.

[34] Ibid., p. 73.

[35] See, for example, Barry A. Windeatt's notes to Geoffrey Chaucer, *Troilus and Criseyde*, ed. B. A. Windeatt (Harlow, 1990), pp. 103 and 401, and Stephen Barney's notes in Chaucer, *Riverside Chaucer*, p. 549.

[36] David Vance Smith, 'Body doubles: producing the masculine *corpus*', in J. J. Cohen and B. Wheeler (eds), *Becoming Male in the Middle Ages* (New York, 1997), pp. 3–19. For other examples of 'swink and sweat' see Langland, *Piers Plowman*, Passus VI, ll. 25 and 128; 'Pearl', in M. Andrew and R. Waldron (eds), *The Poems of the Pearl Manuscript: Pearl, Cleannness, Patience, Sir Gawain and the Green Knight* (Exeter, 1987), l. 586; 'The Song of the Husbandman', l. 20, and 'The Plowman's Tale', in J. M. Dean (ed.), *Six Ecclesiastical Satires* (Kalamazoo, 1991), ll. 29 and 34.

[37] Julian of Norwich, *Revelation of Love*, p. 77.

[38] Ibid., p. 76.

[39] Joan Cadden, *Meanings of Sex Difference in the Middle Ages: Medicine, Science and Culture* (Cambridge, 1993), p. 183.

[40] Bynum, *Fragmentation*, pp. 109–14.

[41] *Middle English Dictionary*, ed. H. Kurath (Ann Arbor, 1956–), 1(c).

[42] Julian of Norwich, *Revelation of Love*, p. 78.

[43] Anne Laskaya, *Chaucer's Approach to Gender in* The Canterbury Tales (Cambridge, 1995), p. 16.

[44] Langland, *Piers Plowman*, Passus XIX, ll. 5–8.

[45] Ibid., Passus XIX, l. 8.

[46] Others have discerned similar associations between representations of workmen and Eucharistic ritual. See, for example, Richard K. Emmerson and P. Jeremy P. Goldberg, ' "The Lord Geoffrey had me made": lordship and labour in the Luttrell Psalter', in Bothwell et al. (eds), *The Problem of Labour*, pp. 43–63 (esp. p. 62).

[47] Siegfried Wenzel (ed. and trans.), *Fasciculus Morum: A Fourteenth-Century Preacher's Handbook* (Pennsylvania, 1989), pp. 400–1.

[48] 'The Life of Adam and Eve', in Nicholas F. Blake (ed.), *Middle English Religious Prose* (London, 1972), pp. 103–18 (116).

[49] See, for example, Liz Herbert McAvoy, ' "The moders service": motherhood as matrix in Julian of Norwich', *Mystics Quarterly* 24/4 (1998), 181–97 (192) and Sarah McNamer, 'The exploratory image: God as mother in Julian of Norwich's *Revelations of Divine Love*', *Mystics Quarterly* 15/1 (1989), 21–8 (26).

[50] Sixten Ringbom, 'Devotional images and imaginative devotions: notes on the place of art in late medieval private piety', *Gazette des beaux arts* 73 (1969), 159–70 (162).

[51] Ian Johnson, 'Auctricitas? Holy women and their Middle English texts', in Rosalyn Voaden (ed.), *Prophets Abroad: the Reception of Continental Holy Women in Late-Medieval England* (Cambridge, 1996), pp. 177–97.

[52] Toril Moi, 'What is a woman? Sex, gender, and the body in feminist theory', in *What is a Woman? And Other Essays* (Oxford, 1999), p. 68.

5

Reproductive Rites: Anne Askew and the Female Body as Witness in the Acts and Monuments

ತಿ

KIMBERLY ANNE COLES

For this my silence neither your law nor any law in the world is able justly and rightly to punish me. (Thomas More)

> this is a personal matter,
> a private affair and God knows
> none of your business.
> (Anne Sexton, 'Jesus Dies')

The woodcut of Anne Askew's execution in Foxe's *Acts and Monuments* is remarkable for its lack of a central figure.[1] The scene pictured is a bird's eye view of the site of her capital punishment at Smithfield: spectators swarm around a central ring in which four figures are bound to stakes, attendants move about them in preparation for their execution, and a preacher (Nicholas Shaxton) delivers a sermon from a pulpit in the top left-hand section of the ring. The far-left figure on the line, bound at the waist, presumably depicts Anne Askew. Although this illustration was not originally commissioned by John Day for the *Acts and Monuments*,[2] its use here to punctuate Foxe's account of Askew's martyrdom is expressive: the woodcut maps the pattern of her corporeal displacement which occurs within the text.

In the martyrologies of Thomas Cranmer, John Hooper or Nicholas Ridley, the verbal record of their bodies in the text is detailed (and often gruesome), echoing in many ways traditional

Execution of Anne Askew. Engraving on p. 1420 of the *Acts and Monuments* by John Foxe (1570). Mason F 143, vol. 2. Reproduced by kind permission of the Bodleian Library, University of Oxford.

representations of the martyred body in medieval hagiographic texts – something which Liz Herbert McAvoy examines in the context of anchoritic privation later in this volume. In contrast to these martyrologies, however, the instruments of Askew's corporeality – her voice and her body – are oddly decentred in her narrative. The story of Anne Askew's examinations and martyrdom is particular within the *Acts and Monuments* because she was a woman who wrote her own account of events (although the status of her autobiographical voice is troubled by the fact that it is redacted by John Bale). What is perhaps most interesting in the account is the extent to which – and the places where – her voice and body are deliberately withheld. When questioned by the English authorities Askew often offers silence as a form of resistance. At moments when the physical fact of her body registers in the text, she works to conceal it from public view. This essay will trace the reasons for this elision of her material subjectivity, and then go on to explore the effect that this rhetorical manœuvre produces within the context of the *Acts and Monuments*.

In her article, 'Pain, persecution, and the construction of selfhood', Janel Mueller notices the doctrinal reformulations by which Marian martyrs articulate the experience of their bodies in pain. Mueller argues (among other things) that the process of trials for heresy – which denied silence as an alternative for the accused, and maintained the legally sanctioned mode of execution, burning at the stake, as a present threat during these exchanges – produced the terms of embodiment that were an integral part of the debate.[3] Askew's account of her trials, by contrast, refuses this construction. The argument that follows is not an attempt to challenge Mueller's outline of the composition of martyred identity, but to extend its boundaries – to explore the construction of martyrdom that occurs when the subject is positioned at the edges of the religious debate.

Askew left her Catholic husband, Thomas Kyme, and two children, and migrated from her home in Friskney, Lincolnshire, to London (for the purpose of seeking a divorce).[4] As a married woman who lacked the protection of her husband, Askew was extremely vulnerable when she was arrested 'for certeyn matters concernying the vi Articles'.[5] She was first detained in March 1545, and subsequently rearrested in June 1546. Although she may have had other detentions (Charles Wriothesley, the Windsor Herald, records another arraignment on 13 June 1545[6]), these two are the subject of her first and latter *Examinations*. She wrote her record of her trials either in separate instalments, or at one time in the intervening days between her condemnation and execution. What is most interesting about these accounts – particularly given the preceding models – is their habit of veiled speech.[7]

As a testament to her faith, Askew's narrative is unsatisfying; she, unlike other (male) martyrs who recorded their ordeals (either in letters or as part of treatises), does not 'publish [her] mynde'.[8] In spite of the public act of authorship, Askew's text registers a radically interior self-construction, and a reluctance to exhibit the private precincts of belief. Religion is the optic through which Askew's distinctive rhetorical habits need to be viewed. This is not to say that her discourse is devoid of gender differentials – in fact, I will suggest the opposite. Her discursive practices (both in the course of defying Henrician religious authority and in how she records the procedure of her examinations) clearly register the convictions of Protestantism at an inaugural moment; these convictions, however, are inflected in her writing by her female position.

The only personal history written from prison during the reign of Henry VIII that bears some resemblance to the *Examinations* is *The articles wherefore John Frith died* (1533) which are annexed to Frith's answer to Thomas More concerning the sacrament. This is quite possibly the treatise that Askew was reading when Archdeacon John Wymesley warned her that 'Such bookes as this, hath brought you to the trouble ye are in'.[9] The appended *articles* give some account of the examinations that Frith underwent, but they are mostly a point-by-point answer to the charges that condemned him. Such a publication of his system of belief, he himself observes, is sure to purchase him a 'moste cruell deth'.[10] It is precisely this kind of exposure which Askew's narrative refuses.

The first *Examination* is confined exclusively to public events; it witnesses the procedures that took place during the course of Askew's detention. Her defence during her interrogations takes two forms: silence or scripture. She manipulates the traditional role of her sex in order to avoid entrapment, and when this tactic fails, she resorts to a textual authority that cannot be assailed. When twice called upon to clarify her meaning concerning the scriptural passage 'god dwelleth not in temples made with hands'

(Acts 17: 24) – the answer to which could secure her conviction – she gestures in both directions during the same interrogation (and in a single response). She tells Doctor Standish, one of the theologians examining her, that it is counter to 'Saynt Paules learnyng, that I beyng a woman, should intreprete the Scriptures, specially where so many wise learned men were'.[11] When Edmund Bonner, the bishop of London, probes her for a more satisfying answer to the question she responds:

> I beleue as the Scripture doth teache me. Then inquired hee of me, what if the Scripture do say that it is the body of Christ? I beleue, sayd I, as the Scripture doth teache me. Then asked he againe, what if the Scripture do say that it is not the body of Christ? My aunswere was still, I beleue as the Scripture informeth me . . . Then he asked me, why I had so fewe wordes? And I aunswered, God hath geuen me the gift of knowlege, but not of vtterance. And Salomon sayth, *that a woman of few wordes is a gift of God, Prou. xix.*[12]

Called 'tanswere to the lawe' for her 'obstinate' opinions in 'matiers of religion',[13] she uses the roles available to her – reformist or female – in order to open space for manœuvre. Rather than the usual interrogations that are played out in 'Foxe's Book of Martyrs' (*Acts and Monuments*), in which both sides assert their contrary formulations of religious meaning, Askew's record of her trials transcribes the system of evasion by which she keeps her meaning indeterminate.[14]

Askew cannot enter the polemical discourse into which John Frith inserts himself – she is barred by virtue of gender, education and Pauline proscription. Upbraided by the 'Byshoppes chaunceller' for 'utterynge the scriptures' counter to St Paul's directive, she tells him that she knows 'Paules meaning as well as he, which is in the Corinthians 14, that a woman ought not to speake in the Congregation, by the way of teaching'.[15] Regardless of her willingness to instruct the members of the quest, her adherence to scriptural regulation would not have allowed her to enter into the public debate concerning transubstantiation being waged in numerous treatises. Rather, her authority rests on the power to interpret scripture for herself. She owns, and asserts her right to own, a private faith. 'I take the . . . most mercifull God of *mine*', she writes, 'to recorde that I hold no opinions contrarie to his most holy word.'[16] The structure of her faith is founded upon an individual grasp of scripture: it privileges local and positional truths. Unlike Frith, or even her fellow martyr John Lascelles, she does not use the platform of her interrogations to answer the articles with which she is charged. Throughout the first half of the second *Examination* she continues her tactic of circumspection, and refuses to locate her position concerning the sacrament. Then the course of the narrative abruptly changes: 'the bishop [Stephen Gardiner] sayd I should be burnt.'[17] Once her condemnation is pronounced, her voice becomes more expansive and takes on the assertions of faith. From the moment of Gardiner's judgment, she is willing to declare openly her opinion concerning sacramental ontology; her confessions of belief, however, still retain a markedly different quality from other narratives contemporary to her (or the testaments of the Marian martyrs that follow). Like the men who wrote accounts of the events that led up to their martyrdoms (or the faith that brought them there), her identity formation is laid on ideological ground; unlike them, it is stylistically privatized. 'I beleue,' she writes in her confession of faith, 'we nede no vnwritten verities to rule his church with. Therefore looke what he hath sayd vnto *me* with hys own mouth, in hys holy Gospell, that haue I with Gods grace, closed up in *my* hart.'[18] Askew does not enter the arena of sermonizing in which Frith or Lascelles, with their masculine privilege, feel free to engage. When she articulates her belief, her disclosure takes the form of scriptural citation; her understanding of God's verity is individually apprehended, and is 'closed up in [her] hart'. She writes from a singular, marginalized position – and the place from which she writes confirms the extent of her isolation: 'Truth is layd in prison.'[19]

The acts of rhetorical self-enclosure that mark Askew's text are continued in her treatment of her body. Just following Gardiner's announcement of his lethal intentions, Askew writes that 'on the sonday I was sore sicke, thinking no lesse then to die . . . Then was I sent to Newgate in my extremitie of sickenes: for in all my life afore was I neuer in such paine. Thus the Lord strengthen vs in the truth.'[20] What is remarkable about this recollection is her profound understatement. She does not concentrate on the natural fact of her bodily suffering, even at a time when illness threatens to carry her off. Pain registers for only a moment in the text – her focus quickly shifts to 'the truth' that allows her to endure it. The construction of selfhood that she articulates here has a dual aspect:

a material element that can be tried, and a spiritual self-possession which sustains her in the midst of physical extremity. The body's torment becomes the means by which faith is fortified. This construction of her body is more pronounced at a later point in the narrative, when its physical limits are tested on the rack. After she was condemned to death, Lord Chancellor Wriothesley and Richard Rich, hoping to gain information that would discredit Queen Katherine Parr, tortured her:

> Then they did put me on the racke, because I confessed no Ladys or Gentle-women to be of my opinion, and theron they kept me a longe tyme. And because I lay stil and did not cry, my L. Chauncellour and [master Rich], tooke paines to racke me with their owne handes, till I was nigh dead.[21]

The remarkable restraint of this passage is often noticed; what I wish to remark upon here is its disembodied quality. We understand her bodily experience obliquely: she does not observe her pain, only her response to it. Until she tells us that she was racked 'till [she] was nigh dead' we have no sense of the extent of her physical suffering. She relates her inability to stand up, and the experience of lying on the floor for hours as Wriothesley works to rob her of her belief:

> Then the Lieftenaunt caused me to be loosed from the racke. Incontinently I swounded . . . After that I satte ii. long hours reasonyng with my Lord Chancellor vppon the bare flore, wheras he with many flattering wordes, perswaded me to leaue my opinion. But my lord God (I thanke his euerlasting goodnes) gaue me grace to perseuer.[22]

Her torture is imparted as a series of sensory events; she admits bodily awareness but not bodily experience. Here (as in the episode of her illness), her consciousness divides into two parts: a corporeal reality, and a realm of experience that she fixes as interior and private. Wriothesley applies physical torment in an attempt to probe and extract the inner recesses of her belief – to (in Elaine Scarry's resonant phrase) 'unmake [her] world'.[23] In denying her body she denies her tormentors access to the interior spaces that they are trying to dismantle; if she disowns the effect of her body-breaking – she lies still and does not cry – she retains the inner truth that torture is designed to discover. At moments of acute bodily suffering, Askew is 'strengthen[ed] . . . in the truth', or endowed with 'grace': rather than her inner world crumbling during physical distress, she perceives in pain the opportunity for the 'making of [her] soul'.[24]

Following her racking, Askew writes that:

> Then was I brought to an house, and laid in a bed with as werye and painful bones, as euer had pacient *Iob*, I thanke my Lord God therof. Then my Lord Chauncellour sent me worde if I would leaue my opinion, I should want nothing: If I would not, I should forth to Newgate, & so be burned. I sent hym agayn word, that I would rather die, then to breake my faith.[25]

She thanks God for her pain. Askew's conception of faith contains a persecutory imagination similar to that of the male martyrs noted earlier. She seems convinced that physical torment marks the members of God's true church – that, as William Tyndale writes, the faithful 'suffer with [Christ] that [they] may also be glorified wyth hym'.[26] But she does not conceive of herself in the spectacular terms of these prominent clerics. For her, it is not a matter of serving as an example by which others will come to comprehend the true meaning of the gospel. It is an exclusively local matter: 'I would rather die, then to breake my faith.' Askew's model of witness depends upon maintaining the integrity of her soul against the disintegration of her body.

Janel Mueller's study records Protestant reconfigurations of union with the divine that serve as a counterpart to Catholic conceptions of real presence. Catholic doctrine affirmed a direct physical communion with God. Protestantism recast the embodied presence of Catholic belief into the abstract terms of rhetoric. As Mueller observes, the activity of establishing an opposing ontology of presence to the Catholic formulation produced in the Protestant debate a pattern of complex figurative relations between the human and divine body.[27] Those reforming churchmen who understood their disputation (both oral and written) as the means of doctrinal formation configured the meanings of the Eucharist so that the whole process could be apprehended differently. The semiotic structure that they plotted is conceived in bodily terms: the process of setting out an alternative system of meaning for the

Protestant community created an embodied rhetoric. In his disputations at Oxford, Thomas Cranmer articulates the Protestant formulation of sacramental presence:

> Christ saith not thus: *Thys is my body, eate ye*: but after he had bydden them eate, then he sayd: *This is my body, which shall be geuen for you.* Whych is to meane, as though he should say: In eatyng of thys bread, consider you that this bread is no common thing, but a mysticall matter: neither do you attend that which is set before your bodely eyes, but what fedeth you with in. Consider and behold my body crucified for you: that eate and digest in your myndes. Chawe you upon my passion, be fed with my death. This is the true meate, thys is the drinke that moisteneth, wherewith you being truly fed and inebriate, shall liue for ever.[28]

Protestant figurations of the mass replaced the Catholic story of communion with the divine – in which Christ's body miraculously inhabits the host and is subsequently ingested by the faithful – with a different method of absorption. Rather, the bread is digested, but the sacrament is not taken in except by an act of mental figuration; an understanding through faith of the signification of the sacrament allows the faithful member to receive its benefits. Nicholas Ridley outlines the way in which the sacrament is to be understood:

> The Analogie of the sacramentes is necessary: For if the sacramentes had not some similitude or lykenes of the things whereof they be sacraments, they could in no wyse be sacraments. And this similitude in the Sacrament of the Lordes Supper, is taken three manner of wayes.
> 1 The first consisteth in nourishing: as ye shall reade in *Rabane, Cyprian, Augustine, Irenee*, & most plainly in *Isodore* out of *Bertram.*
> 2 The second, in the vniting and ioyning of many into one, as *Cyprian* teacheth.
> 3 The thyrd is a similitude of vnlike things: where, lyke as the bread is turned into our body: so we, by the right vse of this Sacrament, are turned through fayth into the body of Christ.[29]

Ridley's system of conversion focuses upon natural processes rather than supernatural intervention. Bread is no longer miraculously transformed, but signifies a miracle once performed. The Protestant project of finding alternative material meanings for the Eucharist created a focus on the natural body. The absence of miracles necessarily carried the material facts of the process down to the level of physical experience (chewing bread, drinking wine, nourishing the body).

It is at this level of experience that we witness the embodied constructions of martyred identity to which Mueller pays extended attention (particularly as it is the bodies of the Protestant ecclesiastics who developed the opposing doctrine of negative presence that served to confirm it). A rhetoric preoccupied with sacramental ontology and the organics of the body was converted into a descriptive discourse of painful witness when human bodies burned. John Frith insists that his death is required so that the 'congregacion of Christe' will not be bound 'by [his] example': perceiving themselves as examples to be followed, these men also seem to have conceived of themselves as spectacles. 'Your cause is Christs gospell,' Tyndale tells Frith in a letter designed to encourage him; 'a light that must be fed with the bloud of faith. The lampe must be dressed and snuffed dayly, and that oyle poured in . . . that ye light go not out.'[30] Tyndale plays upon metaphors of burning to emphasize the proselytizing effect of his fellow reformer's death: Frith will be the light by which others see the meaning of the gospel. Hugh Latimer invokes a similar metaphor in his famous exhortation to Ridley at the stake: 'we shall this day lyght such a candle by Gods grace in England, as (I trust) shall neuer be put out'.[31] These articulations stress the importance that early reformers attached to such spectacles in the project of spreading Protestant doctrine – but by the treatment of their bodies as wicks or raw materials for the consumption of the flames, it also expresses the hideous changes that the body will undergo during its trial by fire.

But Askew does not follow the figurations of male martyrs in which the unstable borders of their bodies give way to transformation; she envisions no alchemical process by which she will be organically converted into the body of Christ. Foxe, however, needs such spectacular bodies. His history of the Protestant struggle against the Catholic Church required a kind of visible record: one that figured bodily sacrifice through words. Askew does not understand herself as a public issue ('a singular example of Christen constancie for all men to folowe'); her discourse is organized at the level of personal faith.[32] It is her acts of self-enclosure that make Askew an 'eccentric subject' within John Foxe's narrative in the *Acts and Monuments*;[33] such an inward self-construction does not fit the design of Foxe's project. Foxe needs to make the enigma of belief readable; his only means of doing this is to tell the story of the body that suffers for faith. Foxe, therefore, brings Anne Askew's body back into the narrative. It is precisely Askew's gestures towards an interiority that Foxe cancels in order to make her subjectivity a textual fact.

In the 1570 edition of the *Acts and Monuments*, Foxe intrudes upon her account at the moment of her racking in order to emphasize the suffering that she will not concede. He describes, in an extended passage, how the rack was stretched 'til her bones & ioyntes almost were pluckt a sonder', and her body so mangled by the instrument that she had to be taken from the Tower in a chair.[34] Foxe feminizes her at this moment as well: according to his scenario, the lieutenant in charge, Anthony Knyvett, 'tenderyng the weaknes of the woman', refuses to torture her further. After he defies their orders, Wriothesley and Rich grab the wheel them- selves. This added moment serves to stress the horror of the scene, and the irregularity of torture performed upon a woman.[35] But Askew makes no mention of this; rather, she says that the two men tormented her because she *did not cry*. It was (according to her) her silent endurance, not her jailer's compassion, that so provoked her persecutors.

Foxe evokes her broken body as it is carried to the stake: 'the day of her execution beyng appoynted, she was brought into Smithfield in a chaire, because she could not go on her feete, by meanes of her great torments'.[36] He tells us that she 'was tied by the middle with a chayne' at the pyre in order to support her body.[37] Foxe's descriptions work to bring Askew's corporeality to the centre. Without a displayed carcass, Foxe has no means to demonstrate the enclosed sphere of faith – the subjects of his stories must be visible bodies. Askew purposefully denies her body and privileges a private realm of experience in her discourse. As his commentary frames her account, this results in a strange distortion of her appearance in the narrative. The effect of their conflicting rhetorical manœuvres is that there is a movement of Askew's body to the borders of her story; the tensions between the inward direction of her discourse and Foxe's aim to make inner truth plain and readable result in the marginalization of her body in the text.

Because Anne Askew does not plot the points of Protestant sacramental meaning, her rhetoric does not assume the embodied terms visible in the writings of dissident scholars. She does not conceive of herself as either example or spectacle for the Protestant cause; her physical body, therefore, does not bear witness. John Foxe's purpose is to make her available to a popular audience. In the discourse of the body that marked the martyrology genre, Foxe writes Askew as a visible subject. These competing intentions produce a dislocation of her body within the text: she both appears, and crucially does not appear, in Foxe's edition of her narrative. As in the woodcut scene of her execution, Askew's bodily presence within the *Acts and Monuments* is incongruous – fractured, decentred, both exhibited and hidden.[38]

Notes

[1] This woodcut appears in all of the sixteenth-century edns of the *Acts and Monuments* (1563, 1570, 1576, 1583, 1596).

[2] It was first used by Day for a 1548 pamphlet by Robert Crowley, *The confutation of xiii. articles wherunto N. Shaxton . . . subscribed*, STC 6083. See John King, *English Reformation Literature: The Tudor Origins of the Protestant Tradition* (Princeton, 1982), pp. 439–40.

[3] Janel Mueller, 'Pain, persecution, and the construction of selfhood', in Claire McEachern and Debora Shuger (eds), *Religion and Culture in Renaissance England* (Cambridge, 1997), pp. 161–87 (165).

[4] *The Examinations of Anne Askew*, ed. Elaine Beilin (Oxford, 1996), p. xix; see also Susan Brigden, *London and the Reformation* (Oxford, 1989), p. 371.

[5] City of London records confirm Askew's first detention on 10 March 1545 (C.L.R.O Repertory 11, fo. 174v).

[6] Charles Wriothesley, *A Chronicle of England During the Reigns of the Tudors: From A.D. 1485 to 1559*, ed. William Douglas Hamilton (London, 1875), I, pp. 155–6.

[7] The antecedent form is the *book of William Thorpe*, a title often cited among the books owned by Lollard suspects (see, for example, *Acts and Monuments* (1570), 969, 1188–9, (1576), 804). Ritchie Kendall notes the importance of the examination within Lollard writing, and locates Askew's narrative within a reformist tradition that worked from these paradigms; see *The Drama of Dissent: The Radical Poetics of Nonconformity* (Chapel Hill, 1986), pp. 123–8.

[8] John Frith, *A boke . . . answeringe unto M. mores lettur*, STC 11381, A2ᵛ.

[9] John Foxe, *The First [second] Volume of the Ecclesiasticall history contaynyng the Actes and Monuments* (London, 1570), 1415.

[10] *A boke made by John Frith*, A2ᵛ.

[11] *Acts and Monuments*, 1415.

[12] Ibid.

[13] *Acts of the Privy Council of England*, ed. John Roche Dasent (London, 1890), I, p. 462.

[14] For more on this, see in particular Paula McQuade, ' "Except that they had

offended the Lawe": gender and jurisprudence in *The Examinations of Anne Askew'*, *Literature and History*, 3rd ser. 3 (1994), 1–14; Elizabeth Mazzola, 'Expert witnesses and secret subjects: Anne Askew's *Examinations* and Renaissance self-incrimination', in Carole Levin and Patricia Sullivan (eds), *Political Rhetoric, Power, and Renaissance Women* (Albany, 1995), pp. 157–71; Thomas Betteridge, 'Anne Askewe, John Bale, and Protestant history', *Journal of Medieval and Early Modern Studies* 27 (1997), 265–84; and Megan Matchinske, *Writing, Gender and State in Early Modern England: Identity Formation and the Female Subject* (Cambridge, 1998), ch. 1.

[15] *Acts and Monuments*, 1414.

[16] Ibid., 1419; my emphasis.

[17] Ibid., 1417.

[18] Ibid., 1419; my emphasis.

[19] Ibid., 1417.

[20] Ibid.

[21] *Acts and Monuments*, 1418. In the 1570 and 1576 edns, 'master Rich' is changed to 'Syr Iohn Baker' (and is subsequently changed back).

[22] Ibid.

[23] Elaine Scarry, *The Body in Pain: The Making and Unmaking of the World* (Oxford, 1985).

[24] Elizabeth Hanson, 'Torture and truth in Renaissance England', *Representations*, 34 (1991), p. 56. Hanson is referring here to the practice of inflicting pain as a form of penance among certain Catholic orders. However, it seems clear to me that the predisposition of religious training is not required to produce this psychology, only the torture of the physical body in an attempt to make the conscience apostatize.

[25] *Acts and Monuments*, 1418.

[26] Ibid., 1231.

[27] Mueller, 'Pain, persecution, and the construction of selfhood', *passim*.

[28] *Acts and Monuments*, 1595.

[29] Ibid., 1610.

[30] Ibid., 1231.

[31] Ibid., 1937. The evidence suggests that Latimer never actually spoke these words (see Thomas Freeman, 'Texts, lies, and microfilm: reading and misreading Foxe's "Book of Martyrs"', *Sixteenth Century Journal* 30 (1999), 42–5). But whether the source of the metaphor was Latimer or Foxe, the point is the same.

[32] Ibid.

[33] Teresa de Lauretis, 'Eccentric subjects: feminist theory and historical consciousness,' *Feminist Studies* 16 (1990), 115–50.

[34] *Acts and Monuments*, 1419.

[35] See McQuade, 'Except that they had offended the Lawe', p. 10.

[36] *Acts and Monuments*, 1420.

[37] Ibid.

[38] Part of this present work appears in an extended article in *Modern Philology* 99: 4. I would like to thank the editors for their thoughtful readings of this essay; I would also like to thank Thomas Betteridge, John Carey, Thomas Freeman, David Scott Kastan, Emma Smith and Nigel Smith whose sound advice helped to shape it.

6

'Such Stowage as These Trinkets': Trading and Tasting Women in Fletcher and Massinger's The Sea Voyage (1622)

TERESA WALTERS

The Sea Voyage, like *The Tempest*, begins with a storm at sea. And like *The Tempest*, in which the storm-wracked ship's troubling gynaecological functions – that make her 'leaky as an unstaunched wench' (*Tempest*, 1. 1. 45–6) – are accorded partial blame for the coming disaster, Fletcher and Massinger's play presents a commonplace attribution of 'trouble at sea' to a woman's presence – and more precisely, to her threatening reproductive/sexual capacities.[1] The ship's master demands that the French pirate Captain Albert take Aminta, whom he has abducted, below deck:

> Carry her down, captain,
> Or, by these hands, I'll give no more direction,
> Let the ship sink or swim. We have ne'er better luck
> When we ha' such stowage as these trinkets with us,
> These sweet sin-breeders. How can heaven smile on us
> When such a burden of iniquity
> Lies tumbling like a potion in our ship's belly?[2]

As well as situating women *per se* as harbingers of ill fortune, this over-determined misogynistic rant positions Aminta confusingly as both precious and worthless, and as both subject and object. It also gives her both male and female body parts, making her a monstrous catalyst in a chain of social, natural and cosmic disruption.

Aminta is 'stowage' or cargo and therefore a surplus-producing commodity;[3] at the same time she is a 'trinket' – a worthless object with only superficial appeal. Oxymoronically, she is a *'sweet* sin-breeder' provoking sexual desire, inviting sin and reproducing more sin from her body. She is both subject to and willing agent of this sexual provocation. And at the same time as being defined by her womb, she is a depraved foetal 'burden' and masculinized as a 'potion' of semen frothing in the ship's womb or 'belly': she is receptacle, contained and penetrating. Not only does her presence disrupt the homosocial order amongst the men, but also the 'natural' order in which men and women keep to their own parts (and the first of six cross-dressing boy actors appearing on the stage could only have intensified this). Even the cosmic order, which ordains whether heaven should 'smile on' them, is unsettled by her presence. In sum, she is defined by and as her sex organs and their functions; and the master wants her put in her place *below* deck.[4]

This initial moment of semantic disruption sets the scene for the main focus of this essay, which is the relations of colonial and sexual exchange. By teasing out the disordered referential chain that this passage sets in motion and that the play, despite its comic resolution, leaves suspended, I will be arguing that *The Sea Voyage* dramatizes, amongst other aspects of Britain's colonial history, anxieties about the early seventeenth-century trade in trinkets with native Americans and the 'traffic' in women between the Virginia Company's London offices and the Jamestown colonists.

Several critics have, in fact, pointed to the colonial contexts and co-texts of the production of Fletcher's travel plays. While Anthony Parr, the play's most recent editor, argues that *The Sea Voyage*'s 'very abundance of analogy' with popular voyage literature suggests that 'the play refutes any attempt to tie it exclusively to a particular place or venture',[5] Gordon McMullan and Andrew Hadfield concur in seeing the play as casting an equivocal or even critical light on the Virginian enterprise in particular, as well as on colonial projects in general.[6] McMullan also draws attention to Fletcher's possible involvement as investor in the Virginia Company.

Before situating the play alongside the 1622 crisis in colonial relations in Jamestown, and the trading history that preceded it, it might be useful to provide a brief summary of the action of *The Sea Voyage*. The French party come ashore on a barren island and discover two stranded Portuguese men, who show them their gold and, while the French fight over it, steal their ship – to return later. Captain Albert swims to the neighbouring and more plentifully supplied island seeking food for Aminta, and is found by members of a commonwealth of Portuguese women who have modelled themselves on the tribe of Amazons who were the island's former occupants. These women agree to rescue the men for the purposes of pleasure and procreation; meanwhile the French gallants and the ship's surgeon threaten to eat Aminta. The women sail across to choose their sexual partners, and are offered the gold that the Portuguese left behind, as a kind of marriage settlement, but recognize the gold to be *their* treasure, lost with their husbands after a pirate invasion, and imprison the French men, pending execution. The Portuguese men then return in the nick of time to prove that they have not been murdered, nor had their gold stolen by these particular pirates. All the couples are either promised in marriage or reunited.

In numerous instances of early trade between Europeans and native Americans, the Europeans claimed advantage. Some, such as Thomas Harriot, register this with a sense of respectful wonder. The 'naturall inhabitants', of Virginia, he notes in 1587, 'for want of skills and judgement in the knowledge of our things, doe esteeme our trifles before things of greater value'.[7] Others see gifts of trinkets as having a pacifying potential in Anglo-Indian relations. In his account of Humphrey Gilbert's 'discovery' of the lands north of Florida, Sir George Peckham recommends that before using violence, the Christian settlers should make the 'savages' understand that they come 'not to their hurt but for their good, and to no other ende, but to dwell peaceably amongst them'.[8] 'To further this', he argues, if language fails them, words should be exchanged for 'deedes'; 'there must bee presented unto them gratis, some kinds of our pettie marchandizes and trifles'.[9]

Captain Gabriel Archer, an early Jamestown colonist, reports of the 1607 meeting with the Algonquian leader, Powhatan, that 'gyftes of dyvers sortes, as penny knyves, sheeres, belles, beades, glasse toyes &c.' pleased Powhatan greatly, and assumes that these proffered trifles provided ample recompense for the food and entertainments freely given by the Algonquians.[10] Most of the early accounts, however, take a more gloating tone as gift-giving is exchanged for explicit bargaining. John Smith explains how, in the interim period before the colony's crops grew and cattle multiplied, 'I durst vndertake to haue corne enough from the Saluages for 300 men, for a few trifles'. However, should this fail, he says, and 'they should bee vntoward (as it is most certaine they are) thirty or forty good men will be sufficient to bring them all in subiection, and make this prouision'.[11]

The exchange of trinkets, then, stood in for, and staved off, more violent means of conquest, functioning to keep the natives in their (subordinate) place and serving as a bolster to the Europeans' often insecure sense of cultural superiority. Joan Pong Linton follows this discursive trend in the journals of Columbus, arguing that while the Indians 'are constructed as gullible consumers', the construction can be contested on the grounds of cultural relativity – what may seem worthless becomes acceptable currency in the process of inter-cultural exchange.[12] As Helen C. Rountree points out, the English 'trinkets' and 'trash' – glass beads, for example – could have been highly desirable because they corresponded with 'the rare or hard-to-make things that had long been a sign of wealth and power in Powhatan Society'.[13]

The downplaying of the gifts proffered may well also betray a disavowal on the part of the English: while they 'crossed the Atlantic expecting to dominate and transform the natives', as Martin H. Quitt notes, 'after landing, they had to rely on trade with the Powhatans for their sustenance'.[14] Without Algonquian corn, they could – and did – starve. Furthermore, the trinkets were not necessarily accepted in the spirit in which they were given: the satisfaction displayed by the natives, argues Quitt, 'was in part obligatory and in part prospective . . . it was not the object itself but the concomitant bond it signified that invested it with value'.[15] Having learned the European bartering system, and realized the minimal part that friendship played within it, Powhatan quickly came to demand not trinkets, but tools and firearms, in exchange for his corn.[16]

On their part, the English – who were rarely specialists in husbandry in the early years, or even willing labourers – were unwilling to accept that the Indian women's virtual monopoly over corn production might have carried high esteem or to give up their dreams of instant wealth in exchange for an emasculating share of the Indian women's work.[17] This left the English ill equipped and highly vulnerable, and their later resort to guns, Quitt argues, was 'a belated recognition that they could not dominate in a free marketplace of cultural exchange'.[18]

In the world of *The Sea Voyage*, the plight of the various stranded parties clearly acknowledges that demand determines value and not intrinsic worth: without food, ships, water or prospects for procreation, gold is merely a useless distraction. Aboard ship, women's exchange value cannot be cashed in. What is one person's trinket is another's treasure; it depends on one's position.

The gallants in the play embody the role of early merchant adventurers, who have converted titles to money, and money to goods, and expect to exchange their goods for land and titles in the New World. Ordered to lighten the ship's load by throwing their possessions overboard, Franville and Lamure resist:

Franville: Will ye throw away my lordship that I sold,
        Put it into clothes and necessaries
        To go to sea with (1. 2. 131–3)

Lamure: Must my goods over too?
        Why, honest master, here lies all my money,
        The money I ha' racked by usury
        To buy new lands and lordships in new countries
                      (1. 2. 115–18)

Despite these hopeful exchanges, titles, clothes and goods all become worthless. What the play insists upon is the need for exchanging the right kind of commodities. While the Portuguese men have plenty of gold, they have nothing to eat or drink:

Sebastian: Here's nothing but rocks and barrenness,
        Hunger and cold to eat. Here's no vineyards
        To cheer the heart of man, no crystal rivers (1. 3. 24–6)

and when the pirates fight over the treasure and lose their ship in the process, they come to occupy the same position. Tibalt mocks the gallants' greed, saying, 'You shall have gold – yes, I'll cram it int'ee' (1. 3. 197), emphasizing the uselessness of gold in the face of hunger.[19]

The worthless treasure is temporarily revalued with the onset of heterosexual exchange, as an inter-gender settlement for the women's sexual favours. But almost immediately it becomes the sign of disorder and greed. French gold-lust, we discover, was the cause of the Portuguese's initial flight from their colony, and the cause of the death of the first wave of pirates – the fathers of Albert's band – who fought to the death over it (5. 2. 90–116).

Albert, chastened by the history of the fathers' demise, recognizes the gold that caused their deaths as the same 'fatal muck we quarrelled for' (5. 2. 30). From medieval times usage of the word 'muck' signified not only dirt or filth, but also dung, as well as worldly wealth or money, an analogy which was still a familiar topos during the early modern period.[20] But despite the treasure's symbolic course – from the (plundered) wealth of the original Portuguese colony, to a pile of trinkets that divert the pirates' eyes, to a tempting bride price and to dangerous excrement – with the play's denouement it is purged of these associations and returned to its original place. With ship, food, heterosexual coupling and the promise of a future, it takes up its original function as currency.

The Sea Voyage satirizes the unpreparedness – in terms of human and material resources, expectations and skills – that characterized the early Jamestown experience. Despite the hopes of Peckham and others, the export of English cloth, England's primary export elsewhere, did not flourish in the Americas. Instead, the English themselves became consumers – of the Spaniards' West Indian tobacco. However, by 1616, the almost exclusive planting of tobacco had established the English James-town colony's commercial viability, while leaving the colonists still dependent for food on English shipments and Algonquian groups.[21]

Another English export achieved slightly more success in Virginia: the trade in English 'maids'. After disastrous attempts at settlement in Roanoke, and the leanest periods in Jamestown, women had been discouraged from emigrating. And some of those who *were* sent (such as the women from Bridewell) were considered by the colonists to be unsuitable.[22]

In the minutes of a Virginia Company court of 3 November 1619, the company clerk reports Edwin Sandys's proposals for the particularly *social* development of the Jamestown colony:

> Lastly he wished that a fitt hundreth might be sent of woemen, Maids young and vncorrupt to make wifes to the Inhabitants and by that meanes to make the men there more setled & less moueable who by defect thereof (as is credibly reported) stay there but to gett something and then to returne for England wch will breed a dissolucon, and so an ouerthrow of the Plantacon. These woemen if they marry to the publiq ffarmors, to be transported at the charges of the Company; If otherwise, then those that takes them to wife to pay the said Company their charges of transportacon, and it was neuer fitter time to send them then nowe.[23]

The reduction in the male colonist's geographical and political 'moveability', it appeared, would accord with the degree of the women's moral or sexual purity, and the degree to which this would *breed* stability rather than dissolution.

In 1619 – when the end of indentured service in Jamestown meant that private tobacco production rose rapidly – ninety women, skilled daughters of artisans and gentry, were shipped by the Virginia Company 'at the publike charge' as wives for the tenants, with the promise of one hundred more to follow. In March 1621 however, a royal proclamation suspended the public funding of the company's projects. In July, company officers proposed that a series of 'magazines' should advertize subscription opportunities for a number of projects, including one charged with establishing a glass furnace in Jamestown to make beads for trade currency, and another with funding the transportation of the promised maids. These would be held in 'joint stock' by 'private adventurers':

> ffower seuerall Rolls were now read and offered to such as would please to vnderwrite The ffirst beinge for a Magazine of Apparell, and other necessary pvisions such as the Colony stood in great need of; The Second for sendinge of 100: mayds to be made wives; The third for the advancement of the Glasse ffurnace as hath been formerly menconed: The ffowerth was for the settinge out of a Voyadge to trade with the Indians in Virginia for Furrs.[24]

Here we see the demand for funding the traffic in women (to placate the Jamestown men) and glass-bead production (to placate the Indians) arising concurrently with, and underwriting, the early market in stocks and shares.[25] In this market, money would soon multiply in symbolic value, accruing a worth determined by confident imaginations in addition to that determined by the market price of goods. In return for capital ventured, any profit would return to the stockholders. Costs for the transport of women were to be reimbursed by any of the Virginian tenants who married the women (together with a healthy profit of 100 per cent); and the currency was tobacco. Their price fluctuated according to the price of tobacco on the English market – between £18 (the value of 150 lb of tobacco) and £22 (for 120 lb) per woman.[26] And as the prices were elevated, so were the company's insistence upon and guarantee of their virginity. After repeated presentation of the Rolls, fifty-seven women, skilled in service or in trade, were finally sent that year – although the adventurers failed to recoup investments, and poorer planters had their bids for wives refused.[27]

Women emigrants were, like Aminta, and like the glass beads with which the *The Sea Voyage* invites us to compare them, converted in this process from worthless 'trinkets' – women of the middling sorts were considered burdens to their families if they remained unmarried – into valuable commodities. Valued by the colonists for the burdens of childbirth and other labours they would bear, and by the Virginia Company for their social influence, potentially they could produce a surplus value to be pocketed by the private adventurers. As contemporary definitions of 'trinkets' suggest – dainty foods, or delicacies, jewellery of little value, but also the tools of a trade – Fletcher's use of the term, in the months following the emigrant women's departure, seems particularly timely.

The gallants' expectations of abundance, like those of the early colonists in North America, have ill-equipped them for even the most basic form of survival – without help from the natives. Unlike the terrain surrounding Jamestown, however, there are no 'natives' in *The Sea Voyage*; instead there is a neighbouring group of women who have food, but no men to reproduce their colony. As Claire Jowitt notes, considering the disastrous effects on the Virginia Company of the 'Jamestown Massacre' of 1622 – in which 347 colonists were killed by neighbouring Indians – it is hardly surprising that the play treats the Virginia context only obliquely, and that the native inhabitants have been removed from the scene.[28]

It is also fair to say, then, as Michael Hattaway does, that the Portuguese 'Amazons' figure as natives. But, while he argues that 'they are merely figurative savages, translations really, on whom, as is customary, can be projected images of what explorers and colonizers take to be evil', I contend that this is no 'mere' or one-to-one translation.[29] The women also stand in inversely for the all-male colonists in Jamestown – a position which challenges my reading of Aminta as convertible trinket, and puts the men's bodies in the exchangeable position she occupied. They also represent the potentially disruptive, potentially pacifying all-female cargoes sent to meet them. In addition, they function quite specifically as the threateningly independent Amazons of antiquity, and the Indian warrior women who were given their name.

When the objects of trade become the agents of trade, and the subjects of their own discourse, the accepted relations of exchange – those considered natural – are soon overturned. Like the gold that cannot be eaten, the Portuguese 'Amazon' women of *The Sea Voyage* temporarily evade the system of exchange during their period of self-enforced separatism – being powerfully unavailable, their sexual and reproductive capacities cannot be converted into assets. Like the gold, however, they appear to return to their 'proper' place by the play's denouement, with their leader, Rosellia, willingly 'discharging' those powers of leadership that had become 'too burdensome' (5. 4. 98). On learning of the men's arrival, Rosellia finally proposes that the women should rescue the men and mix with them on the following terms:

> Each one shall choose a husband, and injoy
> His Company a month, but that expir'd,
> You shall no more come near 'em; if you prove fruitful,
> The Males ye shall return to them, the Females
> We will reserve our selves: this is the utmost
> Ye shall e'er obtain.   (2. 2. 237–42)

This passage draws conspicuously on a vast textual resource of 'Amazon' mythology which had been reproduced in the Western world since the classical era, and which had constantly relocated the Amazons to a place just beyond the spatial edge of the known world.[30] New World discovery narratives relocated the Amazons in the Americas, and by the early sixteenth century they were well established in the Spanish and Portuguese imaginations, attracting desires not just for their wealth, but of the body.[31] Most emphasize the whiteness of the Amazons' skin, their martial prowess, their stores of gold and silver and, above all, their system of selecting sexual partners themselves, for procreative purposes, just once each year.[32] It seems that *because* of their wealth, their whiteness, their 'manly' appearance and behaviour and their position outside the patriarchal system of sexual exchange, real or imagined Amazons became legitimate objects of a conflated desire for colonial and sexual conquest.[33]

Neither 'trinkets' nor commodities of any kind, the Amazon women, as agents rather than objects of exchange, threatened those systems which, on symbolic and material levels, sought to contain women.[34] When women traded *on* their sexuality, rather than being traded *for* it, becoming agents rather than objects, the symbolic economies of both gender and trade collapsed – or collapsed into one.

From the late sixteenth century, theatre-goers saw a proliferation of viragos in the theatre, which, according to Gabriele Bernhardt Jackson, was fuelled by the accounts of Amazons in the New World, and functioned to express a range of gender anxieties that could be contained temporarily on the stage.[35] These stage Amazons evoked a range of responses, from titillation to outrage – made more unsettling perhaps by the fact that these were boy actors cross-dressing as women cross-dressing as men – directed at what Dr John Rainoldes called the 'provocation of men to lust and leacherie'.[36] However, attitudes towards real women who transgressed by stepping outside the established gender economy were met with uniform hostility.[37]

In *The Sea Voyage*, then, during the course of exchange, Aminta appears to stabilize this disorder. The master orders Albert repeatedly to 'Clap this woman under hatches' (1. 1. 51); to 'stow' her (1. 1. 54); to 'Carry her down' (1. 1. 63). As 'stowage' Aminta is, by implication, not only lodged, but also imprisoned and silenced. Contemporary meanings of the verb 'to stow' would, however, have included spending and investment; as an orderly commodity Aminta can be expected to bring in returns. Despite her provocative presence, her most valuable asset appears to be her virginity. Although she has been abducted, her chastity is vouched for by all, including her abductor, and by her bodily marks of chastity – her unstained complexion and blush. Her purity then marks her as a fitting object of exchange between men; should she escape their stowage, however, she could wreak havoc with this economy.

The passage with which I began this paper suggests, as I have already argued, that Aminta's mere presence both invites and stands in for penetrative sex. It also, by positioning her as foetus/ sperm, incorporated within the ship's belly, functions dramatically to forewarn the audience of the threats of ultimate consumption – sexual defilement and cannibalism – that both place her and plague her in her position as commodity.

Images of devouring dominate the play so that, both structurally and thematically, it is driven by the desire to eat. The group of women threaten with unstopped speech and voracious sexual appetites to incorporate the men indiscriminately, making them the 'trinkets' with which to pacify the Amazon natives-colonists. Even love is exploited for its cannibal potential and the bawdy possibilities of the pun on appetites are exploited to the full in the play, with the colony of women desiring to be 'hunted' down and 'eaten',[38] and to hunt down and eat the men.

In Act 3, however, the cannibal puns turn away from the taste for sexual satiation when the language of anthropophagy finally becomes literalized in the desire for a cannibal feast. The starving men turn their attention, ominously, to Aminta, and suggest a solution to their appetites for *both* food and vengeance:

> Morilliat: This thing hath been our overthrow, and all
> These biting mischiefs that fall on us are come
> Through her means.   (3. 1. 80–2)

> Lamure: Why should we consume thus, and starve?
> Have nothing to relieve us, and she live there
> That bred all our miseries, unroasted
> Or unsod! [unboiled].   (3. 1. 90–3)

Morilliat says that 'ere we die . . . we'll have one dainty meal' (3. 1. 124) and Aminta innocently responds: 'Shall I be with ye, gentlemen?', to be told by Lamure, 'Yes, marry shall ye! In our bellies'. The gallants all desire a taste of Aminta's 'hinder parts', at which point the initial pun – on sex suggestive of eating – is reversed. Do they really wish to consume Aminta, or are they considering rape? Tibalt, however, argues that they should eat one of the men instead 'And spare the woman to beget more food on' (3. 1. 156); rape would, it is implied, produce a worthwhile surplus – a supply of babies for future feasts.

As commodity, once consumed, Aminta's worth evaporates. As virgin cargo, her worth diminishes with just one taste. As well as working satirically in relation to reports of cannibalism in the starving Jamestown colony in 1609 and later, the discourse on anthropophagy points self-referentially in other directions: first, to the gross consumption of Indian land and food supplies that the colonists attempted to legitimize with their gifts of trinkets. Second, to the anxious acknowledgement of the Virginia Company's engagement in the 'human auction' of women – 'trinkets' that, given the right markets and the right marketing, could be converted and consumed as wives and profit.[39] Or third, to a reversal: does the play's anxious dramatization of women consuming, rather than being consumed, mirror the Jamestown colonists' anxious realization that the natives (particularly the native women, who controlled grain supplies), who are represented as gullible consumers, were actually in a position of economic superiority? Put another way, did the early relations of colonial exchange threaten a disruption in the economies of both finance *and* gender?

Notes

[1] Anthony Parr observes both of these parallels in *Three Renaissance Travel Plays*, ed. Anthony Parr (Manchester, 1995), p. 22.

[2] John Fletcher and Philip Massinger, *The Sea Voyage*, ed. Anthony Parr, 1. 1. 63–9.

[3] Karl Marx argues that capitalist production produces, in addition to a product or commodity, a '*surplus-value* for capital, and consequently the actual *transformation* of money or commodity into capital'. *Theories of Surplus Value*, Part I (Moscow, 1939), p. 161, cited and emphasis added by Gayle Rubin in 'The traffic in women: notes on the "political economy of sex"', in Rayna R. Reiter, *Toward an Anthropology of Women* (London and New York, 1975), pp. 157–210.

[4] Jonathan Sawday, in *The Body Emblazoned: Dissection and the Human Body*

in Renaissance Culture (London and New York, 1995), describes the typical anatomical image of women's bodies as '[n]o more than the vehicle for a vagina', p. 223.

[5] Parr, *Three Renaissance Travel Plays*, p. 22.

[6] Gordon McMullan, *The Politics of Unease* (Amherst, 1994), pp. 197–256; Andrew Hadfield, *Literature, Travel and Colonial Writing in the English Renaissance 1545–1625* (Oxford, 1998), pp. 254–64.

[7] Thomas Harriot, *A brief and true report of the new found land of Virginia*, in Richard Hakluyt (ed.), *The Principal Navigations Voyages Traffiques and Discoveries of the English Nation* (Glasgow, 1904 [1600, 1st edn 1589]), 12 vols, VIII, 350–84 (375).

[8] Sir George Peckham, *A true Report of the late discoveries*, ibid., 89–107, 98.

[9] Ibid., 97.

[10] Gabriel Archer, *A relatyon of the Discovery of our River, from James Forte into the Maine*, in Philip L. Barbour (ed.), *The Jamestown Voyages under the First Charter, 1606–1609*, 2 vols, II, 80–98, 84.

[11] John Smith, *A Description of New England* [1616], in *Tracts and Other Papers,* collected by Peter Force (Gloucester, Mass., 1963 [1836]), 2 vols, II, 10.

[12] Joan Pong Linton, *The Romance of the New World* (Cambridge, 1998), p. 105.

[13] Helen C. Rountree, 'The Powhatans and the English: a case of multiple conflicting agendas', in Rountree (ed.), *Powhatan Foreign Relations 1500–1722* (Charlottesville and London, 1993), pp. 173–205, 178.

[14] Martin H. Quitt, 'Trade and acculturation at Jamestown, 1607–1609: the limits of understanding', *The William and Mary Quarterly*, 3rd ser., 52 (1995), 225–58 (225).

[15] Ibid., 247.

[16] Ibid., 256.

[17] Ibid., 235–6.

[18] Ibid., 243.

[19] As Parr points out, the reference is also suggestive of Benzoni's account of the Peruvian Indians who forced Europeans to eat the gold they so craved; in De Bry, *Discovering the New World, Based on the Works of Theodore de Bry*, ed. Michael Alexander (London, 1976), p. 137.

[20] See the *OED*, x, 1a and 2.

[21] See Linton, *The Romance of the New World*, pp. 104–30.

[22] David R. Ransome, 'Wives for Virginia, 1621', *William and Mary Quarterly*, 3rd ser., 48 (1991), 3–18 (5).

[23] Susan Myra Kingsbury (ed.), *The Records of the Virginia Company of London*, 4 vols (Washington, DC, 1906), I, p. 256.

[24] Ibid., 513–14

[25] See D. C. Coleman, *The Economy of England 1450–1750* (Oxford, 1977), pp. 55–9.

[26] Linton, *The Romance of the New World*, p. 6.

[27] Ibid., 126–7; see also Ransome, 'Wives for Virginia', and Karen Ordahl Kupperman on the same practice in Roanoke in *Roanoke: The Abandoned Colony* (Maryland, 1984), p. 167. For pricing details see Kingsbury, *The Records*, III, pp. 15, 162, 173–4, 493, 503–4. On the lack of success see Kingsbury, IV, pp. 231–2.

[28] Claire Jowitt, *Gender Politics and Voyage Drama 1589–1642: Real and Imagined Worlds* (Manchester, 2002); McMullan also notes the removal of 'aboriginal inhabitants' from the scene in *The Politics of Unease*, p. 245.

[29] Michael Hattaway, ' "Seeing things": Amazons and cannibals', in Jean-Pierre Maquerlet and Michèle Willems (eds), *Travel and Drama in Shakespeare's Time* (Cambridge, 1996), pp. 179–92, 186, 188.

[30] From Scythia to Libya, Ethiopia to the Far East and the 'Torrid Zone'. Sir John Mandeville locates them beside 'Chaldea', near Baghdad, in 'the land of Amazon', and explains that this wealthy group 'would never let men dwell with them over seven days, ne never suffer knave child be nourished among them', *Mandeville's Travels: Texts and Translations*, ed. Malcolm Letts (London, 1953), 2 vols, I, pp. 111 and 112.

[31] See Nunno di Gusman's account, for example, in Samuel Purchas, *Purchas His Pilgrimes*, 20 vols, XVIII (Glasgow, 1906 [1625]), pp. 52–60.

[32] See, for example, the narratives of Garcilasso Inca de La Vega, Antonia de Herrara and Cristovall de Acuna in C. R. Markham, *Expeditions into the Valley of the Amazons* (New York, 1970 [1859]), pp. 1–20, 21–40, 41–134.

[33] Walter Raleigh, for example, exhorted his queen to conquer the wealthy and powerful 'Amazones' of Guyana, in *The Discoverie of the Large, Rich and Bewtiful Empyre of Guiana* (1595), ed. Neil Whitehead (Manchester, 1997), p. 199.

[34] Gayle Rubin, in 'The traffic in women', describes a 'systematic social apparatus which takes up females as raw materials and fashions domesticated women as products', p. 158.

[35] Gabriele Bernhardt Jackson, 'Topical ideology: witches, Amazons, and Shakespeare's Joan of Arc', in Deborah E. Barker and Ivo Kamps (eds), *Shakespeare and Gender: A History* (London, 1995), p. 151.

[36] Lisa Jardine cites Rainoldes from *Th'Overthrow of Stage-Players* (Middleburgh, 1599), in 'Boy actors, female roles, and Elizabethan eroticism', in D. Scott Kastan and Peter Stallybrass (eds), *Staging the Renaissance: Reinterpretations of Elizabethan and Jacobean Drama* (London, 1991), pp. 57–67 (57).

[37] While Jackson, in 'Topical ideology', documents the persecution of cross-dressing women in the period, Mary Prior focuses on the parallel difficulties faced by urban working women in 'Women and the urban economy: Oxford 1500–1800', in Prior (ed.), *Women in English Society 1500–1800* (London, 1991), pp. 93–117 (108).

[38] Michael Schoenfeldt, in *Prayer and Power: George Herbert and Renaissance Courtship* (Chicago, 1991), points out that eating 'possessed strong sexual connotations even in the Renaissance', p. 261.

[39] For a discussion of the Virginia Company's response to the 'misrepresentation' of the venture as 'a human auction', see Ransome, 'Wives for Virginia', p. 6.

7

'Antipodean Tricks': Travel, Gender and Monstrousness in Richard Brome's The Antipodes

CLAIRE JOWITT

Richard Brome's *The Antipodes* (1638) uses the idea of a voyage to a new world, in this case the fantasy continent of Terra Australis Incognita or the Antipodes, to focus on issues of gender identity and performance, as well as the relationship between new and old worlds.[1] During the sixteenth and seventeenth centuries detailed cartographic representations of a southern continent proliferated, though no certain discovery took place.[2] In the wake of Pomponius Mela's and Ptolemy's arguments that a southern continent was needed to balance the one in the north, increasingly elaborate representations circulated of the land and peoples expected to be found in Terra Australis Incognita. Ortelius's 1570 *Theatrum Orbis Terrarum*, for instance, shows a meticulously drawn Antipodean coastline complete with promontories and local names.[3] This essay argues that the fact that Brome describes an imaginary voyage to an imaginary southern continent rather than engaging with the New World of the Virginia colonies and the Jamestown settlement is important for an understanding of the text's representation of the pointlessness of travel. It also explores Brome's representation of transgressive gender behaviour, specifically in relation to sexual appetite, false pregnancy and monstrousness. Initially, deviant sexual and gender characteristics seem to be associated with exotic fantasy locations but, as we shall see, they are in fact already endemic to Renaissance London.

Brome's text contrasts with other contemporary travel-inspired dramas – for example Fletcher's and Massinger's *The Sea Voyage*

(1622), examined by Teresa Walters in the previous essay, or
Massinger's *The City Madam* (1632) – which are indebted to
popular documentary accounts of travel to and life in the New
World such as Hakluyt's compendium of exploration *Principal
Navigations* (1589).[4] Instead Brome's text follows a different, and
satiric, tradition of writing about imaginary New Worlds. Similar
to Lucian's comic and grotesque fantasy voyage *A True Story*, the
exotic *Mandeville's Travels* (1356),[5] and the more recent text by
Joseph Hall *Mundus Alter et Idem* (1605), in Brome's *The
Antipodes* we have pointless travel, or travel that gets the traveller
nowhere.[6] In other words, Brome's text charts a fantasy voyage to a
fantasy kingdom: hence, it travels nowhere. This is crucial in
switching the focus of the drama from the assimilation of new
ideas and knowledge concerning the New World to the values and
behaviour of the inhabitants of the Old World. Despite being
framed around the idea of travel, the emphasis in this text is very
much on Renaissance London in the 1630s.

The play describes how, following the end of the outbreak of the
plague in London in 1636–7, the Joyless family come to London to
attempt the cure of the son of the family, Peregrine, who has lost his
wits through the reading of exotic travel writing. Indeed, Brome's
text is particularly indebted to Hall's satiric, anti-travel text where,
in 'Terra Australis Incognita', Hall's narrator, Mercurius
Britannicus, travels through a supposedly new continent that
represents in exaggerated form the vices of Renaissance Europe; in
other words he meets 'a world, another and the same'.[7] Because his
parents have not allowed him to become an explorer, Peregrine in
The Antipodes has become so obsessed with imaginary travel that
he is guilty of succumbing to the condition against which Jerome
Turler warned his readers in his influential travel manual *The
Traveiller* (1574). In his chapter 'the preceptes of traveyling',
Turler's principal point was that travellers must not forget the
morals and social customs of their home nation while abroad since
promiscuous cultural intermingling will result in their no longer
fitting into their home society on return.[8] In *The Antipodes* this
is precisely what has happened, since Peregrine has become so
demented through thinking of nothing but strange customs and
countries that he has become a social misfit. He is only interested
in travel and neglects everything else, even his marital duties
towards his young wife Martha so that the marriage remains

unconsummated after three years. Indeed, as the other characters comment, it is Peregrine, rather than his wife, that has conceived since he suffers from a 'tympany'(1. 1. 178), meaning a monstrous swelling or a pregnancy. This condition requires the services of a man midwife, so Peregrine's father, Joyless, consults Hughball, a famous doctor, who undertakes the case. The doctor lives with Letoy, a 'plaine' but 'fantastic lord' (1. 2. 83) who keeps a well-equipped private stage and a group of men-servants who are trained actors.

As part of Peregrine's cure, the doctor and Letoy orchestrate the presentation of a series of scenes from the Antipodes before Peregrine, who, through a drug-induced sleep, is persuaded that he has travelled there. In the midst of scenes of supposed inversion concerning life in the Antipodes, designed to restore Peregrine to his wits by making him recognize the natural and correct order of things, Peregrine invades the property-room backstage, and, after a fight with pasteboard monsters, makes himself king of the Antipodes. He intends to reform Antipodean manners, but is persuaded to take an Antipodean wife, Martha in disguise, as his queen. The couple retire to bed and emerge hours later cured of their maladies since they are now sexually satisfied. The plot is also concerned with the curing of Joyless's excessive jealousy of his young wife, Diana. In order to effect Joyless's cure, he is placed in a position from which he overhears Lord Letoy amorously proposition Diana, who firmly repulses Letoy, maintaining her love for her husband. Joyless is further convinced of Diana's chastity by Letoy's revelation that he is Diana's father. After all these explanations, the play ends with a masque of Discord replaced by Harmony and, super-ficially at least, correct relations are re-established for the inhabit-ants of Renaissance London.

Perhaps unsurprisingly, given that the first performances of this play were when the theatres reopened after a plague outbreak, *The Antipodes* is obsessed with ideas of disease and contagion.[9] But *The Antipodes* is also concerned with false, male pregnancy, as well as with issues of paternity, gender and sexual relations more generally, and these concerns cannot be explained as merely a reflection of the recent London health crisis. Nor, as critics such as Ian Donaldson, Martin Butler and Ira Clark have argued, should *The Antipodes* be seen as a meditation upon the strengths and weaknesses of Caroline rule and society.[10] In contrast to these readings, then, in what follows the focus is on the representations of gender in this text and I examine the ways these ideas impact upon debates about the resemblance between the Antipodes and Renaissance London. Brome's treatment of sexuality and appetite and the connections between these issues and the text's representation of the apparent pointlessness of travel through its staging of a pretend voyage to a fantasyland are also explored.

In *The Antipodes*, Brome represents the characters' various social problems and health issues as types of madness or moral sickness: Peregrine is travel mad, Martha is full of love melancholy, Joyless is horn-mad, etc. But, as becomes apparent, it is not just the Joyless family that is suffering from different forms of madness: virtually all the characters are in one stage or another of psychological ill health. The married couple Blaze and Barbara, mutual friends of Letoy and the Joyless family, have themselves previously been through Doctor Hughball's somewhat radical cure for a husband's horn-madness which involves accepting that he has already been cuckolded and ceasing to worry about it. Even Letoy, at the end of the play, explains that his marriage with Diana's mother was soured through his belief in her unfaithfulness, and that his doubts about his daughter's paternity were laid to rest only on his wife's death-bed. All these illnesses, then, are to do with problems regarding gender behaviour or sexual relations in one form or another

The most striking image in this play and the one upon which the plot of *The Antipodes* revolves is the removal of Peregrine Joyless's 'tympany'. The sexually experienced Barbara asks Doctor Hughball in his role as 'man midwife' to deliver the travel-obsessed and sexually dysfunctional Peregrine of his 'tympany'. She asks that he be delivered of his fantasies of:

> monsters,
> Pygmies and giants, apes and elephants,
> Griffins and crocodiles, men upon women,
> And women upon men, the strangest doings –
> As far beyond all Christendom as 'tis to't.
> (1. 1. 178–82)

According to seventeenth-century definition, 'tympany' meant pregnancy or a disease of the belly and could refer to both a literal and a metaphorical condition.[11] 'Tympany' here uses all of these meanings and the image is part of the text's gender play and debate about resemblance between the Antipodes and Renaissance London.

Gender play is clearly present in this passage since, rather ironically, Barbara asks Doctor Hughball to take the specifically female role of midwife in order to deliver a man, that is Peregrine, of his 'strange', non-Christian interests in exotic and salacious 'monsters' and hermaphrodites: 'men upon women, And women upon men'. Though 'men midwives' were to become common in the eighteenth century as men took over the profession, in the seventeenth century they were not welcome at births. Indeed, the taboo against male attendance was such that in 1552 a physician in Germany was condemned to death when it was discovered that he had attended a birth cross-dressed, and in 1646 in Massachusetts Francis Rayus was fined 50 shillings 'for presuming to act the part of a midwife'.[12] Hence Hughball, as a male midwife, is inverting accepted gender roles just as much as Peregrine is with his tympathic pregnancy. In terms of appropriate gender behaviour, therefore, there is no difference between patient and doctor as both are transgressive figures. Furthermore, Barbara's speech – which asserts that Peregrine has digested exotic travel literature that has made him sick – shows the potentially destabilizing nature of the influence of New Worlds. Accounts of New World life will, as Barbara's comments about 'news' or information make clear, of necessity affect those left at home. More particularly, when those accounts are fantastic ones – 'of the strangest doings' – then their effects will be particularly acute. Peregrine's tympany is just an extreme manifestation of a common condition; it is, crucially, one from which the doctor also suffers.

Peregrine's 'tympany' not only represents a physical condition, then, but also a moral one: it is 'A swelling, as of pride, arrogance, self-conceit, figured as a disease'.[13] Like Falstaff's tumescent belly in *Henry IV, Part II*, Peregrine has become 'puffed up'.[14] He has internalized or consumed the strange and exotic travel stories he has read so that he is unable to pay his marriage debt. And his disease is contagious in the world of the play. Martha, his sex-starved and still virgin wife, meanders through scenes making embarrassing, misdirected sexual remarks as she tries to discover the secrets of married love. Indeed, when Martha appears in the play

almost immediately after Barbara's earlier speech, both Martha
and her situation are described as 'monstrous' (1. 1. 202–4). It appears that Peregrine's obsession with travel and his lack of
attention to his wife have driven her out of her wits. The lure of the
exotic and unknown is so strong that established social and sexual
relations are undermined and inverted for the travel-obsessed
individual, for those with whom he comes into contact and for the
characters who attempt his cure: the worlds of seventeenth-century
London and the Antipodes are not so far apart, it would seem.

The play goes on to problematize the superficially easy identification of the character who caused the contagion. As Martha
tries to find out information about sex from all who will listen to
her, she starts to ruminate on her past experiences:

> For were I now to die, I cannot guess
> What a man does in child-getting. I remember
> A wanton maid once lay with me, and kissed
> And clipped and clapped me strangely, and then wished
> That I had been a man to have got her with child.
>
> (1. 1. 252–6)

The woman-to-woman sexual relationship described here is
obviously not a celebration of same-sex desire; rather, it is predicated on the need of an absent man to father children and thus
fulfil women's biological and social roles. Desire flickers here
between Martha and the 'wanton maid' because of the absence of
any available man. Such a situation is strikingly similar to the one
in which Martha now finds herself as she wants Peregrine to father
a child on her confessing to having searched 'Parsley beds, Straw-
berry banks, or rosemary beds' in the hope of finding elusive offspring, 'Because I would fain have one' (1. 1. 242–4). Moreover, she
then asks Barbara whether she can share a bed with her: 'I'll lie
with you and practise, if you please. Pray take me for a night or
two' (1. 1. 264–5). Martha's desires for pregnancy or 'tympany',
which were awakened by the wanton maid, are emblematic of the
moral disorder of Renaissance London. Peregrine's disease should
thus be viewed as a consequence rather than a cause of the moral
malaise described in the text. The contagion, represented in
Martha's case as same-sex desire, was already fully present prior to
Peregrine's reading of travel accounts. Indeed, as the play

progresses it becomes clear that the character who attempts to be moral and sexual arbiter in the world of the play, the 'fantastic' Lord Letoy, is in fact the most deviant and excessive.

With Doctor Hughball, Lord Letoy organizes a dramatic production to cure Peregrine of his 'tympany'. This play-within-a-play – where Peregrine thinks he has indeed travelled to the Antipodes – tries to present the Antipodean world as a place of inverted class, gender and sexual relations, but it soon becomes apparent that such a discrete separation cannot be maintained. In fact, the character of Letoy in particular who, since he sets himself up as the instigator of Peregrine's cure, would be expected to be morally inviolate, is by far the most socially, sexually and morally ambiguous. For example, during the play-within-the-play in Act 4 we are confronted with a knock-about, satirical scene between three Antipodean courtiers concerning sodomitical relationships, which attempts to condemn such practices (4. 167–205). However, for much of the play, Letoy himself is obsessed with one of the actors, his servant Byplay, a name which, as Anthony Parr comments, means 'action carried on aside . . . while the main action proceeds'.[15] Letoy insistently talks of his 'love' for Byplay and his other male servants, dresses effeminately in the manner of Richard II (5. 2. 15–18), employs the gender-inverting male mid-wife Hughball and, at the end of the play, describes his unhappy marriage. These factors undermine Letoy's position as self-proclaimed guardian of normative sexual and gender relations. Peregrine's tympany – his phantom pregnancy, his morbid swelling and the moral malaise it figuratively represents – is symptomatic, then, of a much more widely held condition. Significantly, it does not appear to be a disease that originated in the Antipodes. Rather, the moral and social decay that the tympany represents was already endemic to Renaissance London.

Indeed, at the end of the play, it appears to be Letoy who is suffering from a moral 'tympany'. The final act contains a strange twist where Letoy admits that he is the father of Diana. For most of the play he has been relentlessly sexually pursuing her, claiming to be attempting to cure Joyless's jealousy. The revelation and miraculous delivery of Diana as Letoy's daughter – another blood-less male birth which echoes Peregrine's tympany – is unprepared for by the text and hence comes as a complete surprise to both Diana and the audience. Indeed, the sense of disquiet caused by

this disclosure is especially strong since Letoy's confession
immediately follows an attempted seduction of her that seems
serious in tone. In fact, Letoy threatens Diana with financial and
social ruin if she will not succumb to his charms:

> I'll . . . not spare
> To boast thou art my prostitute, and thrust ye
> Out of my gates, to try't out by yourselves.
>
> (5. 2. 117–18)

Letoy's tympany, then, represents an excessive and indiscriminate
sexuality – he incestuously tries to seduce his daughter, the text
makes it clear he has already had an affair with Barbara, and his
relationship with his servants, especially Byplay, is sexually
orientated. Brome's play urges its audience and readers to question
where anti-establishment social and sexual practices originate. The
play makes it clear that the excessive and monstrous sexuality
associated with foreign parts is, in fact, rather tame compared with
the activities of the inhabitants of seventeenth-century London.

   This analysis demonstrates that London and the Antipodes are
identical in Brome's drama. In contrast to other travel and travel-
inspired plays, such as Heywood's *The Fair Maid of the West* (Part
I 1599–1604; Part II 1631), Shakespeare's *The Tempest* (1610),
Fletcher's *The Island Princess* (1619–22), Fletcher's and Massinger's
The Sea Voyage (1622) and Massinger's *The City Madam* (1632),
this voyage drama does not actually travel anywhere in the sense of
engaging with the reality of new worlds in an experiential way.[16]
These other voyage dramas are all either set in the New World,
juxtapose Virginia or Virginia-inspired locations against London,
or engage with the hardships and vicissitudes of mercantile
adventuring and sea-life in ways that Brome's text deliberately
avoids. In these other 'geographic' plays, of course, the locations
with which they engage have to be read against the culture out of
which they emerge, but *The Antipodes* is unusual in that the only
meaning of travel is as a lens to focus on the behaviour of the
population of Renaissance London. In *The Antipodes*, the fantasy
new world Peregrine visits is merely an exaggerated version of
Britain: Antipodean natives are recognizably European since,
though their customs are supposedly inversions of British ones,
these practices are derived from the same conceptual framework.

The discovery of lawyers that are honest in the Antipodes, for instance, is not a representation of radical difference. Consequently, Brome's play demonstrates virtually no interest in contemporary America or any other current British territorial ambitions or spheres of interest. In fact, there is only one direct reference to New England where Peregrine debates asking the American Puritan regime for advice on the reformation of Antipodean manners:

> Peregrine: Before I reign
> A month among them, they shall change their notes,
> Or I'll ordain a course to change their coats.
> I shall have much to do in reformation.
> Doctor: Patience and counsel will go through it, sir.
> Peregrine. What if I craved a counsel from New England?
> The old will spare me none.
> Doctor: [Aside] Is this man mad?
> My cure goes fairly on.   (4. 260–7)

Peregrine's request for counsel from New England marks a stage in his return to something approximating to psychic health. The remark satirically attacks Charles' government since Peregrine says 'the old will spare me none': in other words, the butt of the joke is Britain's undemocratic rule, since under Charles I no parliaments were called in the 1630s and hence it was impossible to get any sort of counsel at all in Renaissance London. Because British colonies were from the start administered by a governor and council, New England is here represented as more democratic than Charles's Britain. However, Peregrine's request for New World counsel should not be seen as praise for the Puritan regime. Peregrine may be on the journey back to psychic health when he makes this request, but, as both Letoy and Hughball make clear in their commentary and explanations on the actions of the inset play to the other characters and the audience, Peregrine is still at the 'folly' stage of mental health (4. 495–506). Consequently, Peregrine's request for New World counsel while a fool needs to be seen as a satiric attack on the Puritan reformers and their government in New England as well as an attack on the Stuart monarchy. At no other time in the drama does this play engage with the harsh realities or perceived sexual excesses of British colonial life in the

1630s or the kinds of issues that specifically and particularly affected New World colonists and with which other texts engage.[17] In Massinger's *The City Madam*, for instance, the Virginian plot does not appear until late and involves British men (disguised as native American *sachems*) threatening the proud and unruly Lady Frugal and her daughters with becoming enforced New World colonists. Massinger casts aspersions on colonists' sexual morality. The native Americans' mission to England is necessary only because female virginity 'was not to be purchas'd' in the New World.[18] Female virginity, like any other form of goods, is represented here as a commercial property whose price becomes inflated when demand exceeds supply.[19] Instead, in *The Antipodes*, we have a bowdlerized version of travel in which by falling asleep a would-be traveller can awake painlessly on another continent, and where, paradoxically, the traveller finds solely his own culture.

This conflation of new and old worlds means that this travel drama does not explore any culture apart from a British one. The main result of Peregrine's sojourn is that as a couple he and his wife become sexually active, but this merely enables them to become part of the deviant and unwholesome sexual atmosphere Brome represents as Renaissance London. Peregrine's Mandevillean-derived interests and fears are no more strange or bizarre than the behaviour of the rest of the characters outside the inset play. For example, when Peregrine meets Martha in disguise as a native Antipodean Queen, he is initially reluctant to couple with her because he is worried that she is a Mandevillean Gadlibirien that 'stings oft-times to death' the man she has married (4. 468). But on being assured by Hughball 'She's no Gadlibirien, sir, upon my Knowledge' (4. 469), (presumably a boast designed to announce that he has had sexual knowledge of her) Peregrine is persuaded to further the relationship. Here Peregrine's virginity – his lack of, as Diana puts it, 'the real knowledge of the woman' (4. 514) – makes him vulnerable to believing Mandevillean stories concerning the practice of hiring 'another man to couple with his bride, To clear the dangerous passage of a maidenhead' (4. 464–5). This practice of sexual surrogacy was necessary, according to Mandeville, because Gadlibirien women had 'within them nadders [snakes], that tanged [stung] the husbands on the yards [penises] in the women's bodies; and so were many men slain'.[20] Peregrine's sexual inadequacy – his failure to consummate his marriage earlier

– makes him prone to believing fantastic and exotic stories about women's threatening sexuality. Similarly, his desire to allow another man to have sexual relations with his wife – his positive willingness to be cuckolded – marks Peregrine as an example of failed masculinity.[21] Yet, Peregrine's inadequacy is no more striking – in fact somewhat less so – than the strangeness of Letoy attempting to seduce his own daughter. Brome does not encourage the audience to have any faith in the moral conclusion of his drama; Diana is reunited with her father, Peregrine and Martha have had sex, Joyless and Diana are reconciled, as are Barbara and Blaze. Nevertheless there is a sense of pointlessness about the whole text since what the characters are moving towards through Hughball's and Letoy's machinations is not necessarily better than their previous situations. Martha and Peregrine may have finally consummated their marriage, but the examples of married life around them are not ones that recommend the condition. Just as in the inset play nobody actually travels anywhere, the play's resolution is equally pointless. This play represents a paradox, then; it is a travel drama that is not about travel and it offers a resolution where supposed normative values are re-established which turn out, on closer inspection, to be as strange as the ones they replaced. The fantasy of the Antipodean New World is in this drama, then, filled with the Old World; there is nothing new about it.

Notes

[1] Richard Brome, *The Antipodes*, in *Three Renaissance Travel Plays*, ed. Anthony Parr (Manchester, 1995). All references are to this edn.

[2] On the history of the discovery of Australia see Robert Hughes, *The Fatal Shore: A History of the Transportation of Convicts to Australia 1787–1868* (London, 1988), pp. 43–6.

[3] For discussion of the satiric exploitation by writers of the inconsistency between the representation of a detailed Terra Australis Incognita on maps and certain knowledge of the continent see Richard McCabe, *Joseph Hall: A Study in Satire and Meditation* (Oxford, 1982), pp. 85–8.

[4] On the representation of the New World in this period see Mary Fuller, *Voyages in Print* (Cambridge, 1995); Andrew Hadfield, *Literature, Travel and Colonial Writing in the English Renaissance, 1545–1625* (Oxford, 1998); Joan Pong Linton, *The Romance of the New World: Gender and Literary Formations of English Colonialism* (Cambridge, 1998); Claire Jowitt, *Gender Politics and Voyage Drama 1589–1642: Real and Imagined Worlds* (Manchester, 2002).

[5] For a discussion of Mandeville and his influence in the period see Stephen

Greenblatt, *Marvellous Possessions: The Wonder of the New World* (Oxford, 1988), pp. 26–51; see also Mary Baine Campbell, *The Witness and the Other World: Exotic European Travel Writing 400–1600* (Ithaca, NY, 1988), pp. 122–62.

  [6] See Joseph Hall, *Mundus Alter et Idem*, ed. and trans. Joseph Millar Wands (New Haven, 1982), Introduction, pp. xxvii–xxxii.

  [7] For discussion see Claire Jowitt, 'Old worlds and new worlds: Renaissance voyages of discovery', unpublished Ph.D. dissertation (University of Southampton, 1996), pp. 133–52; Ruth Gilbert, *Early Modern Hermaphrodites: Sex and Other Stories* (London, 2002).

  [8] Jerome Turler, *The Traveiller*, ed. D. E. Baughan (Gainesville, FL, 1951), pp. 19–22. For a more recent consideration of the traveller's iconoclastic potential see Wayne Franklin, *Discoverers, Explorers, Settlers? The Diligent Writers of Early America* (Chicago, 1979), pp. 1–12.

  [9] For information about the history of stage performance in this period see Andrew Gurr, *The Shakespearean Stage 1574–1642* (Cambridge, 1980), pp. 21–2. See also Ann Haaker, 'The plague, the theater and the poet', *Renaissance Drama* 1 (1968), 283–306.

  [10] Ian Donaldson, for instance, has seen Brome's play as essentially conservative: Peregrine's exposure to the inverted world of the Antipodes, 'presenting to him the things he imagined he most wished to see, forces him to see them not as desirable but as repugnant, drives him steadily back to normality' (p. 94). In Donaldson's view the drama stages a reassuring catharsis where the characters emerge purged of their unhealthy humours through their sojourn in anti-London. However, other critics persuasively argue that the 'normality' of the play's representation of London is not as assured as Donaldson suggests. Martin Butler, for instance, sees the play as an attack on Charles I's autocratic rule in which any demarcation between anti-London and London is unstable. Brome's anti-London draws attention to Charles's financial abuses and the corruption of monarchical rule without a parliament, but at the same time makes it clear that there are aspects of anti-London (honest lawyers, merciful sergeants, cultured aldermen and paid poets) from which Caroline London could profitably learn (pp. 216–17). Ira Clark's account also argues that the play demonstrates the need for 'healing reform' in social, political and familial arenas of 1630s London, but suggests that Brome does not specify what exactly these reforms should be, instead exemplifying 'a process of extemporaneous free play, of improvisation, of vicarious trial of potential reforms' (p. 183). According to Clark, the play is not programmatic since it fails to suggest a direct course of action to be followed, but it shows the processes by which change and reform become possible. See Ian Donaldson, *The World Turned Upside Down: Comedy from Jonson to Fielding* (Oxford, 1970), pp. 78–98; Martin Butler, *Theatre and Crisis 1632–1642* (Cambridge, 1984), pp. 211–20; Ira Clark, *Professional Playwrights: Massinger, Ford, Shirley and Brome* (Lexington, 1992), pp. 155–96; see also Anthony Parr's introduction to *Three Renaissance Travel Plays*, pp. 34–52.

  [11] *OED*, 2nd edn, XVIII, pp. 783–5.

  [12] The generally accepted explanation of the origin of man midwifery is that it began for the lying in of Louis XIV's mistress Louise de Vallière in 1663 when the King's need for secrecy led to the exclusion of the 'gossiping' midwives. See Jane B. Donegan, *Women and Men Midwives: Medicine, Morality and Misogyny in Early America* (London, 1978), pp. 18–19; see also Elaine Hobby (ed.), *Jane Sharp's The Midwives Book* (Oxford, 1999), introduction, pp. xi–xxxv.

[13] *OED*, XVIII, p. 785, and Hobby, 'Gender, science and midwifery: Jane Sharp, The Midwives Book (1671)', in Claire Jowitt and Diane Watt (eds), *The Arts of Seventeenth-Century Science: Representations of the Natural World in European and North American Culture* (Aldershot, 2002).

[14] Falstaff in *Henry IV, Part II*, also seems to be an example of a character suffering from a tympany: 'I have a whole school of tongues in this belly of mine, and not a tongue of them all speaks any other word but my name. And I had but a belly of any indifferency, I were simply the most active fellow in Europe: my womb, my womb, my womb undoes me' (4. 3. 18–23). For a reading of Falstaff's sexual ambiguity – which is reliant on the dual meaning of 'womb' as both uterus and stomach – which was available at the end of the sixteenth century – see Colin MacCabe, *Theoretical Essays: Film, Linguistics, Literature* (Manchester, 1985), pp. 116–17. I am grateful to Andrew Hadfield for this reference.

[15] Brome, *The Antipodes*, p. 220.

[16] For readings of these travel dramas see Jean-Pierre Maquerlet and Michèle Willems (eds), *Travel and Drama in Shakespeare's Time* (Cambridge, 1996).

[17] See Nicholas Canny, 'The permissive frontier: the problem of social control in Ireland and Virginia 1550–1650', in K. R. Andrews et al. (eds), *The Westward Enterprise: English Activities in Ireland, the Atlantic, and America, 1480–1650* (Liverpool, 1978), pp. 17–45.

[18] Philip Massinger, *The City Madam*, ed. Cyrus Hoy (London, 1964), 5. 1. 9.

[19] For a fuller discussion of this text see Claire Jowitt, ' "Her flesh must serve you": gender, commerce and the New World in Fletcher's and Massinger's *The Sea Voyage* and Massinger's *The City Madam*', *Parergon*, ns 18/3 (2001), 93–117.

[20] Malcolm Letts (ed.), *Mandeville's Travels: Texts and Translations* (London, 1953), 2 vols, I, p. 200.

[21] On appropriate masculinity in this period see Anthony Fletcher, 'Manhood, the male body: courtship and the household in early modern England', *History* 84 (1999), 419–36.

II

Monstrous Bodies

8

Monstrosity and the Mercurial
Female Imagination

MARGO HENDRICKS

Described by its translator as 'one of the most curious books of the French Renaissance,' Ambroise Paré's *On Monsters and Marvels* gives visual and graphic substance to the imaginary fears haunting medieval and Renaissance conceptualizations of the monstrous.[1] Images such as those represented on medieval and Renaissance maps or suggested in the narratives of travellers such as John Mandeville and Leo Africanus, the drama of William Shakespeare or the sermons of Protestant ministers, helped to define the nature of the monstrous. Figures such as Caliban and Duessa denoted an acute awareness of (and anxiety about) the permeability of the human body, and its susceptibility to corruption. Nowhere is this notion more evident than in the obsession over human reproduction, which is of central concern to Paré's text. *Monsters and Marvels* begins with very little preamble: 'Monsters are things that appear outside the course of nature (and are usually signs of some forthcoming misfortune), such as a child who is born with one arm, another who will have two heads, and additional members over and above the ordinary' (3). Prodigies, or 'marvels,' on the other hand, are 'things which happened that are complete against Nature as when a woman will give birth to a serpent, or a dog, or some other thing that is totally against Nature' (3).

Paré claims that there are 'several things that cause monsters': the 'glory' or the 'wrath' of God; too much or too little 'seed'; 'imagination'; 'posture'; 'hereditary or accidental illnesses'; 'rotten or corrupt seed'; or the 'mixture or mingling of seed' (4). Important is the subtle yet necessary distinction Paré makes in his reiteration of the words 'outside the course of' and 'against' in relation to whether a birth is to be seen as a violation of natural laws, and thus 'monstrous'. According to Paré, the child born with 'one arm' or 'additional members' appears as a result of natural intervention in the generative process and thus signals 'some forthcoming misfortune'. These individuals are to be viewed as 'monsters'. 'Marvels', on the other hand, occur because a woman or a couple engage in some form of abomination, such as:

> disorder in copulation, like brutish beasts, in which their appetite guides them, without respecting the time or other laws ordained by God and Nature: as it is written in Esdras the Prophet (Ch.5, Book 4), that women sullied by menstrual blood will conceive monsters. (5)

Marvels, therefore,

> astonish us doubly because they do not proceed from the above mentioned causes but from a fusing together of strange species, which render the creature not only monstrous but as to be marveled at, that is to say, which is completely abhorrent and against Nature. (5)

For Paré, as for most theorists who write about reproductive aberration, the female imagination is one of the principal causes of monsters and marvels. Paré views the power of the female imagination as extraordinary, calling it the 'fifth cause of monstrosity'. As an example, Paré invokes the tale of the physician Hippocrates and the princess

> who had given birth to a child as black as a Moor, her husband and she both having white skin; which woman was absolved upon Hippocrates' persuasion that it was [caused by] the portrait of a Moor, similar to the child, which was customarily attached to her bed (38).

Paré's use of this myth – one which is echoed in Heliodorus' account of the birth of a white child to the black Persina after gazing on a picture of Andromeda, versions of which are examined by Sujata Iyengar in the final section of this volume – is part of a larger didactic aim. As he argues, 'it is necessary that women – at the hour of conception and when the child is not yet formed (which takes thirty to thirty-five days for males and forty or forty-two, as

Hippocrates says, for females) – not be forced to look at or to imagine monstrous things' (39–40).

The explicit and racialist/racist figuration of Moors as 'monstrous things' is something considered in detail by Kirstie Gulick Rosenfield in the final section of this volume. But in the context of the 'Monstrous Bodies' with which I am dealing here I would like to draw attention to Paré's belief in the absolute power of woman's imagination over the generative and reproductive process – despite a long-standing presumption of the contrary which reaches back to Aristotle. Contrary to traditional arguments about the superiority of the male body and its 'seed', Paré's instructions to pregnant women appear to highlight a complex and persistent anxiety about the need for regulation of the female body. On the one hand, as the essays in this section illustrate, women are crucial to 'generation' or the reproduction of the species, yet the ease with which a woman's imagination controls her body marks the female as a particular danger to the stability of patriarchal societies.[2] More importantly, Paré blames the mercurial nature of female imagination on woman's inability to control her 'appetites', especially her sexual appetite. Women who are prone to excessive frivolity, he suggests, or who engage in gluttonous behaviour, or those who behave wantonly, inevitably produce monstrosities or, more pertinently, are viewed as monstrous themselves. It is just such an alliance between appetite, the body and the monstrous which the essays comprising this section seek to investigate.

What emerged from these traditional medical discourses about generation and reproduction, however, were not just 'elaborate systems of metaphors'. These discourses, predicated as they were upon the female body and imagination, also provided a ready terminology for those wishing to adumbrate social categories of difference and belonging. Conceptually, generation or procreation is the process whereby race becomes socially constituted, and the female body the place of that constitution. Figuratively cast in agrarian rhetoric, the womb becomes the synecdoche for property and its transmission allows for a repressive 'reinvention' of women's bodies as a site for 'masculine activities' and, I would add, masculine 'appetites'. It is significant, then, that each of the essays included in this section in some way engages with the theoretical implications of the monstrous female body as a metonymic understanding of human appetites. While only Marion Hollings frames her analysis in relation to larger questions of racial or ethnic identity, each of the essays is nevertheless marked by the racializing 'otherness' of the female body, even in its absence.

In many ways, Emma Rees's 'Sheela's voracity and Victorian veracity' sets the stage for this type of reading. In her analysis of Victorian reaction to 'Romanesque' architecture, Rees examines the uneasy tension between Victorian aesthetics and the architectural representation of female sexuality in sacred spaces. One such space, Kilpeck Church, Rees argues, created something of an aesthetic dilemma for George Robert Lewis in his attempt to articulate general rules for architectural aesthetics and design. Prominent on the church was the 'figure of a Sheela-na-Gig' or a woman depicted 'with her legs akimbo and vulva stretched open'. Sheela apparently served a 'minatory function, to castigate lust; any fertility or apotraopaic – that is talismanic – rites popularly ascribed to her were a later invention'. For Lewis however, Rees argues, the Sheela-na-Gig was a disappointing and morally inappropriate figure to adorn a church. Rees cogently demonstrates that readings of this 'monstrous' symbol of female sexuality do not necessarily reflect what she may have signified to the medieval culture that produced her. Sheela, Rees suggests, may actually have been designed to 'be read as Christian and didactic', her open body a 'metaphorical' one and a 'warning against sexual promiscuity'. This didactic aim, effective perhaps in medieval Christianity, clearly lost its significance to Protestant Victorian England. Sheela-na-Gig's 'uncompromising physicality' forces Lewis to exclude her corporeal body; 'the feminine can only exist in his discourse as idealized and metaphorical'.

If Lewis's female body is an idealized and metaphorical site where male anxieties are played out, and which is subject to changed inscription over time, then the sexualized female body for medieval writers Mechthild of Magdeburg, Pseudo-Albertus Magnus and Der Stricker is perhaps too corporeal. Bettina Bildhauer's essay 'Bloodsuckers: the construction of female sexuality in medieval science and fiction' provides a timely reminder that the narrative history of the monstrous vampire or bloodsucker and its connection to female sexuality is a long one. The metaphoric locus for this concern is the fluid which sustains the human body, blood. In each of these texts we discover that 'these early bloodsuckers . . . are . . . gendered female; more precisely, they can be seen as embodiments of female sexual appetites'. Bildhauer's analysis traces the variant representations of bloodsucking in Mechthild's mystical text, *The Flowing Light of the Godhead*, the scientific treatise *Secrets of Women*, and the Arthurian romance *Daniel of the Blossoming Valley*. The representations of blood-suckers range from the monstrous bodiless creatures in *Daniel* to the Christian soul drinking the blood of Christ to the womb 'sucking' the male semen in order to conceive. Despite their distinctive generic differences, these texts all share a concern with female sexuality and its ability to affect – indeed, often to threaten – male identity.

Liz Herbert McAvoy returns our attention to the idealized female body, one that is cloistered and passive. However, as McAvoy contends, this representation may not be as accurate as many scholars assume. In her exploration of what she terms 'the female impulse toward anchoritism', McAvoy looks to texts written for and/or by medieval female mystics and anchorites. In their writings, the female mystics frequently explain their decisions to leave the 'worldly' and embrace the divine in terms of a desire for mystical union with Christ. Crucially, according to McAvoy, these moments of union often come when the woman experiences or has experienced a life-threatening illness. McAvoy's reading of Julian of Norwich's writings assesses the complex and often puzzling link between illness and suffering and a woman's entrance into the anchoritic existence. What is striking about the writings is the deeply ingrained acceptance of the monstrous female (the desiring and consuming womb, the problematic menstrual blood and the suffering associated with pregnancy). For Julian, as for other female anchorites, the enclosed life becomes both an articulation and a redemption of the monstrous female body which, when redefined within the context of divine love, becomes an expression of the divine itself. For Julian and others, the female body thus becomes a site of potential empowerment and agency as it 'provides direct access to the Divine [and] a series of redeeming hermeneutics to explicate the insights provided by that access'.

The essays of Marion Hollings and Margaret Healy deal with a somewhat later temporality, the sixteenth and seventeenth centuries, yet identify a similar conceptualization of the monstrous (female) body. In her discussion of the destruction of Acrasia's Bower in Book 2 of Edmund Spenser's *The Faerie Queene*, Hollings redirects our critical gaze away from the 'New World' thinking exemplified in recent new historicist readings of Book 2 (particularly that of Stephen Greenblatt) and towards the 'Orient' that in fact was a familiar and oft-used locus in Renaissance discourse on monstrous appetite and its site. Hollings contends that the tendency to look to the New World to explain Spenser's representation of 'monstrous female sexuality' occludes the more immediate canvas which the Middle East and Islamic art provided for Christian writers. Hollings argues persuasively that the context for the homoerotic and excessive sensuality that Acrasia represents is better sought in narratives such as that of William Lighthow, whose description of Christian Armenian women may have been one of the 'Eastern contexts for Acrasia's sexuality'. Acrasia's 'otherness', then, not Guyon's temperance, has its basis in the troubling and unruly East, and especially its women.

Margaret Healy focuses on the banquet rather than the female body as the source of political and social instability. In a discussion that looks at English obsessions with the potentially detrimental effects of lavish feasts and hospitality, Healy highlights the particular anxiety that shaped sixteenth- and seventeenth-century English culture. The lavish banquet, Healy contends, becomes a tool of interrogation, a symbol of extreme licentiousness, and the harbinger of political dysfunction. Among Protestants, especially the more radical groups, the Stuart court was emblematic of England's fall into incivility and decay. What becomes clear to writers such as John Preston, John Ponet and John Milton is the monarchy's inability to mend its own 'diseased body' and thus the need for the true Christian Englishman to provide a just remedy, tyrannicide. While the other essays in this section concentrate on the female body as a source of excessive and threatening appetites, this essay attends to the satirical and conscious mobilization of gluttonous *male* bodies as metonymies for the state of the nation. Here, the banquet or feast becomes linked to excess, wanton behaviour and, in the end, to a descent into barbarism. Competition among Stuart courtiers created greater and greater demands for more costly luxury items and foods; little or no thought was given to the effect these 'games' were having on the body of the nation. In the end, for England to survive, the diseased head must be 'severed to save the health and liberty of the English commonwealth'.

Apart from Healy's, the essays in this section of the volume highlight one of the increasingly problematic issues in medieval and Renaissance studies: the over-determined female body as the exemplum of 'appetite' and its excesses. Yet, curiously, none of the essays directly 'speaks to' another. This apparent 'discontinuity' signals the immense scope of the topos considered. These five essays draw attention not only to the very complex ways in which patriarchal concerns over 'excess' in general, and sexual excess in particular, become manifested in literary, architectural, scientific and political discourses, but also to how they are articulated by the indefinable monstrous body that is imagined solely on the page. What becomes clear in these essays, then, is the fact that the monstrous was not a single body nor easily defined. It was, rather, a fluid and changeable entity and in their attempts to define it, patriarchal cultures needed to invent 'elaborate systems of metaphors' which could then easily be adapted to any threatening situation which might arise. These essays therefore suggest that medieval and Renaissance discourses provided a ready lexicon and iconography for those wishing to adumbrate social categories of difference – particularly the 'monstrous' – and the status of belonging. Conceptually, as Paré posits, the human body is the site where gender becomes socially constituted, and the female body the place of constitution. Not surprisingly, the womb becomes the synecdoche for the reproducibility of masculine perfection and, appropriately, its disfigurement. Even more significant is the realization that the female body supersedes the male body as the place where power originates.

Mary Fissell, in a recent essay, reminds us of the importance of metaphors to early modern medical discussions on the female body and sexual reproduction. Fissell traces the significance of the use of such metaphors in seventeenth- and eighteenth-century medical treatises dealing with generation or reproduction.[3] In these texts, she contends, 'three overlapping sets of metaphors dominate discussions of reproduction. Figures of speech are drawn from arable farming, from orchard-keeping, and from craft-work'. Strikingly, it is the sites associated with land – 'arable farming' and 'orchard-keeping' – that provide the ideological context from which most of the metaphors are taken. Fissell contends that one reason for the dominance of this series of metaphors is, of course, that early modern England was still by and large an agrarian society and these metaphors speak to that social formation. An additional factor is that early modern writers, in their engagements with the theories posited by classical and medieval physicians, perhaps saw no need to invent new terminology. Whatever the incentive, these 'elaborate systems of metaphors in discussions of sex and reproduction', Fissell argues, allow for a repressive 'reinvention' of women's bodies as a site for 'masculine activities'.

I began this response with a brief discussion of Paré's text for two reasons: first, *Monsters and Marvels* is clearly indebted to classical and medieval medical theories for its rhetoric on the monstrous. Second, as part of a larger work that was deeply influential within Renaissance and early modern medical discourse, Paré's text, with its union of empiricism and the fantastic, locates the monstrous decisively within domestic space, in both its familial and national signification. What is also relevant to the general aims of this volume is the deep-seated gender anxiety that produced the inextricable link between the female body and the idea of the monstrous both in the Middle Ages and the Renaissance, suggesting that the monstrous is a concept inherently predicated upon the female and manifested primarily through the female body. Thus, though men occasionally may be described as 'monstrous', as other essays in this volume lucidly illustrate, their monstrosity is frequently derived through their interactions with or enslavement to the female body. The effect of this is a continual destabilization of social hierarchy, aesthetic truths and the security of patriarchal institutions and ideologies.

Thus, all five of these essays illuminate the powerful imaginative hold the monstrous had on medieval and Renaissance cultures. Taken as a whole, they provide a cogent reminder of societal attempts to regulate human behaviour by controlling the appetites and drives of the human body. The impossibility of this goal, however, is nowhere better demonstrated than in Spenser's *Faerie Queene*, Book 2. The destruction of Acrasia's Bower does not eliminate the threat that her representation highlights. The Bower and its steady production of 'appetites' is, after all, not in any sense a 'real' place. It is an imaginary space, which like the female body itself, becomes the uncontrollable site where a series of male anxieties are projected and played out, from both within and without the text.

Notes

[1] Ambroise Paré, *On Monsters and Marvels*, trans. Janis L. Pallister (Chicago, 1982), p. xv.

[2] Janet Adelman, *Suffocating Mothers: Fantasies of Maternal Origin in Shakespeare's Plays, 'Hamlet' to 'The Tempest'* (New York, 1992). Adelman notes that 'patriarchal society depends on the principle of inheritance in which the father's identity – his property, name, his authority – is transmitted from father to son . . . But this transmission from father to son can take place only insofar as both father and son pass through the body of a woman' (106–7). It is especially significant in the case of 'monstrous births'. As Marie Hélène Huet reminds us, 'in a political culture where the notions of inheritance, name, title, and lineage [i.e. gender] were reinforced by multiple rights (birthrights, rights to inheritance, entails, and so forth), the question of paternity had considerable urgency. The uncertainty of legitimacy also explains the success of a theory that attributed a lack of resemblance to the power of the mother's imagination.' *Monstrous Imagination* (Cambridge, MA, and London, 1993), p. 34.

[3] Mary Fissell, 'Gender and generation: representing reproduction in early modern England', *Gender and History* 7/3 (1995), 435.

9

Bloodsuckers: The Construction of Female Sexuality in Medieval Science and Fiction

୬

BETTINA BILDHAUER

In his essay on Lacan and the uncanny, Mladen Dolar makes the claim: 'Ghosts, vampires, monsters, the undead dead, etc. . . . are something brought about by modernity itself'.[1] Dolar is not alone in such seeming unawareness of any medieval concepts of vampires: the abundant research on vampire films, folklore and fiction has focused on Bram Stoker and his successors (and, to a lesser extent, on his eighteenth- and nineteenth-century predecessors), and almost completely excluded medieval bloodsuckers.[2] The present essay, therefore, will examine some of the forgotten medieval creatures in German literature that display the same monstrous appetite for blood which is a defining characteristic of the modern concept of vampire. In particular, it will focus on the women who 'suck' out semen (understood as men's blood in its purest form) in the gynaecological treatise *Secrets of Women*, the feminized soul sucking the blood from Jesus' wounds in the mystical text of Mechthild of Magdeburg, *The Flowing Light of the Godhead*, and finally, the monsters without bellies which appear in Der Stricker's Arthurian romance, *Daniel of the Blossoming Valley*.[3] What is common to all of these early 'bloodsuckers' is that, unlike familiar depictions of Dracula and many other modern vampires, they are all explicitly or implicitly gendered female; more precisely, they can be seen as embodiments of female sexual appetites. Thus they form part of the history not just of monsters and consumption, but also of the role played within that history by female sexuality and its literary representation. However, as I shall demonstrate, the fear of female sexuality evident in the *Secrets* and in *Daniel* follows a standard and recognizable pattern, whereas in *The Flowing Light*, its treatment illustrates how stereotypical – and negative – conceptions of female desire could be modified and revalued to more positive ends.

According to medieval medicine, as synthesized in the *Secrets of Women*, all women are considered to be vampiristic insofar as they constantly suck out men's 'life-blood' (semen), with their vaginas during intercourse.[4] Semen, the male seed, is described as being a specially processed kind of blood; in turn, blood is claimed by this text to be made from food that has been digested and purified in several stages.[5] Semen is far superior to its female equivalent, menstrual blood, since men are hotter and can thus process the blood to a higher degree of purification.[6] Semen also contains moisture and heat, considered to be the essence of life. Women, however, too cold to produce this precious liquid themselves, must obtain it through sex in order to gain strength, but as a result they leave men drained and cause them to die prematurely:

> And thus the seed, being further ejected by the men, dries the body from which it comes, for the seed has the power to make moist and warm. But when the body is dried up and the moisture extracted from the body, there occurs an illness of body and life, and thus the human being dies. And this is why those [men] do not live long and die early who often and vigorously fornicate.[7]

From the perspective of the male partner, the life-threatening nature of this extraction of semen by women during conception is described in terms of being sucked:

> The second sign [of conception] is that when the man embraces the woman, he feels that his penis is being pulled and stretched by an enclosure and a press. Just as a baby sucks a little breast and pulls the breast, so the penis is pulled by the woman's vagina.[8]

This extraordinary male fear of having one's life-blood sucked out by women during intercourse can be understood in terms of the fundamental gender opposition which structures this text.[9] Such discourses, of course, allocate to femininity the role of a hostile 'other', a negative foil against which the male subject is defined;[10] being permanently deprived of this powerful substance herself, it would follow that the woman would constantly crave it. Any contact with this 'other' is thus risky for the male, and hetero-sexual intercourse (especially if leading to conception) is a prime instance in the *Secrets* of close physical contact with the other sex as presenting a danger of merging. Moreover, this danger is unavoidable, since sex in moderation is necessary and desirable for reproduction.[11] According to this text, however, the risk can be kept within limits if the man is firmly in control, regulating the woman's desire through stimulation of the breasts and the vagina.[12] Thus, it is only unchecked, insatiable female desire that jeopardizes this guarded contact and encroaches upon the masculine subject, both physically and by usurping his active, dominant position. A further risk of intercourse leading to con-ception derives from the perception of the foetus as an extension of the male seed, that is, a part of the man that is absorbed into the hostile female body. Man and his semen, and the foetus which it produces, are therefore represented as a continuum under threat of infection and injury from the woman.[13] Throughout the pregnancy too, the foetus remains under threat from its mother through potential attempts at abortion, her eating habits and her move-ments.[14] Even after birth, the baby is still presented as threatened by a woman's body, for example, by her 'evil eye', which, in turn, is linked to her menses.[15]

The choice of the term 'sucking' to describe how women drain men's vitality expresses the pull, the force, of female desire and her greed and hunger for semen, and it correlates with the concept of human beings as containers of fluids which characterizes medieval medicine. But, as the comparison between the vagina sucking the penis and the baby sucking the breast in the extract quoted above would suggest, there is also a strong parallel drawn between sexual intercourse and breast-feeding.[16] Milk, like semen, was also thought to be processed blood (in this case, menstrual blood).[17] Logically, then, one might consider breast-feeding as also being a comparable moment of dangerous bloodsucking during which the mother is in danger of having her own life-blood drained by the baby. In this scenario, however, what we find is that if anyone is endangered it is again the suckling baby who is also considered to be threatened by the polluting substances of the mother.[18] What is common to both situations, then, is that during sex, and to a lesser extent breast-feeding, it is the male or male-identified party who is threatened, whether sucking or being sucked, whether in contact with a mother or a sexual partner, or whether the exchanged fluid is nourishing or reproductive. However, whereas the role of woman as nursing mother seems to limit her threatening potential, her adoption of an active 'vampirism' in her extraction of male life-blood is highly frightening.[19]

Such connections between bloodsucking, breast-feeding and female desire are not restricted to medical texts, however. In many of the writings of the medieval mystics images of bloodsucking, nursing and sexual desire abound.[20] For example, Mechthild of Magdeburg's *The Flowing Light of the Godhead* depicts the mystic's soul specifically as a bloodsucker – as drinking Christ's blood from his wounds. Like many other mystical texts too, the *Flowing Light* represents the soul of the narrator as female (often a lover or bride), longing for and uniting with a male God.[21] In her depiction of this episode of bloodsucking, for example, Mechthild of Magdeburg describes the relationship between the soul and God in terms of sexual contact: kissing, loving gazes, close embrace in the bed of love.[22] A dialogue between the soul and the Virgin Mary follows, in which no less than the history of salvation is told in terms of Mary's breast-feeding: first she nurses the prophets and sages, then Jesus, then the personification of Christendom and the apostles, and finally she gives suck to the soul and all Christians up until Judgement Day.[23] More significantly, also inserted into this conversation is the description of the soul being breast-fed by both Mary's breasts *and* Jesus' wounds: 'Then both his wounds and her breasts stood open, the wounds poured, the breasts flowed, so that the soul became alive and very healthy, when he poured the bright red wine into her red mouth.'[24]

By representing the feminized soul as drinking a life-giving fluid directly from the wound of her masculine sexual partner, the text invokes the same image of the bloodsucking woman which we saw in the *Secrets*. But the act here is less one of aggressive female sucking than of deliberate male (and female) giving suck: both

Mary and Jesus offer their blood freely.[25] Not only is the feminized soul's desire reciprocated, but God's growing lust is also mentioned in this chapter,[26] and their mutual yearning is a main theme throughout the *Flowing Light*.[27] In fact, in another episode, it is the woman whose own heart is sucked by Jesus.[28] Therefore, in this account written from a woman's perspective, female desire is not seen as a threatening encroachment upon the male, but as fully reciprocated by the man's similar urge to give. By representing the female soul as a bloodsucker, therefore, Mechthild utilizes and perpetuates this particular conception of femininity, as well as modifying and revaluing it as a predominantly positive way of becoming one with God.[29]

Turning now to Der Stricker's Arthurian romance *Daniel of the Blossoming Valley*, we find that bloodsucking is apparently separated from the female body and projected on to fantastic monsters resembling modern vampires. In this text, these creatures have usurped the Country of the Light Fountain, and its distressed countess begs the passing eponymous hero for help. The leader of these monsters has, she explains, a gigantic head so heavy that two men could not carry it, with huge eyes and a mouth more than a yard wide. As this creature lacks a belly and intestines (and by implication is devoid of sexual organs), its arms and legs are directly attached to the head, the chin reaching down to the knees. Leading an army of identical creatures, this monster has come from the sea and occupies the country with the help of a magic weapon it carries around, a kind of Medusa-head which kills anyone who looks it in the eye.[30] And, crucially, like modern vampires, these monsters live exclusively by sucking blood straight from the bodies of their numerous victims: 'Whomever he has killed, has his blood sucked out by them. They keep it in their mouths for a short while and let it flow back out again. So they all live. They do not have any other food.'[31]

As in the previous examples, blood is synonymous with life; it is essential nourishment for those who drink it and death for those who lose it. These bloodsuckers, however, in their display of the same lust for life-blood as the women in the *Secrets*, can again be read as representations of life-threatening female desire in spite of their apparent lack of gender credentials. Apart from their bloodsucking, they also share several other characteristics with the desiring women of the *Secrets* and other medieval texts: their possession of the evil eye, for instance.[32] More significantly, it is a lady's desire that leads Daniel into confrontation with these monstrous bloodsuckers (although, contrary to generic convention, she has to persuade him to help her in a long humiliating plea), and the bloodsucking monsters and female desire thus become further conflated in this text.[33] Similarly, it is only the men (Daniel and the countess's husband) who are actually at risk from the bloodsuckers, whereas the women (the countess and her forty maids) are represented as being elsewhere, in a position of safety.

This reading of the bloodsuckers as inherently female, or as projections of female desire, is corroborated by the repetition of this pattern in the other two episodes which constitute part of Daniel's personal quest.[34] Both episodes again feature ladies desirous of the hero's help who cause him to become involved in fights with monstrous opponents. One lady, Sandinose, literally entraps him in a magical net and forces him to fight against another version of the bloodsucker – a sick man with a hypnotic gaze and voice who periodically cuts the throats of a hundred men so that he can bathe in their blood to cure his unnamed disease.[35] On another occasion, the daughter of the Duke of the Country of the Dull Mountain ensnares Daniel in a fight against a violent dwarf, again simply by being a lady in distress. As Daniel muses at length, as a knight he is obliged to help her,[36] and as the text emphasizes by means of crude terminology, this latter lady's appetites are also clearly sexual, a fact that makes Daniel beg for leave rather than attracting him to the task.[37] In this text, therefore, women are presented not as the passive objects of men's desires which we would normally expect to find within the romance's ideal of courtly love, but, as we have seen in the *Secrets*, as having desires of their own that ultimately pose a danger to men.

In all three of these texts, therefore, we can recognize how the depiction of female desire is conditioned by an institutionalized gender imbalance. Just as women in the *Secrets* are constructed as biologically lacking the superior semen of the male, so in *Daniel* they are perceived to lack the ability to fight and defend themselves against the usurpers. This lack is addressed by a demand to share in men's power, a demand which is met in Mechthild of Magdeburg's *Flowing Light* by a reconfiguration of female desire, as we have seen, and its use as a means of merging with the divine. In the *Secrets* it is met by the fact that men are obliged to have sex in order to reproduce; and in the gender system intrinsic to romance as evidenced in *Daniel*, a moral code binds the man to give his physical service to ladies. In all three scenarios the danger arises when women disrupt accepted gender roles by enforcing their own desires, by taking control or by actively manipulating the system. The happy ending characteristic of most romances, of course, indicates that this threat posed by active female desire is usually just about contained, with a return to the status quo.

The bloodsuckers in *Daniel*, the soul in the *Flowing Light* and the women in the *Secrets* thus embody a whole web of connections between the concepts of femininity, bloodsucking and desire. These connections are further emphasized by the use of two highly common motifs within these texts: that of the evil eye and the mirror. It is with an examination of these images and how they relate to monstrous female appetite that I would now like to conclude.

As I suggested in my discussion of the *Secrets*, such medical texts promoted the idea of women as having an evil gaze and as able to pollute children in their cradles by means of the poisonous menstrual blood evaporating out of their eyes: 'It should be noted and kept in mind that the old women who thus have retained their period, and also other women whose menstrual blood is fresh, poison the children when they are looking at their child lying in the cradle.'[38] In this text, at least, the female gaze is another way in which women impinge upon and endanger men, or more precisely here, the baby as the male 'semen-extension'. Moreover, this evil eye of the female can again be seen as representative of female sexual desire in particular, since evaporated menstrual blood emitted through this gaze is described in the *Secrets* as the cause of women's sexual desires. Explicitly, it is the matter that 'will itch her so that she must desire to lie with the men'.[39]

Equally threatening in this text is the associated image of the mirror, an object also particularly vulnerable to pollution from the female 'menstrual' gaze. In this case, the potentially lethal menstrual gaze is explicitly compared to the monstrous – the dragon-like basilisk.[40] However, in some versions of the *Secrets* the mirror also, paradoxically, plays a more positive role as a protective device against the female gaze:

In the same way [as a 'menstrual' woman], a basilisk is infected by seeing himself, because he emits poison. And if you take a mirror that will reflect the humours back to the place of the basilisk, he will be killed or infected by them.[41]

Ironically, in this instance the mirror *protects* against the female-identified basilisk's poisonous emissions by returning them and their ill effects back to the source. In other words, the turning of the gaze of the threatening female 'other' back on itself neutralizes the danger it poses to the male subject. It would thus appear that the female 'other' is only dangerous as long as the male subject needs it as a negative foil against which to define himself. If he dispenses with his need to be reflected by the female, then in turn she becomes self-reflective and no longer poses a threat to him.[42]

The mirror, however, is not always a foolproof way of rendering women harmless or passive; in their crucial role as foil for male identity and, of course, as partners for reproduction, they are not as easily defeated as the fantastic basilisks. Thus, in the *Flowing Light*, the reflected gaze is reinterpreted not just as a way of desiring, but actually becomes a means of achieving direct access to God. The reciprocity between the mystic and God invokes and redefines the mirror as a means of connecting through reflection: both looking and reflecting are now reciprocal actions, with the soul looking at God and acting as his mirror, and vice versa. Both lover and beloved become simultaneously 'same' and 'other'. Both parties, too, perceive this interaction as predominantly blissful, rather than posing a one-sided threat to the male object of female desire, as we saw in the *Secrets*.[43] Likewise, in *Daniel* the protagonist is also depicted as using a mirror, this time to locate and observe the leader of the blood-suckers without having to look directly at the lethal Medusa-head carried as a weapon. At one point he is represented as walking backwards towards the creature until he is close enough to decapitate it:

> Daniel watched in the mirror how he went about it . . . and walked backwards very quickly . . . Daniel unsheathed the sword . . . and dealt a blow behind him. He poured him a bitter memorial drink by cutting his legs in two under the chin.[44]

In this text, the motif of the mirror as reflecting a threat back to its source has been slightly displaced, in the same way as the dangerous bloodsucking was also displaced from a specifically female body onto ungendered creatures devoid of torsos. However, as I have argued in the case of these seemingly ungendered creatures, the end result of these displacements is essentially the same: the containment of the original threat which is closely allied to dangerous and destructive female desire. Similarly, the fact that Daniel's decapitation of the monster is necessarily also a violation of what presumably is the monster's (absent) genital region, draws the reader's attention back to the 'blind spot' or the female-associated 'lack', and thus betrays what is really the issue behind all these conspicuous displacements: the fighting of female desire.

Contrary to modern scholars' assumptions, then, about the absence of vampires in pre-modern consciousness, the Middle Ages did create their own bloodsuckers. Their presence seems to have been particularly prevalent in science and in fiction where masculinity is frequently defined as being that which is non-feminine. This feminine is thus constructed as the 'other', which is then established as the object of fear. Nor is this pattern of demonization restricted merely to women – Jews and other outsiders were similarly stigmatized – nor to the Middle Ages. It could well be that the notions of bloodsuckers as discussed here, combined with similar ideas of bloodthirsty, child-eating and man-eating women helped to lay the foundations for the persecution of millions of women as witches in early modern Europe.[45] Even modern vampires, if female, often still show striking parallels to these medieval bloodsuckers, particularly those represented in the *Secrets of Women*, in their sexual thirst, their draining of energy, their choice of children as victims and their connections to menstruation, disease and witchcraft.[46]

Notes

[1] M. Dolar, ' "I shall be with you on your wedding-night": Lacan and the uncanny', *October* 58 (1991), 5–23 (7).

[2] Even histories of vampirism rarely mention medieval literature; and if they do, they tend to concentrate on revenants rather than bloodsuckers, for example, R. Petzoldt, 'Vampire', in C. Lindahl et al. (eds), *Medieval Folklore: An Encyclopedia of Myths, Legends, Tales, Beliefs and Customs* (Santa Barbara, Denver, Oxford, 2000), pp. 1016–19; T. Schürmann, *Nachzehrerglauben in Mitteleuropa* (Marburg, 1990); J. C. Holte, 'The vampire', in M. South (ed.), *Mythical and Fabulous Creatures: A Source Book and Research Guide* (New York,

Westport, London, 1987), pp. 243–64. The historical Dracula, a fifteenth-century Wallachian ruler also known as Vlad the Impaler, has received some critical attention, but ironically, in late medieval accounts, Dracula was not a bloodsucking vampire as such, but only metaphorically bloodthirsty; see, for example, R. T. McNally and R. Florescu, *In Search of Dracula: The History of Dracula and Vampires* (London, 1995 [1972]); D. Harmening, *Der Anfang von Dracula: Zur Geschichte von Geschichten* (Würzburg, 1983).

[3] Der Stricker, *Daniel von dem Blühenden Tal*, ed. M. Resler (Tübingen, 1995 [1983]), c. 1210–25; Mechthild of Magdeburg, *Das fließende Licht der Gottheit*, ed. H. Neumann (Munich and Zurich, 1990), c. 1250–80; Pseudo-Albertus Magnus, *Secreta mulierum cum commento Deutsch*, ed. M. Schleissner (unpublished thesis, Princeton, 1987), a fifteenth-century trans. into German of an unedited thirteenth-century Latin treatise of German origin. Published English trans. of the first two works and Latin versions of the *Secrets* are available, but I have used my own literal trans.

[4] The *Secrets* represents an amalgamation of common medieval medical ideas about sexuality and reproduction in the traditions of Galen and also Aristotle, summarized, for example, by D. Jacquart and C. Thomasset, *Sexuality and Medicine in the Middle Ages* (Cambridge, 1988 [1985]) and J. Cadden, *Meanings of Sex Difference in the Middle Ages: Medicine, Science and Culture* (Cambridge, 1993).

[5] Pseudo-Albertus Magnus, *Secrets*, ll. 2760–86; 2885–2908.

[6] Ibid., ll. 186–214.

[7] Ibid., ll. 2909–43, here 2909–14, cf. ll. 2922–5.

[8] Ibid., ll. 2093–7.

[9] This image is reminiscent of the typology of the *vagina dentata* as perpetuated by writers such as John Mandeville. As Claire Jowitt similarly points out in ch. 7 above, Mandeville claimed of Gadlibirien maidens: '[they had] within them nadders [snakes], that tanged [stung] the husbands on the yards [penises] in the women's bodies; and so were many men slain'. *Mandeville's Travels: Texts and Translations*, ed. Malcolm Letts (London, 1953), 2 vols, I, p. 200.

[10] This way of constructing a subject was most extensively described by Jacques Lacan, who also stressed the importance of the gaze and the mirror (discussed below) for the development of identity. However in the context of this essay, the terms 'subject', 'mirror', 'gaze', 'other' and 'desire' are used more colloquially. For easy access to Lacan's definition of these concepts, see D. Evans, *An Introductory Dictionary of Lacanian Psychoanalysis* (London and New York, 1996).

[11] It is also important for male identity as defined in this text; because only through close contact with the 'other' can men assert their identity as different. This identity is often imagined spatially in the *Secrets*, with femininity depicted as physically surrounding masculinity and always potentially invading its space, engulfing, intruding on, eating or polluting it.

[12] Pseudo-Albertus Magnus, *Secrets*, ll. 1862–9.

[13] For example, the question arises whether male seed that was intended to become a boy can be polluted by thunder at the moment of conception so that it becomes a female embryo. This implies both that the male seed here is perceived to be the sole constituent of the foetus (while female seed is not mentioned), and that the offspring is male by default. Ibid., ll. 1566–73, cf. ll. 1458–1596, 1584–94, 1632–6, 1922–30, 2383.

[14] Ibid., for example, ll. 1448–55, 2153–66, 2610–57.

¹⁵ The belief in the damaging power of gazes, esp. of women's gazes for babies, and related superstitions can be found in many medieval texts and will be examined below.

¹⁶ Throughout the extensive range of medieval German literature collected in Bowling Green State University's electronic Mittelhochdeutsche Begriffsdatenbank, 'to suck' seems to be most commonly used in the context of breast-feeding.

¹⁷ Pseudo-Albertus Magnus, *Secrets,* for example, ll. 1621–47.

¹⁸ Concern for the safety of the child at the breast is voiced, for instance, by Ortolf of Baierland in his *Arzneibuch*, ed. J. Follan (Stuttgart, 1963), p. 89.

¹⁹ Woman's relationship to food could also be an issue here, of course: it is considered natural for women to adopt the role of food-providers (for babies). However, for women to become active in satisfying their own appetites is considered threatening. For other references to women's appetites for strange food see Pseudo-Albertus Magnus, *Secrets,* ll. 2153–66, 2610–57; see also C. W. Bynum, *Holy Feast and Holy Fast: The Religious Significance of Food to Medieval Women* (Berkeley, Los Angeles and London, 1987).

²⁰ C. W. Bynum's famous studies, especially *Fragmentation and Redemption: Essays on Gender and the Human Body in Medieval Religion* (New York, 1991), *Jesus as Mother: Studies in the Spirituality of the High Middle Ages* (Berkeley, Los Angeles, London, 1982) and *Holy Feast*, illustrate the widespread devotion of women mystics to Jesus' wounds and, to a lesser extent, how this parallels a devotion to Mary's breasts. See, for example, the case of Catherine of Siena, *Holy Feast,* pp. 165–80.

²¹ Soul, narrator and author, and even other characters such as Mary in the chapter under discussion, sometimes blur into one character in the *Flowing Light* (another instance of positive, non-threatening merging of identities).

²² Mechthild, *Flowing Light,* I, 22, ll. 18–34.

²³ Ibid., I, 22, ll. 50–77.

²⁴ Ibid., I, 22, ll. 56–8.

²⁵ Unlike the men in the *Secrets* who are unwilling to share their limited resources of semen, God's and Mary's blood/milk/wine supplies seem to be endless and even increase, paradoxically, when consumed. However, God is incomparably superior and powerful in relation to the female soul (Mechthild, *Flowing Light,* I, 22, l. 30). The use of wine as a synonym for blood here recalls the identity of Jesus' blood with the Eucharistic wine (for example, *Flowing Light,* II, 7 and II, 24), moving the image of bloodsucking even further away from a physiological draining of men.

²⁶ Mechthild, *Flowing Light,* I, 22, l. 26.

²⁷ For example, ibid., I, 17–20.

²⁸ Ibid., I, 4, ll. 100–1.

²⁹ This 'tamed' image of the female bloodsucker is, however, still problematic, potentially raising fears of queer sexuality, cannibalism and the dissolution of the bodies involved.

³⁰ Stricker, *Daniel,* ll. 1876–1916. These features highlight the monstrosity of the creatures; their big eyes draw attention to the issue of the gaze, their mouths to eating and drinking (see below).

³¹ Ibid., ll. 1917–23.

³² D. Jacquart and C. Thomasset also regard the link to the sea as a menstrual feature in *Sexuality and Medicine*, p. 74. For an overview of the history of the evil eye see David Williams, *Deformed Discourse: The Function of the Monster in Mediaeval Thought and Literature* (Exeter, 1996), pp. 149–55.

[33] Stricker, *Daniel*, ll. 1787–1876.

[34] This quest is intertwined with a story line of a challenge to the Arthurian court as a whole.

[35] Stricker, *Daniel*, ll. 4146–4214, 4376–4443.

[36] Ibid., ll. 1115–1200, 1343–94.

[37] Ibid., ll. 1739–82.

[38] Pseudo-Albertus Magnus, *Secrets*, ll. 2315–18.

[39] Pseudo-Albertus Magnus, *Secrets*, l. 239, cf. ll. 2146–9.

[40] See, for example, Pseudo-Albertus Magnus, *Secrets*, ll. 626–32.

[41] Pseudo-Albertus Magnus, *Libellus de formatione hominis in vtero, vel ut notiori Titulo, Secreta mulierum* (Antwerp, 1538), ch. 10.

[42] It is worth noting here that modern vampires do not have a reflection in the mirror, perhaps because they are nothing but 'others'; they do not exist independently as subjects and accordingly have no 'other'. A similar explanation, but given within the framework of Lacanian psychoanalysis, is offered by J. Copjec, 'Vampires, breast-feeding, and anxiety', *October* 58 (1998), 24–43 (27).

[43] For a list of images of eyes and mirrors in this text see G. Lüers, *Die Sprache der deutschen Mystik des Mittelalters im Werke der Mechthild von Magdeburg* (Munich, 1926), pp. 129–31, 245–8.

[44] Stricker, *Daniel*, ll. 2086–2109.

[45] Compare, for example, N. Cohn, *Europe's Inner Demons: The Demonization of Christians in Medieval Christendom* (London, 1993 [1975]), esp. pp. 162–6.

[46] See, for example, S. Macfie, ' "They suck us dry": a study of late nineteenth-century projections of vampire women', in P. Shaw and P. Stockwell (eds), *Subjectivity and Literature from the Romantics to the Present Day* (London, New York, 1991), pp. 58–67 (58–61).

10

Sheela's Voracity and Victorian Veracity[1]

EMMA L. E. REES

When the French critic Hélène Cixous asked in her 'Sorties' of 1975 'Where is she?', she illustrated her response by means of a series of binaries in which the 'she' is discursively – and, by extension, culturally – inscribed as the absence, or shadowy other, which is effectively eradicated by the presence of a dominant 'he':

> Activity/Passivity
> Sun/Moon
> Culture/Nature
> Day/Night
> . . .
> Head/Heart
> Intelligible/Palpable.[2]

'Either woman is passive', argued Cixous, 'or she does not exist. What is left of her is unthinkable, unthought.'[3] A similarly compelling series of binary oppositions structures the transhistorical gendered relationship at the centre of this essay. For want of a better term, a 'dialogue' is at the heart of my analysis; a dialogue between two equally intransigent figures separated by some 700 years, and one which prompts the reader to reiterate Cixous's 'Where is she?' This dialogue functions as the locus for a clash of, on the one hand, censorial eradication and, on the other hand, bodily exhibitionism. Binaries of mendacity and veracity, restraint and voracity, silence and volubility, also feature. To put it another way, it will be shown what happens when the extrinsic pieties of Victorian gentility meet the explicit genitalia of Romanesque piety.

George Robert Lewis (1782–1871) was an early exponent of an architectural tradition which included, among others, the Pugin family.[4] Victorian Gothic revivalism was arguably not so much an aesthetic as a didactic movement fuelled – as A. W. N. Pugin's *Contrasts* of 1836 suggests – by a vehement religiosity.[5] It is significant that these Victorians, in naming their movement, were drawn more to the geometric orderliness of the 'Gothic' than to its near historical cousin, the rather haphazard 'Romanesque'. Pugin's theory was predicated on paradox and reversal; he reread the Christian 'Dark Ages' as in fact radiating light and inspiration. Following the repeal of the Test and Corporation Acts in 1828, and the passing of the Catholic Emancipation Act of 1829, the 1830s and 1840s rapidly became the era of the gentleman ecclesiastical architect in whose person and psyche discourses of religion, art and socio-economic reform converged.[6] In his 1841 *True Principles of Pointed or Christian Architecture*, Pugin delineated a model of a perfect balance of style, ornament and utility distilled into his 'two great rules for design': '1st, that there should be no features about a building which are not necessary for convenience, construction, or propriety; 2nd, that all ornament should consist of enrichment of the essential construction of the building'.[7]

That G. R. Lewis shared such sympathies with Pugin is suggested by the inclusion in the 'List of Subscribers' to his 1842 *Illustrations of Kilpeck Church*[8] of one 'Pugin, Alvelly, Esq., Architect, Cheyne Walk, Chelsea' (7).[9] The *Illustrations* contains an *Essay on Ecclesiastical Design*, central to which is Lewis's belief that 'the stone, the wood, and the glass of His places of worship' represent and reflect God's word, so that the physical materials of an ecclesiastical building function as 'symbolic, emblematic, or hieroglyphic representations of . . . Holy Writ', becoming 'vehicle[s] of communication upon the Sacred Writings' (ii). His stated aim is to uncover what motivated church designers of the Middle Ages who 'must have had some other end in view than the inner appropriated spaces for religious worship' (ii).

Unambiguous in his condemnation of, among others, Henry VIII, 'the great Spoliator' whose 'tyrannous acts' destroyed the Church, Lewis charts the decline of, and tries to reintroduce, his ideological touchstone, 'intelligent Design' (iv).[10] 'Intelligent Design' is explicitly and repeatedly opposed to an impious 'animal mode of dealing with intellect', such as was exhibited at the

Reformation (iv). This constant predication of the rational over the bodily is reminiscent of the stark binaries with which this essay opened. In such a discourse, as will be seen, an exhibitionist female figure is necessarily allied with the corporeal or non-rational. As Lewis reminds his readers, 'The wages of sin is death, and he who prefers animal gratification to those of intellect, must expect it' (6). However, in what will be shown to be his *eradication* of the non-rational, exemplified by his confrontation with the figure of a Sheela-na-Gig at Kilpeck Church, this essay interrogates whether Lewis was actually moving closer to his politico-aesthetic philosophy of 'intelligent Design'. In her intentional symbolism, the Sheela-na-Gig is central to the original church architect's *own* 'intelligent Design'; for Lewis's argument to function, she must, by extension, be central to that, too. As Foucault argues in his *History of Sexuality*, eradicating something is to acknowledge that there exists something to be eradicated, and Sheela haunts Lewis's thesis from the margins of eradication, her solid, stony presence troubling and silently confrontational.[11] It will be seen how Lewis's denial of female sexuality, therefore, goes far deeper than facile propriety; it is actually necessary for the maintenance of Lewis's deeper religious, cultural and aesthetic beliefs, which reflect and are set up in his thesis against an impious, unruly and anti-intellectual wider society.

The parish church of St Mary and St David in Kilpeck is an isolated three-cell Romanesque building situated about eight miles south-west of Hereford.[12] For Lewis, it is the archetype of 'intelligent Design', a crucially important 'work of high imagination' combined with 'pure Christianity' (xvi, xvii). In its '66 feet by 26, the Designer has conveyed religious information sufficient to guide us through the whole course of our lives' (18). A touch of what has been termed Pugin's 'inspirational bigotry' is in evidence as Lewis deplores the deterioration he sees in the late 1830s in the condition of Kilpeck church, however.[13] The inference is that any renovation work must, of course, be executed by an adherent to Lewis's own philosophy:

> These important matters must be taken in hand by the highly educated, for to expect parishioners of an obscure village to be aware of the

beauties and intelligence that are in the works of imagination, is more than we have any reason to do, as their minds are wholly directed to their calling – agricultural pursuits. (xvii)[14]

Lewis continues in this vein, condemning the destruction of the original apsidal roof, and of the frescos which he recalls seeing during his visit in 1818, and the obliteration of much of the building by 'unsightly coatings of white, buff, and grey wash' (xviii).[15]

Built by Hugh of Kilpeck on land given to his father by William the Conqueror, the church was probably completed by 1134 when it was given to St Peter's Abbey, Gloucester.[16] Because Lewis believed that the designers of the earliest churches were also their ministers, he easily allies form and function. In fact, the designer of Kilpeck church was probably not a minister but a patron eager for bricks-and-mortar evidence of his power and piety. Hugh of Kilpeck was a kinsman of the lord of Wigmore, Hugh Mortimer. Mortimer's steward, Oliver de Merlimond, followed the pilgrimage routes to the shrine of St James at Santiago de Compostela, returning with Victorine monks to commence the building of a church at nearby Shobdon for Mortimer.[17] Hugh of Kilpeck then probably employed the same masons on his church. The architectural influences are Norman, strictly speaking, but the cultural cross-fertilization of the pilgrimage routes through western Europe means that Kilpeck is actually highly eclectic – in places, unique – as Celtic, Saxon, Scandinavian and even Oriental images and styles are united into a capricious Romanesque whole.[18]

One of the most striking features of Kilpeck Church, and one to which Lewis devotes much space, is its elaborate table of eighty-nine corbels. The corbel is primarily a structural necessity, often highly decorative. Deriving from the Latin *corbis*, meaning 'basket', it was designed to support weight. As is the case at Kilpeck, 'outside, corbels are best seen in a long row underneath the parapet wall or cornice. This is known as a "corbel-table"'.[19] The corbels are essential 'vehicle[s] of communication upon the subject for which they were made' and Lewis describes them carefully, stressing their didactic functions (13). The assertion of the anonymous author of the modern *Guide* to the church, claiming that '[o]ut of over seventy grotesque carvings on the corbel [*sic*] only two can be said to have any religious significance', is inaccurate.[20] Of the corbels, however, one is of particular

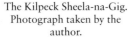

The Kilpeck Sheela-na-Gig. Photograph taken by the author.

Drawing of the Kilpeck 'fool' by G. R. Lewis.

importance here: that depicting the Sheela-na-Gig. This exhibitionist female figure is by no means unique to Kilpeck; there are other mainland examples – some texts list as many as twenty-four, from Sussex to Derbyshire – as well as many in Ireland and, of course, in France and into Spain along the pilgrim routes.[21]

Use of the term 'Sheela-na-Gig' entered antiquarian circles in Ireland in the 1840s.[22] Its origins are unclear, but it could derive from the Irish 'Sighle na gCíoch', meaning 'the old hag of the breasts', or 'Síle-ina-Giob', 'sheela (an old woman) on her hunkers'.[23] It has already been seen how pilgrimage routes into north-west Spain, to Santiago de Compostela in particular, were responsible for introducing Romanesque architecture into Britain from the middle of the tenth century.[24] Pilgrimages, of course, such as that taken by Oliver de Merlimond, would take a long time, and temptations of the flesh were many along the well-established pilgrim routes. The Sheela-na-Gig may have become one of many Romanesque church symbols designed to deter potential sinners from fornication. Sheela, it would seem, has always suffered at the hands of a patriarchy unwilling to accept the multiple possible interpretations of her pose with legs akimbo and vulva stretched open. The Kilpeck Sheela is actually rather benign and challenges the highly questionable and subjective assertions of modern (male) critics who dismiss all such sculptures as 'grotesque, hideous and ugly', or 'particularly terrifying', removing them from the realm of the erotic.[25] Of pagan Celtic icons it has been said that 'the symbolic content would be a matter of conscious choice by people who were fully cognizant with the means best employed in endowing a cult-object with the greatest potency', and this would seem to be the case with the Kilpeck Sheela.[26] As Weir and Jerman, authors of *Images of Lust: Sexual Carvings on Medieval Churches*, are forced to conclude:

> the weight of testimony is overwhelmingly in favour of didacticism as the mainspring of Romanesque carving. In the face of cumulative evidence we find it impossible to believe that medieval carvers could adorn religious edifices with every nuance of lewd designs unless they had had the approval of their ecclesiastical patrons. The Church *must* have been in consonance with the masons, and vice versa, and both worked with a view to showing mankind the error of its ways.[27]

A Romanesque archetype, then, Sheela was probably intended to have a minatory function, to castigate lust; any fertility or apotropaic – that is, talismanic – rites popularly ascribed to her were a later invention.[28] Given the expense and effort involved in building a church as ostentatious and elaborate as Kilpeck, and in spite of the fact that it derived from secular not religious patronage, it is unlikely in the extreme that Sheela is there on a stonemason's mischievous, pornographic whim; to make such a claim is to deny her her power as a deeply religious Christian figure. Lewis's disapproval of Sheela continued a long history of clerical misogyny, and it may be the case that 'monastic fulminations against Eve were also at the very heart of sheela-na-gig invention . . . Her provenance is to be sought in the anti-feminism of the twelfth-century Church.'[29] Thus, if we follow the didactic line of argument as to the function of the Sheela figure, Lewis would actually have been emphasizing – rather than detracting from – his own didactic Christian argument had he incorporated Sheela truthfully. Instead, he is guilty of an excess of propriety and denies her her seriousness, writing her out of what he apparently perceived to be 'otiose sculptural graffiti'.[30]

There is no possibility that Lewis did not realize or understand what Sheela was about. For a start, he could not plead a failure to see the corbel clearly since he records being loaned scaffolding so that he could 'approach the different portions of the edifice sufficiently near to delineate with accuracy equal to portraiture' (36). The figure of Sheela is described thus in his work: '26 represents a fool – the cut in his chest, the way to his heart, denotes it is always open and to all alike' (15). If Lewis really thought that what he could see from his scaffold was this 'fool', then why not represent it as it appears? Instead, considerable alterations have been made, leading to the description of the representation as being 'a Victorian bowdlerised version'.[31] In Lewis's drawing, the arms point away from the body; the hands are freely visible. The legs are practically indistinguishable, and the vagina resembles an elongated heraldic shield in shape. As Andersen puts it, 'any suggestion of immodesty has been removed from the figure'.[32] In reality, Sheela's elbows form two angles of a roughly equilateral triangle, the third point of which is formed by the base of the vulva. The arms point in towards her body, and her hands almost disappear into her stretched-open vagina. The splayed legs, with knees drawn up, are clearly visible. In summary, then, she is not a 'fool', and the 'cut' is – put crudely, perhaps, but suggestively, given Lewis's choice of words – a 'cunt'. Whilst acknowledging that the corbels 'are evidently the result of different minds and times', Lewis cannot entertain the possibility that an accurate representation of Sheela's pose could be anything other than unsuitable for his subscribers (15).[33]

Lewis's beautifully executed lithographs of Kilpeck are explained in a commentary which, if it serves its intended purpose, would mean that readers 'should then have the *truth* placed before [them]' (1; my emphasis). 'Truth', however, is a slippery term, and from the outset there are suggestions that, if Kilpeck does not conform in actuality to Lewis's thesis, in representation it will be made to. The 'common-place and vulgar bell-box mutilation', for example, is replaced in his lithographs by 'the Apex and Cross as it was formerly', but Lewis admits to not knowing for certain whether this indeed was how the church was 'formerly', and in a footnote he assures his readers that these 'are the only alterations that I have made' (2 and 3).[34] As this essay has illustrated, this is not the case. Lewis's stated intention is to show the church as it originally appeared so that 'its shameful mutilations may be seen and reprobated accordingly' (3). However, the authorial guarantee of truthfulness and authenticity is undone some pages later when, ironically in a diatribe against social hypocrisy whereby modern churches resemble 'hideous Gin Palaces to call us to sobriety and a healthful state of body', Lewis reiterates his 'chief aim', to

> endeavour to ascertain why things are as they are, and *not to make them appear what they were never intended for.* We should always compare the object with the subject it was intended to illustrate, and endeavour to ascertain to what extent it approximates in its design. (18; my emphasis)

The central structural paradox is that, for Lewis's doctrine of truthful design to work, Sheela must be, untruthfully, excluded. So, in her exclusion, his doctrine must fail. The historian cannot fit the corporeal female into a thesis of cerebral, or 'intelligent Design'. Through her uncompromising physicality, the sexualized female silently disrupts hegemonic values. In his revision and trans-mutation of Sheela, Lewis ignores that she may actually be read as Christian and didactic – the very qualities he desired in his own argument. The man who loftily declares that 'we should then have our minds free, open, and ready to examine every new subject that may be presented' (xii), closes his own mind to Sheela. It is thus Lewis's own hypocritical re-presentation of Sheela which overturns the entire authenticity of his polemic. The re-presenting of Sheela is especially problematic since every detail of the church's fabric apparently has some significance in Lewis's architectural exegesis, functioning as it does as part of a larger, apodictic, spiritual design. Tellingly, the feminine can only exist in his discourse as idealized and metaphorical, not as realistically bodily.[35] The church, for example, is a 'she', ravaged by 'plastering quacks and light-age utilitarians' who have erected a porch, the 'conceit and ignorance' of which clearly infuriates Lewis who describes it in lan-guage which reveals both his social concerns and feelings of vulnerability: 'Who can divest themselves of the impression of smoking and drinking which the porch must make upon the mind of every beholder; it being in its appearance a public-house porch[?]' (16).[36]

In the ensuing discussion of 'taste', rhetorical recourse is made once more to the feminine. The moralizing and sexualized under-tones are unmistakable, as taste becomes a gaudy whore, 'twin sister of fashion or caprice, ever thrusting herself forward', dangerous because 'Women follow her advice and lace in their waists to meet the form that *taste* has laid down' (18). Lewis's society's preferment of taste over scripture has resulted in the lamentable fact that human beings, instead of 'walking steadily on in the path of truth', are 'travelling at a railway pace on the road of error' (37). Modern society – here epitomized by that exemplar of Victorian progress, the locomotive – clearly terrifies him.

Sheela does not change. Readings of her do. Hence the possibility that she was revered as a pagan goddess of fertility by the Celts, was a moral and didactic Christian emblem for Kilpeck's builders, warning against sexual promiscuity, became imbued with apotropaic qualities in the later Middle Ages and was erased generations later by Lewis.[37] From the female body each culture takes what it needs and attempts to eradicate what it does not. So Sheela becomes a chaotic site of cultural expectation and imbrication, freighted with the compelling needs and desires of her observers. She is the locus for psychological contestation, putting Lewis into something of a quandary: should he represent her in her authentic, challenging pose, or re-present her as desexualized and inauthentic? In the end, social mores (and, no doubt, sensitive subscribers) made up his mind for him and he bowed to their demands. In this act of duplicitous cultural complicity he effectively undid much of the underpinning of his 'truthful' project as a whole. So, just as this essay began by positing that the reader of G. R. Lewis's work on Kilpeck Church would be justified in reiterating Cixous's question, 'Where is she?' I conclude by suggesting that ultimately it should be more a question of 'Where is *he*?'[38] Unlike many of his contemporaries – Pugin, for example, and, later, Ruskin – G. R. Lewis is almost anonymous and unread. In stark contrast, Sheela's lapideous legacy endures – she remains tenacious and very much 'open to all and to all alike'.[39]

Notes

[1] My thanks are due to Jon Cooke of English Heritage for his assistance, and to John Harding for his electronic Sheela discussion forum on which contributions from Abby, Jack, Shae and Keith have been of particular interest. Thanks too to

Richard E. Wilson for 'discovering' Kilpeck with me one serendipitous summer afternoon in 1995.

[2] Hélène Cixous, 'Sorties', in *The Hélène Cixous Reader*, ed. Susan Sellers (London, 1994), pp. 37–46 (37).

[3] Ibid., p. 39.

[4] On Lewis's background see *The Grove Dictionary of Art*, ed. Jane Turner, 34 vols (London, 1996), ix, 284.

[5] A. Welby Pugin, *Contrasts; or, A Parallel Between the Noble Edifices of the Fourteenth and Fifteenth Centuries, and Similar Buildings of the Present Day; showing the Present Decay of Taste* (London, 1836).

[6] For more on the social impact of Victorian church-building projects, see Chris Brooks and Andrew Saint (eds), *The Victorian Church: Architecture and Society* (Manchester, 1995), pp. 20–4.

[7] A. Welby Pugin, *The True Principles of Pointed or Christian Architecture* (a reprint of the 1st edn with a foreword by Marina Henderson, London, 1973), p. 1. Henderson's assessment of Pugin is mixed. While she acknowledges his importance, her final assessment is that he was a 'fanatic' (foreword, unnumbered).

[8] G. R. Lewis, *Illustrations of Kilpeck Church, Herefordshire: In a Series of Drawings Made on the Spot. With an Essay on Ecclesiastical Design, and a Descriptive Interpretation* (London, 1842).

[9] The majority of listed subscribers have either nobiliary or ecclesiastical titles, and few of them are women – 'Atherton, Miss Eleonora, Kersall Cell, Manchester (4 copies)' is an exception (5). Geographically, the distribution was wide, as this entry suggests: 'Jennings, B., Esq., Sculptor, Rome' (6). While I have been unable to find biographical details for 'Alvelly Pugin', the Pugin family did reside briefly in Cheyne Walk in 1841, and the possibility that 'Alvelly' is a transcription for 'A. Welby' is compelling. For biographical information on the Pugins see the entry for 'Augustus Welby Northmore Pugin' in *The Catholic Encyclopedia* (June 1911); Online edition 1999: *http://www.newadvent.org/cathen/12558b.htm*

[10] The Reformation is a recurrent preoccupation in Lewis's treatise; he returns to the 'irretrievable ruin' and 'vain and unmanly quality' of conceit, a characteristic which he unhesitatingly attributes to both Henry VIII and Cromwell (xi, xii). Pugin, too, criticizes 'the rapacious tyrant Henry' and 'his lamentable schism', *True Principles*, p. 36.

[11] Michel Foucault, *The History of Sexuality* (Harmondsworth, 1990), I, p. 8. Here Foucault maps the processes by which repressive discourses wield power.

[12] For a more detailed technical description of the church, see Malcolm Thurlby, *The Herefordshire School of Romanesque Sculpture* (Herefordshire, 1999), esp. ch. 4, 'Kilpeck', pp. 37–70.

[13] For more on Pugin's 'inspirational bigotry' see Brooks and Saint (eds), *The Victorian Church*, p. 8.

[14] The sophistication of the iconographic representations might threaten to exceed the intellect of Kilpeck's rural congregation, and later Lewis asks his readers to be patient with 'those who have not the power to perceive the meaning' (28). He is aware of the importance of conveying often complex ideas to an illiterate populace, declaring that 'art can be made a vehicle of communication as well as letter press, and as it possesses powers of form and colour which metal type does not, they should not be neglected' (35).

[15] In his anxieties over heavy-handed 'restoration' work, Lewis is here an early advocate of what came to be termed the 'Anti-scrape' movement. The Society for

the Preservation of Ancient Buildings, or the Anti-scrape Society, was founded in 1878 and numbered William Morris among its founders. See Bernard Denvir, *The Late Victorians: Art, Design and Society, 1852–1910* (London, 1986), pp. 132–3; Chris Miele, ' "Their interest and habit": professionalism and the restoration of medieval churches, 1837–77', in Brooks and Saint (eds), *The Victorian Church*, pp. 151–72. Miele discusses the career of the antiquarian-architect Lewis Nockalls Cottingham, who restored Kilpeck's apse in 1849, putting new glass, designed by Pugin, into the window. See the anonymous *Guide to the Parish Church of SS. Mary and David, Kilpeck* (revised 1989), p. 3.

[16] See Thurlby, *The Herefordshire School*, p. xiii.

[17] For the importance of Shobdon in the development of English Romanesque art, and for an assessment of the value of the record made of Shobdon's sculptures by Lewis in the 1850s, see Joe Hillaby, *The Sculptured Capitals of Leominster Priory* (Leominster, 1993). For information on the dating of Merlimond's pilgrimage, see George Zarnecki, 'The future of the Shobdon arches', *Journal of the British Archaeological Association* 146 (1993), 87–92, especially 88. Andersen also discusses the importance of the pilgrimage in ch. 3 ('The Romanesque Motif') of *The Witch on the Wall*.

[18] On how elements of Kilpeck's sculptures are 'only superficially similar to proper Viking forms', see James F. King, 'The parish church at Kilpeck reassessed', in David Whitehead (ed.), *Medieval Art, Architecture and Archaeology at Hereford* (Leeds, 1995; *The British Archaeological Association Conference Transactions* 15), pp. 82–93 (84). King also details the possible influences on Kilpeck's architecture of the twelfth-century papal legate Henry, abbot of St Jean d'Angely. King, 'Kilpeck reassessed', p. 89.

[19] Thomas Maude, *Guided by a Stone-Mason: The Cathedrals, Abbeys and Churches of Britain Unveiled* (London, 1997), p. 143.

[20] Anon., *Guide to the Parish Church of SS. Mary and David, Kilpeck*, p. 3.

[21] For maps showing the geographical distribution of Romanesque sexual carvings throughout Europe, see Anthony Weir and James Jerman, *Images of Lust: Sexual Carvings on Medieval Churches* (London, 1986), esp. pp. 116–22. Weir and Jerman identify four categories or types of poses into which Sheela sculptures fall, pp. 12–13. The Kilpeck Sheela is a 'Type I'. For the locations of the twenty-four 'female exhibitionists' see Weir and Jerman, *Images of Lust*, pp. 116–17.

[22] See Eamonn P. Kelly, *Sheela-na-Gigs: Origins and Functions* (Dublin, 1996), p. 5. Kelly claims that the name was in use as early as the seventeenth century.

[23] Ibid., p. 5. For more on possible etymology, see the idiosyncratic but astute online article by Kathryn Price Theatana, 'Síla na Géige: Sheela na Gig and sacred space': *http://ourworld.compuserve.com/homepages/moonstone/Sheela.htm*

[24] See Kelly, *Sheela-na-Gigs*, pp. 9–10.

[25] Ibid., p. 35. Not all observers find the figure of Sheela so minatory. *The Kilpeck Anthology*, ed. Glenn Storhaug, for example, contains celebratory poems by Jonathan Williams ('Serenade', which has the line: 'Sheila-na-gigg, the Celtic Pussy Galore'); Seamus Heaney ('Sile Na Gig'), and Fleur Adcock (whose 'Kilpeck' has the lines: 'the Whore of Kilpeck. / She leans out under the roof / holding her pink stony cleft agape / with her ancient little hands'), among others. See Glenn Storhaug (ed.), *The Kilpeck Anthology* (Five Seasons Press, 1981), pp. 13, 18–19, 40.

[26] Miranda Green, *Symbol and Image in Celtic Religious Art* (London, 1989), p. 6. Green analyses why features of Celtic sculptures are exaggerated and

produces a convincing argument central to which is the idea that schematism functions as 'a kind of divine shorthand, where reduction to the essentials of imagery has taken place' (p. 214). Sheela is not a Celtic image but has attributes such as exaggeration and didacticism in common with Celtic religious art. As Weir and Jerman succinctly put it: 'the Celts made no use of female sexual symbols', *Images of Lust*, p. 29.

[27] Weir and Jerman, *Images of Lust*, p. 152.

[28] Weir and Jerman add further evidence to their anti-apotropaic argument by declaring – in a rather suspect way – that the vulva, 'receptive [and] passive' is not as frightening as a phallus. Lewis, presumably, would disagree. See Weir and Jerman, *Images of Lust*, p. 146.

[29] Ibid., p. 20.

[30] Ibid., p. 99. Thurlby, too, favours the didactic interpretation of the corbels, writing that their 'rich variety of types reflects that variety of human experience, the struggle between good and evil . . . The evils of sexual promiscuity are blatantly displayed'. See Thurlby, *The Herefordshire School*, pp. 51–2.

[31] Weir and Jerman, *Images of Lust*, p. 22.

[32] Jørgen Andersen, *The Witch on the Wall: Medieval Erotic Sculptures in the British Isles* (London, 1977), p. 10. As my essay suggests, however, I depart from Andersen's assertion that, at the time at which Lewis was writing, 'the motif cannot have been recognized' (p. 10).

[33] Again, Lewis's erasure of Sheela calls to mind Cixous: 'She does not exist, she can not-be; but there has to be something of her. He keeps, then, of the woman on whom he is no longer dependent, only this space, always virginal, as matter to be subjected to the desire he wishes to impart'. Cixous, 'Sorties', p. 39.

[34] In the same footnote Lewis admits to other 'alterations' such as 'filling in' a recently added door and lights (3).

[35] Pugin adopts a similar mode of gendered personification. In its imposing buttresses, pointed architecture 'does *not conceal her construction, but beautifies it*'. Pugin, *True Principles*, p. 4.

[36] An engraving showing the wooden porch, bell-tower and original apsidal roof may be seen accompanying a letter written by T. L. Parker published in *The Gentleman's Magazine* (May 1833), pp. 392–4. Pugin was, of course, equally class-conscious – also with an emphasis on sobriety and morality – criticizing 'hotel and tavern keepers' for abusing Gothic elements in their wall-coverings. See Pugin, *True Principles*, pp. 29–30.

[37] On Sheela as fertility symbol, see Kelly, *Sheela-na-Gigs*, p. 38. See also Ann Pearson, 'Reclaiming the Sheela-na-gigs: goddess imagery in medieval sculptures of Ireland', *Canadian Woman Studies/Les Cahiers de la Femme* 17/3 (1997), 20–4.

[38] I am, of course, acutely aware of the paradox that in appropriating and rewriting Cixous's question I am guilty of a similarly self-serving – but I hope ultimately less pernicious – poetic licence to that of which Lewis here stands accused.

[39] Lewis's statement here is ambiguous; 'all alike' could mean either 'everyone', or 'in the same way'. The latter, as this essay demonstrates, is inaccurate.

11

'Ant nes he him seolf reclus i maries wombe?': Julian of Norwich, the Anchorhold and Redemption of the Monstrous Female Body

LIZ HERBERT McAVOY

In her exhaustive study of the English anchoritic movement Ann Warren has identified an extraordinary predilection amongst women to embrace a life of anchoritic enclosure during the later Middle Ages in England.[1] During the centuries which she surveys, namely the twelfth through to the early sixteenth century, it would appear that women were consistently more likely than men to enter the anchorhold. At one point during the thirteenth century, for example, there were four times as many female recluses as male. Even in the fourteenth and fifteenth centuries, when a burgeoning profit-driven economy was actually opening up opportunities for women in the developing urban areas of England, there were still substantially more women than men enclosed. To be precise, the ratio of 5:2 was sustained in the fourteenth century and 5:3 in the fifteenth.[2] Similarly, Warren's findings would suggest that, unlike their male counterparts who were usually from a religious order or clerics (24), the women who entered the anchorhold during this period were overwhelmingly laywomen who had lived in the outside world rather than the cloister prior to enclosure (22).

In an attempt to explicate the extraordinary impetus behind the popularity of female anchoritism in England during the twelfth through to the fifteenth century, Warren hazards the following explanation: 'a woman might have wanted to become an anchorite to escape an unattractive marriage, to avoid the dangers of childbirth, to have a private home, because she had no husband, because there was no place for her at the local nunnery' (123). As an all-encompassing explanation for the phenomenon of female anchoritism, however, Warren's claim seems overly simplistic and offers an image of the anchorhold primarily as a means of escape from the other options available to a woman in the world, rather than as a location which could actively empower her. This essay will interrogate Warren's assertion by examining the extent to which discourses of enclosure intersected with female bodily inscription of the monstrous in the Middle Ages, and will suggest that such an intersection was central to female anchoritic subjectivity. It will argue that, by means of a recontextualization – reinscription even – of the cultural narratives of monstrosity to which her body was subject, the anchoress could achieve a measure of empowerment, something which may also offer an alternative suggestion as to why so many more women than men felt called to the anchoritic life.

The following passage, taken from the shorter version of Julian of Norwich's *Revelations of Divine Love*, comes from one of the few extant female-authored texts written in the English vernacular which we know for certain to have been associated with the anchorhold. It is an extract from a passage which foregrounds the female body and presents us with a subtle glimpse of one of the possible motivations behind the female impulse toward anchoritism, evidence which has hitherto been entirely overlooked in Julian's writing:

> Aftyr this my syght byganne to fayle, and it was alle dyrke abowte me in the chaumbyr, and myrke as it hadde bene nyght; save in the ymage of the crosse there helde a comon lyght, and I wyste nevere howe. Alle that was besyde the crosse was huglye to me as ʒyf it hadde bene mykylle occupyede with fendys. (42)[3]

One could be forgiven for reading this extract as documenting a moment leading up to mystical union between the anchoress and her heavenly lover, Christ. As the anchorhold grows increasingly dark, the only light evident is that emanating from the animated crucifix hanging before her eyes and, as all awareness of the bodily and the worldly is relinquished, so the anchoress becomes privy to a direct experience of God. In truth, however, far from documenting a mystical experience within the anchorhold, this passage forms part of an early account by Julian of a life-threatening illness which she suffered as a young woman in 1373. Not only that, but the setting is almost certainly a domestic one – that of Julian's own bedchamber – and it is within this domestic environment and during this dangerous illness that the author experiences the series of mystical visions of Christ which were to dictate the course of her life and become the source of two highly complex texts. I suggest it is highly likely that Julian's experience of sickness within that dark and enclosed bedchamber and her subsequent mystical encounter there generated within her a desire for a perpetual re-enactment of those experiences. In turn, this desire found its literary expression in the production of her two mystical texts, and its physical expression in the author's own anchoritic enclosure in the 1390s. Similarly, I argue that within this encounter with bodily suffering and abjection lies a paradigm for an understanding of the inordinate and sustained popularity of the anchoritic life for women during the period in question.

The domestic nature of the location of Julian's illness is further corroborated by the reference to Julian's own mother who is sitting at the bedside keeping watch over her daughter (ST 54). At one point, in a poignant gesture of maternal love, Julian's mother reaches over to close the eyes of her daughter, whom she now deems to be dead. The inert Julian is helpless to respond to this gesture, but it precipitates in her a meditation on the Virgin's love for *her* child. In fact, all primary protagonists in that dark bedchamber – distraught mother, dying daughter, weeping Virgin and dying Christ (who, of course, is identified as specifically maternal in Julian's Long Text) – become conflated, identifying this dark and enclosed location of abjection as a specifically feminized space.[4]

In the context of *physical* space, of course, feminine spaces tended to be the enclosed and strictly policed locations of home or cloister. In that sense the containment of both sickroom and anchorhold would appear to adhere firmly to those spaces deemed most appropriate for women to occupy within contemporary society. *The Book of Margery Kempe*,[5] for example, is one text which testifies explicitly to the over-determined reactions of patriarchal society to the dangerous body of the uncategorizable woman who transgresses the domestic boundaries which it has laid down for her. On one occasion at Canterbury Margery is told explicitly by a monk whom she has infuriated with her scriptural homilies: 'I wold þow wer closyd in an hows of ston þat þer schuld no man speke wyth þe' (27). In this ambiguous reference to stone walls of containment we see paradigmatically represented the main choices open to women in society – either to rest content behind the walls of the domestic residence, or else embrace those of the cloister. To wander freely at will simply was not a socially accept-able option, and it would seem that the only appropriate space for a woman and her problematic body was that which was enclosed by walls of stone. Indeed, one of society's solutions to Margery Kempe's usurpation of public space is on several occasions to lock her up within the stone walls of a prison or keep her under house arrest.[6]

This desire on the part of society to confine women to domestic or religious enclosure was, of course, closely related to the need to police and control a perceived incontinent sexuality. This is clearly a subtext within popular iconographic and literary representations of the Annunciation in which the Virgin Mary is frequently depicted as enclosed within the walls of a domestic residence.[7] It is just this domesticated setting of the Annunciation which is foregrounded by Aelred of Rievaulx in his *De Institutione Inclus-arum*, an influential treatise on the anchoritic life written for his enclosed sister between 1162 and 1164.[8] The Middle English version of this text specifically identifies the scene of the Annunci-ation as being the Virgin's private bedchamber, which Aelred then proceeds to liken explicitly to her sealed womb (and, by implication, the sealed womb of his sister): 'And ferst goo into þy pryue chaumbre wit our lady Marie wher schee abood þe angel message . . . þanne, sustre, wundre gretly in þyn herte how þilke lord . . . was iclosed witynne þe bowelys of a smal gentil mayden' (39).

Such a domesticated location for the transcendent religious experience is again echoed both by Margery Kempe in her descrip-tion of her first encounter with Christ whilst locked up in her own bedchamber (8), and indeed by Julian in the account of her sickroom experiences already examined. Thus, it would seem that the most perfect expression of woman (and one which also served to contain and control her potentially monstrous sexuality, of course) was inseparable from the four walls which surrounded her. In this way, like the Virgin herself, the anchoress could be regarded as both subject to and expression of that same enclosure-induced perfection. Such an association can also be read as the site of a potential 'blind-spot' which evades the controlling gaze of patriarchal policing: whereas society implicitly regarded the anchorhold as a place of control and containment for the unruly female body, it could actually provide a space within which a woman could herself redefine and recontextualize that construction of femininity for her own purposes, as we shall see. As Bettina Bildhauer suggests in relation to Mechthild of Magdeburg in her essay in this volume, such a recontextualization of cultural discourses could allow for an unprecedented level of intellectual and creative freedom for the woman. At the same time, however, it would allow for an appearance of compliance with − even *performance* of − society's most explicit need to contain her potentially insatiable appetites. In effect, therefore, enclosure could offer a woman access to what Luce Irigaray has identified in her essay on female mysticism as '[e]ndless open space, hung emptily between here and there, dizzying height, steep ascent, even retreat'[9] − in essence, the type of unpoliced physical and intellectual space which would be largely unavailable to her whilst remaining in the world.

This paradox of expansiveness within enclosure is epitomized by the series of images of enclosure within enclosure with which Julian presents us in her sickroom narrative: like so many concentric circles, building, walls, room, body, womb, soul are all depicted as leading both inwards and outwards to the very seat of an immanent divinity. In turn, this divinity in its humanity is famously represented as specifically female and maternal by Julian in the Long Text, a shift from traditional patriarchal representations of God to one which serves to place the disparaged female body at centre stage and redefine it as a potent and crucial salvific entity.

As I have already suggested, this incorporation of the problematic female within the hermeneutics of enclosure is introduced by

Julian early in both of her texts by means of her placing a suffering self at the forefront of her sickness narrative. Here, Julian describes how her inert body is wracked with pain, following which a gradual paralysis engulfs her and threatens to take away her eyesight. Although a common topos in the writing of religious women, it would seem likely that in this self-depiction, Julian is indirectly engaging with the commonly held beliefs about perceived female ontology as disseminated in popular medical treatises, particularly *The Knowyng of Woman's Kynde* and the other so-called *Trotula* texts, which were now becoming available in the vernacular.[10] These texts, informed as they also were by the theological notion of the transgression of Eve, are everywhere suggestive that woman was born to suffer as part of a monstrous ontological legacy.[11] Indeed, *The Knowyng of Woman's Kynde* categorically tells its audience that 'whomen ben more febull . . . be nature þan men been and have grete travell in chyldyng'.[12] Elsewhere the author suggests a similar legacy of hideous suffering by cataloguing the medical disorders to which the woman is subject: namely the pains of childbirth, uterine disorder and menstruation.[13] In literary works the belief in such a legacy of suffering is also evident, but is perhaps nowhere more explicit than in the early thirteenth-century treatise on virginity, *Hali Meiðhad*.[14] This work, written specifically to extol the virtues of the sealed female body, is associated, along with the *Ancrene Wisse*, with the so-called *Katherine Group* of texts written for a group of anchoresses in the early thirteenth century, but whose popularity attests to a much wider audience from the early four-teenth century onwards.[15] Here the author makes clear to his female audience what monstrous suffering lies in store for a woman who does not opt for virginity and, more specifically, for the multifaceted virginity of the enclosed recluse:

Ga me nu forðre, ant loki we hwuch wunne ariseð þrefter i burþene of bearn . . . Þi rudie neb schal leanin, ant of þi breines turnunge þin heaued aken sare. Inwið i þi wombe, swel in þi butte þe bereð þe forð as a weater-bulge, þine þearmes þralunge ant stiches i þi lonke, ant i þi lendene sar eche riue; heuinesse in euch lim; þine breostes burnþene o þine twa pappes, ant te milc-strunden þe þerof strikeð . . . Þe cares aȝein þi pinunge þrahen bineomeð þe nahtes slepes. Hwen hit þenne þerto kimeð, þet sore sorhfule angoise, þet stronge ant stikinde stiche, þet unroles uuel, þet pine ouer pine, þet wondrinde ȝeomerunge . . . (30–2).

Let us now go further, and see what happiness comes to you afterwards
during pregnancy . . . Your rosy face will grow thin, and turn green as
grass; your eyes will grow dull, and shadowed underneath, and because
of your dizziness your head will ache cruelly. Inside, in your belly, a
swelling in your womb which bulges you out like a water-skin,
discomfort in your bowels and stitches in your side, and often painful
backache; heaviness in every limb; the dragging weight of your two
breasts, and the streams of milk that run from them . . . Worry about
your labour pains keeps you awake at night. Then when it comes to it,
that cruel distressing anguish, that fierce and stabbing pain, that
incessant misery, that torment upon torment, that wailing outcry . . .

Although at no point in either of her texts does Julian resort to
such didactic rhetoric in connection with her *own* bodily suffering,
nevertheless there is evidence very early on in the Short Text that
she is identifying with a similar discourse of ontological – and
monstrous – female suffering, which, like traditional pseudo-
Bonaventuran Passion narrative, is characterized by copious blood-
loss:

And aftyr this I sawe bahaldande the bodye plentevouslye bledande,
hate & freschlye and lyfelye . . . and this ranne so plenteuouslye to my
syght that me thought ʒyf itt hadde bene so in kynde for þat tyme, itt
schulde hafe made the bedde alle on blode & hafe passede on abowte
. . . botte ʒit lykes hym bettyr that we take fullye his blessede blode to
wasche vs with of synne. (ST 50)

By means of its unstaunchable flow, its threatened incursion into
her own bed, its association with her own bleedings and bodily
suffering as a woman, the blood of Christ serves to relocate Julian's
perceived female ontology from the realm of the monstrous
(m)other to the very heart of the salvific process. In so doing, it is
freed from its traditionally negative frame of reference, and its
potentially monstrous female excess is transformed into something
altogether more authoritative and subversive, whilst still appearing
to adhere to orthodox representation.[16]

The question of the subjectivity and empowerment of the female
recluse has recently been addressed in different contexts by

Susannah Chewning, Rosalynn Voaden and – more controversially – David Aers.[17] Taking up an Irigarayan stance, Chewning and Voaden have suggested that women were in a more advantageous position for the achievement of a mystical apotheosis which was dependent upon the *relinquishment* of self because – arguably – they had already given up their own subjectivity for that constructed by hegemonic patriarchal socio-religious ideology. Aers, on the other hand, questions the plausibility – even the possibility – of such female empowerment within late medieval culture, speculating that a use of the feminine in their writings, far from being subversive, merely echoed and reinforced a 'divinization of maternity as the essence of "woman" ' (35). For Aers, these women were only ever operating within 'specific discursive regimes with specific technologies of power' (35), and therefore were always unable to escape the hegemonic influence of these regimes. What Aers fails to take account of, however, is that, according to his own argument of culturally constructed difference, cultural discourses concerning the female body and the feminine would have been received differently by women (who were in possession of that body) from men (for whom it remained a representation of the 'other'). If the female body, albeit one constructed by cultural narratives and mediated by systems of patriarchal power, was what was 'known' and 'experienced' by the woman, then regardless of the origins of that construction, it presented her with an experiential authority unavailable to men. Thus, her body became a location of contested meanings which could be filtered and manipulated expediently by the woman herself. Looked at in the context of Julian, the gynaecentric metaphors contained within a suffering and bleeding Christic body could be absorbed into her own body and corroborate her own lived experience of it, just as that lived experience could also be transferred back on to Christ in a never-ending process of reciprocity. I therefore argue that for Julian and her sister anchoresses a sense of empowerment lay not in a relinquishment of a discursively constructed monstrous feminine subjectivity, nor in an unquestioned internalization of social stereotypes, but in a highly subtle manipulation of their hegemony. This manipulation was achieved by means of a *strategic* acceptance and incorporation – whether explicit or implicit – of the hitherto monstrous 'feminine' into the pattern of their literary and meditative practices, and into their perceptions of the physical conditions which characterized the enclosed way of life. In other words, for those women who chose it, the anchoritic life provided a type of *continuum* of the same female subjectivity as had operated for them previously whilst in the world. Now, however, it could be transformed into an empowering subjectivity ideally suited to redirection towards the divine by means of an exploitation of its hermeneutic potential, as we have seen in the case of Julian. As a consequence, enclosure could appeal directly to these women and their bodies in a way in which it could not do for men.

In further support of this claim, it is useful to consider how the concept of enclosure is dealt with in other anchoritic literature directed at women, and to examine the extent to which, like the concept of female suffering, it also draws upon popular contemporary discourses concerning the female body. In the *Ancrene Wisse*, an early thirteenth-century handbook for anchoresses, the author is consistently keen to extend the fundamental image of enclosure in order to engage with a wealth of contemporary beliefs about the danger of women's leaky bodies. Here women are exhorted to close up their various orifices lest corruption enter them and contaminate their surroundings.[18] On one occasion, the anchoress is instructed not to open 'ower muðes flodȝeten' (39: the floodgates of your mouth) because 'þe feond of helle mid his ferd wend þurh ut te tutel þe is eauer open in to þe heorte,' (40: the fiend of hell with all his army goes straight through the mouth which is always open into the heart). Similarly, in the same way as she is exhorted to close her ears and fasten the windows of the anchorhold against the evil speech of the world, she must close up her own 'eiþurles' (eye-windows) which, in a homophonic play on words, are also referred to as 'eilþurles' (harm-windows).[19] These types of analogies are ubiquitous throughout the male-authored literature directed at anchoresses during the period under scrutiny; time and time again the audience is reminded that anchoress and anchorhold, like a castle or fortress, must equally be shut, sealed, closed, covered, guarded, fastened, bolted up, locked up, blindfolded, intact, to use just some of the terminology employed by the *Ancrene Wisse* author alone. Like the female body, the anchorhold is always under threat of penetration and must therefore be shut up and sealed. It could be argued perhaps that such analogies do arise naturally out of the location in which the audience of this literature is captive, providing a ready and obvious metaphor.

Nevertheless, in view of the fact that the audience of such works was primarily female and its authors male, the preponderance of references to enclosure and the threat of penetration takes on a decidedly more gendered tone. It also provides another powerful pointer to explain the popularity of an enclosed reclusive life for women during the period in question. It is likely that the notion of having to protect the body and internal living spaces from external penetration was one which was more directly applicable to the experiences of women than men. Within a socio-religious climate of compulsory heterosexuality which conceptualized men primarily as penetrators rather than penetrated and women as inherently open, receptive, seductive and dangerous, it is likely that men would have responded to such textual imagery largely as allegory or metaphor rather than as experiential reality.[20]

A second area eminently exploitable by the female recluse was the notion of woman as actually *embodying* enclosure as well as needing herself to be enclosed. Again this is a concept which is recurrent in anchoritic literature and is a theme which also draws upon medieval medical and anatomical discourse for its validity.[21] According to traditional Aristotelian anatomical belief, woman was created primarily for her powers of procreation and her naturally cold, moist body needed constant union with the hotter, dryer male, hence her inherently monstrous appetite for sexual satiation. Within this sexual economy her womb and, by implication, woman herself, became a voracious vessel for consumption of the male seed.[22] In theological terms, too, it was woman in her reproductive capacity who was to receive the full impact of God's punishment for the transgression of her appetite-driven Edenic foremother Eve, as I have already suggested. According to another popular medical belief, in their imagined propensity to wander uncontrollably, if not harnessed by pregnancy and childbirth, women and their wombs were actually considered synonymous.[23] Indeed, this Platonic reification of a monstrous wandering womb was taken up enthusiastically by medical theorists in the Middle Ages. For example, two Middle English versions of Gilbertus Anglicus' *The Sekenesse of Wymmen* dedicate fourteen chapters alone to an examination of this problematic organ, and for this writer the womb, rather than being the site of female sickness, *is* the sickness of women. As he tells his audience: 'the moder *id est matrix*'[24] – woman *is* her womb. Within other male-authored texts, such as

Hali Meiðhad and the *Ancrene Wisse*, references to the female womb are also largely negative, as we have seen. At this point, therefore, we might ask how such discourses could ever be rendered positive or attractive for women contemplating enclosure? However, if we examine the discourse of enclosure with which anchoritic literature is saturated, it becomes evident that enclosure could have presented itself as a feminine concept that would ultimately reassure the potential anchoress of her ability to attain a Marian – even Christic – state of *salvific* virginity (or *neo*-virginity), by means of a sealed female body within a sealed womb-like space, as indeed Aelred suggested to his sister. Such an assertion is further corroborated by the *Ancrene Wisse* author's representation of Christ himself as a recluse in Mary's womb: 'Ant nes he him seolf reclus i maries wombe' (192: and wasn't he himself a recluse in Mary's womb). Such an image, of course, now offers the anchoress a monopoly on salvation by transforming her into both Christ *and* Mary by means of her own newly (re)sealed womb *and* the womb-like location of her own enclosure. The potential here for recontextualization of the perceived biological destiny of the female is evident and provides a powerfully attractive counter-discourse with which to parry the misogyny more often associated with representations of a monstrous and unruly womb. Similarly the *Ancrene Wisse* author links the analogous anchorhold/womb to the concept of the tomb, again by means of a reference to the destiny of Christ:

> Beo ȝe ibunden inwið fowr large wahes? He in a nearow cader i neilet o rode i stanene þruh bi cluset hete faste. Marie wombe & þis þruh weren his ancre huses (192–3).

> Are you constrained within four wide walls – and he in a confined cradle, nailed on the cross, closed in tight in a stone tomb? Mary's womb and this tomb were his anchor-houses.

Here the depictions of womb, cradle, tomb, anchorhold, invoked by the author inscribe a powerful *imitatio Christi* upon his female audience and incontrovertibly produce a hermeneutics of the feminine which renders the central milestones of human experience – those of birth and death – as indisputably gynaecentric. Not only that, but the human body too (and in the context of the womb–tomb analogy which has just preceded it, it is a paradigmatically *feminized* body), becomes the ultimate anchorhold in which is housed the precious soul. What we are left with again (and as we saw earlier in the Julian narrative) is a series of concentric circles of containment, each one of which is characterized by its own liminal and feminine specificity and each one of which serves as a powerful affirmatory discourse which endorses the anchoress as the embodiment of apotheosized and salvific female ontology. Such an elevated expression of female liminality and her transformation from monster to mediatrix is perhaps best summed up in the lyrical thirteenth-century paean to Christ, *Þe Wohunge of Ure Lauerd*, in which the indubitably feminized narrative voice, presumably that of the anchoress, cries out to her divine spouse:

> Mi bodi henge
> wið þi bodi neiled o rode sper-
> red querfaste wið inne fowr
> wahes & henge i wile wið þe
> & neauer mare of mi rode cu
> me til þ(at) i deie. For þenne sch-
> al i lepen fra rode in to reste.[25]

My body hangs with your body, nailed to the cross, enclosed within four walls, and I will hang with you and never come from my cross until I die. For then I shall leap from the cross into rest.

The conflation here of the four-walled anchorhold with the four points of the cross itself confirms for the anchoress (who figuratively and literally lies fixed upon and within it) her role as liminal Christic redeemer. Now the anchorhold is both womb and cross, further emphasizing the role played by the anchoress as central yet liminal embodiment of the salvific process.

This interconnectedness of imagery incorporated within the economy of enclosure can be seen as the culmination of all that I have examined in this essay. Now the potentially monstrous female is able actually to become Christ the redeemer by means of her own recontextualized and hyperbolized femininity. Her enclosed and enclosing body echoes that of Christ enclosed within the flesh and yet himself enclosing the Word of God; her womb enclosed within her body is likewise that of Mary enclosing the Son of God within her female flesh; the liminal death-within-life space of the inescapable four-cornered anchorhold becomes the paradoxically liminal but centralized location of the cross through which humankind is offered eternal salvation. In effect it is the space of the divine womb from which God's redemption of the world's sins emerges.

Thus, just as we have seen illustrated in the writing of Julian of Norwich with which this essay began, enclosure becomes a specifically feminine phenomenon which not only provides direct access to the divine, but also provides a series of redeeming hermeneutics to explicate the insights provided by that access. For a woman, access to these insights was readily available by means of a renegotiation of the cultural narratives written upon and of her body and her lived experiences of its presumed ontology. Men, on the other hand, were excluded from it on an experiential level and (as is clearly evident in the writing of the fourteenth-century mystic, Richard Rolle, for example[26]) had to seek to transform themselves by means of a relinquishment of their masculine subjectivity and the appropriation of the feminine perspective. In Irigaray's words, they had to relinquish self 'in order to speak woman'.[27]

In the light of this, perhaps we can now begin to reassess the extent to which cultural narratives concerning the female body could yield up major counter-discourses able to consume the misogynistic discourses so prevalent within socio-religious culture and intrinsic to much of the literature directed at enclosed women. Perhaps, too, the prevalence of such counter-discourses and their transformation of the monstrous female into a central player in the salvific drama can offer us clearer insights into the extraordinary popularity of the anchoritic life amongst women for over 400 years during the later Middle Ages than has hitherto been offered.

Notes

[1] Ann K. Warren, *Anchorites and their Patrons in Medieval England* (Los Angeles and London, 1985).

[2] Ibid., 19. On the new opportunities for women see R. H. Britnell, *The Commercialisation of English Society, 1000–1500* (Cambridge and New York, 1993), p. 168.

[3] *Julian of Norwich's Revelations of Divine Love*, ed. Frances Beer (Heidelberg, 1978). This text is generally known as the Short Text (ST). Julian's Long Text (LT) provides a much developed and more exegetical account, begun

perhaps twenty years after her experiences. In this account, too, she systematically attempts to eradicate all domestic allusions.

[4] On the gendered nature of space in the Middle Ages see Roberta Gilchrist, *Gender and Material Culture: The Archaeology of Religious Women* (London and New York, 1994).

[5] *The Book of Margery Kempe*, ed. Sandford Brown Meech and Hope Emily Allen, EETS os 212 (London, New York, Toronto, 1997).

[6] For example, ibid., pp. 112, 130.

[7] Even when this scene is depicted as taking place outside, it is often enclosed within the stone walls of a garden – another strong symbol of the sealed female body.

[8] Aelred of Rievaulx, *De Institutione Inclusarum*, ed. John Ayto and Alexandra Barratt, EETS 287, (London, New York, Toronto, 1984). This edn contains both the Vernon text and the Bodley text, which are Middle English trans. of the original Latin text. For an account of the differences between the original and the Middle English versions see Ann Clark Bartlett, *Male Authors, Female Readers: Representation and Subjectivity in Middle English Devotional Literature* (New York and London, 1995).

[9] Luce Irigaray, 'La Mystèrique', in *Speculum of the Other Woman*, trans. Gillian C. Gill (New York, 1985), pp. 191–202 (194).

[10] On the discourse of women as the 'weaker vessel' in the Middle Ages see Laurinda S. Dixon, 'The curse of chastity: the marginalization of women in medieval art and medicine', in Robert R. Edwards and Vickie Ziegler (eds), *Matrons and Marginal Women in Medieval Society* (Woodbridge, 1995), pp. 49–74. On these texts see Monica H. Green, 'Obstetrical and gynecological texts in Middle English', *Studies in the Age of Chaucer* 14 (1992), 53–88, and 'The development of the *Trotula*', *Revue d'histoire des textes* 26 (1996), 119–203. Both essays have been reproduced in Monica H. Green, *Women's Healthcare in the Medieval West: Texts and Contexts* (Aldershot, 2000).

[11] See Alexandra Barratt, ' "In the lowest part of our need": Julian and medieval gynecological writing', in Sandra McEntire (ed.), *Julian of Norwich; A Book of Essays* (New York and London, 1998), pp. 240–56.

[12] Oxford, Bodley MS Douce 37, *The Knowyng of Woman's Kynde*, fo. 1, as cited by Barratt in 'In the lowest part', p. 241.

[13] *The Knowyng of Woman's Kynde*, fo. 5ᵛ, as cited ibid., p. 242.

[14] *Hali Meiðhad*, ed. Bella Millett and Jocelyn Wogan-Browne, in *Medieval English Prose for Women from the Katherine Group and Ancrene Wisse* (Oxford, 1990), pp. 2–43.

[15] The original text of the *Ancrene Wisse* was written for a group of three anchoresses, as testified to in its original version, a copy of which is to be found in British Library, MS Cotton Nero A. xiv. This has been edited by Mabel Day in *The English Text of the Ancrene Riwle*, EETS os 225 (London, 1952). The anonymous author, however, later revised the text to create a version which has survived only in MS Corpus Christi College, Cambridge 402. This has been edited as *The English Text of the Ancrene Riwle: Ancrene Wisse* by J. R. R. Tolkien, EETS 249 (Oxford, 1962). Unless otherwise stated, all references will be to this text. In this version we learn that the group of recluses had grown to twenty or more. Later, it would seem that it was a work which was adapted for nuns, male religious, laymen and a general audience of the faithful (Millett and Wogan-Browne (eds), *Medieval English Prose for Women*, Introduction, p. xii).

[16] For a much more detailed account of Julian's use of birth imagery and blood, see my article, '"The moders service": motherhood as matrix in Julian of Norwich', *Mystics Quarterly* 24/4 (December 1998), 181–97. For a useful and detailed discussion of the potential of the anchoritic text directed at the female recluse to render up positive 'counter discourses' see Bartlett, *Male Authors, Female Readers*.

[17] Susannah Chewning, 'Mysticism and the anchoritic community: "a time of veiled infinity"', in Diane Watt (ed.), *Medieval Women in their Communities* (Cardiff, 1997), pp. 116–37. See also Rosalynn Voaden, 'All girls together: community, gender and vision at Helfta', ibid., pp. 72–91 for a similar discussion of the women of Helfta; and Elizabeth Robertson, 'Medieval medical views of women and female sprituality in the *Ancrene Wisse* and Julian of Norwich's *Showings*', in Linda Lomperis and Sarah Stanbury (eds), *Feminist Approaches to the Body in Medieval Literature* (Philadelphia, 1993), pp. 142–67. Also, David Aers, 'The humanity of Christ: reflections on orthodox late-medieval representations', in David Aers and Lynn Staley (eds), *Powers of the Holy: Religion, Politics and Gender in Late Medieval English Culture* (University Park, PA, 1996), pp. 15–42 (35). I am also grateful to Catherine Innes-Parker for pointing me towards her essay, 'Fragmentation and reconstruction: images of the female body in *Ancrene Wisse* and the Katherine Group', in which she examines the transfiguration of the female flesh by the anchoress's redirection of its narratives within the context of Christian salvation, in *Comitatus: A Journal of Medieval and Renaissance Studies* 26 (1995), 27–52.

[18] For an examination of the dangers attached to women's bodies and the construction of gender differences in the Middle Ages see Joan Cadden, *Meanings of Sex Difference in the Middle Ages* (Cambridge, 1993), esp. pp. 167, 185, 223.

[19] This section is missing from MS Corpus Christi College, Cambridge 402, presumably having been included on the lost leaves before fo. 15a. It does, however, appear in MS Cotton Nero A. xiv, ed. Day (see n.15 above), p. 27. It is also present in MS Merton College 44, a Latin text of the *Ancrene Riwle*, which has been edited along with British Museum MS Cotton Vitellius E. vii by Charlotte D'Evelyn, EETS 216 (Oxford, 1944), p. 15.

[20] An examination of the responses of male recluses to their enclosure is beyond the scope of this essay. However, in the few extant rules directed specifically at men, very different patterns of imagery emerge. For example, in the vernacular trans. of the fourteenth-century *Speculum Inclusarum*, referred to as the *Myrour of Recluses*, the main pattern of imagery seems to be connected to the threat which extension or projection poses to the anchorite. He is advised, for instance, not to heed the 'diuerse fantasies' of visitors or listen to 'tydynges & auentures þat fallen in diuerse contrees' (6). In this text too, the anchoritic life is depicted more as an abstract *withdrawal* from the world rather than as a physical condition of walled-up enclosure. Thus, rather than sin penetrating his own body, as is the case in the rules written for the female recluse, the body (and its senses) is depicted as actively 'enclynynge vnto synne' (12). Rather than being exhorted to seal up the body against diabolic invasion, the anchorite is exhorted to become 'Cristes knyth' (14), in connection with which masculine images of body armour, wounding and assault abound. *Myrour of Recluses*, ed. Marta Powell Harvey (Madison and London, 1995).

[21] Rosalynn Voaden has briefly examined the use of images of enclosure in the writing of the Helfta visionaries in 'All girls together', pp. 83–4, as does Catherine Innes-Parker in the context of the *Ancrene Wisse*, 'Fragmentation', pp. 46–8.

[22] On this see Cadden, *Meanings of Sex Difference*, pp. 21–6, and also Bildhauer in ch. 9 above.

[23] Cadden, *Meanings of Sex Difference*, p. 14. For a useful and informative study of this particular belief in the context of iconographic representation in the Middle Ages, see Dixon, 'The curse of chastity'.

[24] Green, 'Obstetrical and gynecological texts', p. 74.

[25] *Þe Wohunge of Ure Lauerd,* ed. W. M. Thompson (London, 1958), p. 36.

[26] Rolle is best known for his lyrical expression of nuptial mysticism. The most authoritative study on Rolle to date is Nicholas Watson, *Richard Rolle and the Invention of Authority* (Cambridge, 1991).

[27] Irigaray, 'La Mystèrique', p. 191.

12

Fountains and Strange Women in the Bower of Bliss: Eastern Contexts for Acrasia and her Community

MARION D. HOLLINGS

Stephen Greenblatt draws our attention to echoes in sixteenth-century European culture of significant aspects of the destruction of Acrasia's Bower at the end of Book 2 of *The Faerie Queene*. One such 'reiteration by the culture' of this destruction is, for Greenblatt, 'the European response to the native cultures of the New World'.[1] In setting up his case, Greenblatt quotes Columbus's response to the 'New World': ' "I am completely persuaded in my own mind", writes Columbus in 1498, "that the Terrestrial Paradise is in the place I have described" '.[2] Greenblatt observes that 'descriptive terms' of the New World's abundance are 'shared' and 'mutually reinforc[ed]' in the Renaissance by travellers' accounts and by literary romance, among which figure those by Tasso and Spenser.[3] But Greenblatt's study of Book 2 tends to obscure in its focus on New World contexts the impact that contemporary European assumptions about the East had on descriptions by Renaissance writers of these new-found lands.

New World explorers like Columbus believed they had discovered the 'Indias', which in the European imaginary was conceived of as multiple areas (consisting for Westerners since ancient times of 'high', 'middle' and 'low'); thus it makes sense that the land Columbus encountered, as well as the 'New World' imagined in sixteenth-century romance, would promise 'Paradise', for Eden was thought to be located in the Orient.[4] European travellers like Columbus recreated the continents of North and South America, at least in part, as projections of their expectations for the Orient they sought and believed they had found. In this essay, I wish to explore Eastern contexts for the Bower of Bliss episode provided by travellers' accounts to India and the Middle East. If, as Greenblatt suggests, Acrasia reflects early modern Europe's construction of New World 'Indian' women, then that construction owes something to assumptions about Oriental women and their sexuality that Europeans carried with them to the New World and projected on to it.[5]

Acrasia's name, from the Greek *acrasia*, meaning 'intemperance' or 'self-indulgence', a concept discussed by Aristotle in the *Nicomachean Ethics*, invites us to see her character as foil to Guyon, who is presented as the 'Knight of Temperaunce'. For Aristotle, the virtue of temperance primarily stipulates a 'mean' with regard to bodily pleasures, explaining that men who love honour and learning, delights of the soul or mind, 'are called neither temperate nor self-indulgent'.[6] Acrasia, in her powerful and sensual appeal, like her counterpart Duessa in Book 1, embodies a Persian or 'Orientalized' threat to Guyon's Spartan stoicism and asceticism.[7] Since classical times, Greeks associated that which came from the East with the strange and dangerous. Ellen D. Reeder notes that in an ancient Greek vase painting of a scene from the *Odyssey*, Circe is depicted in Oriental garments, which belie her Eastern origins. Reeder adds that Circe's clothing 'reinforces her identity as a woman of magical powers, which were usually ascribed [by Greeks] to foreigners'.[8] Scholars point to Circe as a figure strongly informing Spenser's Acrasia, variously called a 'witch' (1. 54. 2) and an 'enchaunteresse' (1. 51. 3; 55. 1), as well as Tasso's Armida and Ariosto's Alcina, for reasons including especially their abilities to transform wandering warriors into beasts. But in a more general sense, Acrasia represents much that is Eastern, augmenting Spenser's exploration, begun in the character of Duessa, of theological and ideological threats from Eastern cultures to the Protestant Christianity championed in his poem.

The Bower of Bliss episode is drawn directly from Spenser's Italian sources, themselves informed by the *matière de france* of medieval romance. Because the Middle East is obviously present in Torquato Tasso's *Gerusalemme Liberata*, set as it is during the time of the Crusades and focusing on Christianity's battle to recover the Holy Land from Islam, it is not surprising that many of these elements would be retained by Spenser in adapting them to his Legend of Temperaunce.[9] My consideration of the women of

Spenser's 'Paradise', for so the narrator calls Acrasia's grounds (12. 58. 1; 70. 4), reads them as 'strange women' informed in part by the type of the biblical strange woman, who comes from the East and whose sexual threat is connected to apostasy. Attributes of this early 'strange woman' are amplified by sixteenth-century European perceptions of Middle Eastern, and more broadly 'Oriental', women's sexuality, including women of India and South-east Asia, as these women are encountered more frequently by Europeans during the expansionism enabled by the spice trade. The trope of women bathers, seen in multiple contexts including those provided by accounts of bathing exercises and rituals recorded in early modern travel narratives to the East, leads me to a re-examination of the community of women populating Acrasia's paradise and more generally to a reconsideration of the intricate cultural and religious dynamics at work in Book 2.

Sheila T. Cavanagh reads Acrasia in the context of an early modern 'fascination with female spirits of the night'.[10] For Cavanagh, the threat Acrasia poses is associated with fears surrounding 'depletions of male life forces'.[11] Cavanagh suggests that this threat to men's sexual and martial potency, figured in Acrasia's 'life-sucking predilections', may help explain the 'rigour pittilesse' with which Guyon destroys Acrasia's Bower and which has been the focus of much critical attention (2. 12. 83. 2).[12] But the focus of Cavanagh's analysis slights a treatment of the other women of Acrasia's environs. The fountain 'damzelles', for instance, are referred to only briefly as representative of Guyon's 'susceptibility to . . . sensual temptations', presenting for Cavanagh an example of 'the voyeuristic delight and danger available in the Bower'.[13] However, Spenser's 'damzelles' retain in their bathing exercises a subjectivity based on personal pleasure and agency even in their exposure to the male gaze which would objectify and consume them for its own ends. In this they share an affinity with portrayals of female exposure in the practices of bathing found in Eastern art such as that from the early Mughal period, which employs the theme of women bathing in garden settings quite extensively.[14]

Created during a period in which local Hindu artists were recruited to work under the tutelage of Iranian masters brought to India by Humayan in 1555 and Akbar in 1556, Mughal art merges the natural and artifice.[15] Significantly, depictions of women bathers in Mughal art limit exposure to the waist up. A common-place convention of Islamic art, the covering of female nudes from the waist down is a visual treatment also employed by Spenser in his portrayal of his fountain 'damzelles'. Fifteenth- and sixteenth-century Occidental art tends to objectify female bathers, portraying them often as solitary figures and rendering them quite passively displayed in full nudity, their delight in their natural surroundings eclipsed by the male pleasure of the erotic gaze that dominates them. Botticelli's *Birth of Venus* (*c*.1482) provides a serviceable contrast, while *The Golden Age* (*c*.1530) of Lucas Cranach the Elder as well as the anonymous fifteenth-century *Bathsheba Bathing* offer other examples. In Mughal paintings such as *Slave Girls Sporting in a Stream* (*c*.1567–70), *Water Play: Krishna Sports with the Gopis in the Jumna* (*c*.1560), and a later Mughal painting, *Harem Night-Bathing Scene* (*c*.1650), character-istic qualities of the depicted women, in addition to that of the lower half of their bodies being concealed by the waters in which they frolic, are the self-absorbed enjoyment they radiate, combined with a casual, even amused, consciousness of the viewer. It is this trait, along with the pleasure the women take in each other's company, that reveals in the Mughal theme a surprising similarity to Spenser's 'wanton' maidens.

Guyon's perception moves from the wanton 'damzelles' and their qualified retention of subjectivity to the exaggerated and monstrous sexuality of Acrasia. In the movement of Guyon's perception of the eroticized female, we see dramatized the process by which the strange woman is made barbarically other and subdued. Europeans employ a rhetoric of barbarism to transform Eastern women into erotically charged monsters which function, in Jane Gallop's words, as the 'clitoris of the text'.[16] The medieval and early modern European tendency to see women in general as in possession of inherently voracious sexual organs, exaggerated in depictions of witches and succubi, as various essays in this volume testify, often becomes projected with a vengeance on to women whose otherness is enhanced by ethnicity.

Travelling through the Holy Land, William Lithgow recounts an incident in Nazareth meant to illustrate, among other details recorded about them, the moral deficiencies of the Christian Armenians he has encountered on his pilgrimage. In doing so, Lithgow demonizes the Middle Eastern women on grounds of their 'impudent' sexuality, as it is constructed through his European eyes. Observing the habits of his travelling companions in satisfying their sexual appetites, Lithgow describes 'sixe women' the travellers 'used':

> Truly if I would rehearse the impudency of these Whoores, and the brutishnesse of the Armenians, as it is most ignominious to the actors; so . . . it would be very loathsome to the Reader.
>
> Such is the villanie of these Orientall slaues vnder the Turkes; that not onely by conuersing with them, learne some of their damnable Hethnick customes, but also going beyond them in beastly sensualnesse, become worse then bruite beasts . . . such base and beastly Christians, these wretched Armenians, committed with these Infidelish Harlots a twofold kind of voluptuous abomination, which my conscience commands me to conceale: least I frequent this Northern world, with that which their nature neuer knew, nor their knowledge heard hearing of the like.[17]

The discourse of barbarism, which in this passage and elsewhere in Lithgow, includes such terminology as 'heathen', 'pagan' and 'infidel', especially as it is in association with concepts of 'filthinesse', 'brutishnesse' and 'beastly sensualnesse', creates the 'Orientall' women, as well as the Christian Armenians, as monstrous in a strategy typical of the representational politics of the 'Northern world', which advances its own moral superiority within it. In his attempt to set off Christians from the 'Infidel', Lithgow's categories collapse in on themselves, as the Christian Armenians become indistinguishable from 'the Turkes'.[18]

In part, the origins of the 'strange woman' as potentially threatening in her sexuality, especially as it is representative of morally corruptive energies, is biblical. In Hebrew scripture the perceived physical (sexual) promiscuity of the strange woman symbolically represents spiritual promiscuity or idolatry, the worshipping of gods other than the god of Hebraic tradition, the God of Abraham. Like the biblical strange woman, Acrasia's 'otherness' is dependent on her presentation as a sexual dominatrix, established initially through her association with Circe. Gail Corrington Streete has examined in antique Judaism the relationship between apostasy and sexual behaviour that goes beyond what is determined by the culture as appropriate. The discourses of communities privilege societal values and institutions, which then become 'codified' in literature; the literary code, understood as a divine code, in turn promulgates the 'appropriate behaviour' of the society.[19] Unsanctioned sexual behaviour becomes an offence and a transgression tantamount to apostasy, a concept closely related to idolatry: in worshipping strange gods, a member of the community would be perceived as abandoning the sanctioned religious faith. Both idolatry and apostasy involve an element of spiritual wandering or spiritual promiscuity figuratively represented in sexual terms. The 'strange woman' (*issah zarah*) of Proverbs 1–9 becomes a 'symbol of heterodoxy and apostasy in an equation of "wrong" religious behaviour with "wrong" sexual behaviour'.[20] Patriarchal cultures fashion a double bind in regard to the female body: ideally fully open to a husband's sexuality, a woman's body is thus also perceived as naturally susceptible to unsanctioned openings or promiscuity.[21] Such a form of potential moral shape-shifting accrues for the female body (in various cultural projections) the cast of the monstrous.

Mark Taylor argues that 'intellectual and moral' hegemonic power is acquired and maintained through the dominant culture's ability to create a 'dialectic between monster-making and monster-slaying'. Political and civil hegemony, the attainment of one group's predominance, often entails the 'process of making the other monstrous' and exaggerating its threat to such a degree that it must be destroyed: 'there is a kind of accenting of the other that moves the perceiver . . . from otherness to strangeness, from "the other" to exoticized or wild creature', 'to a determinate point where that process also becomes a life-depriving one'.[22] Because it is often the control of female sexuality and reproductive power that is at stake in a patriarchal culture's constructions of its identity of power, achieved through definitions of masculinity, the feminine becomes the elided other on which masculine identity and its empowerment depend.

In Book 2 of *The Faerie Queene*, we see how Spenser enlists the control of Acrasia's sexuality in representing 'appropriate' defini-tions of masculinity, such as that found in association with the Graeco-Roman virtue of temperance.[23] For Spenser, 'temperance', allegorized in the figure of Guyon, requires the control of a sexuality represented as monstrous and female. Women are 'represented as demonic', notes Streete, when they make their own choices of partners, not for marriage or the preservation of male life, the male line, or the continued interests of the male-dominated household or community, but for what can only be the satisfaction of their own desires, the fulfillment of their own pleasures on their own terms.[24]

In her self-pleasuring (the witch 'solaces' 'her selfe' at 12. 72. 2, for instance), Acrasia poses a threat to the control of female sexual behaviour demanded by a community ultimately dependent on it for the structure of patriarchal institutions and masculine identity. Such female self-pleasuring registers as aggressively destructive of the patriarchal family organization and institutions of power that would press feminine desire into their service.

While the anxiety provoked by 'women's rule' has been addressed in the context of Elizabeth's reign by a number of recent studies of *The Faerie Queene*, a look at the sexual practices of a certain group of women mentioned repeatedly by early modern travellers to India adds to the task of contextualizing it and, more specifically, Acrasia's behaviour.[25] The Nayre women, who practise a kind of female rule, capture the attention of early sixteenth-century Portuguese travellers Fernao Lopez de Castanheda and Duarte Barbosa. In Nicholas Lichefield's 1582 English translation of de Castanheda's *Historia do descobrimento e conquesta*, 'kings' of 'the house of Nayres' do not marry but give their succession to a brother, if they have one, or if not, to the children of their sister, who never marries but has socially sanctioned sexual relations with a number of different Nayre men.[26] The Nayre women are well provided for by the Nayre men with whom they maintain liaisons, and many accounts note the extraordinary 'libertie' afforded them: they 'doe not marry, neither haue any certaintie of husbands. They bee very free and at libertie, to choose . . . whom they lyke, and . . . such as are best esteemed'.[27] Barbosa's account of the 'nairs of Malabar', described as the region's 'gentry', also discusses their unusual practices of qualified matrilineality and female sexual freedom, observing that 'nair women are all accustomed to do with themselves what they please with bramans or nairs' ; 'the more she has the more highly she is esteemed'.[28]

In my attempt to amplify the Eastern contexts for Acrasia's sexuality, I wish to return more particularly to the fountain in her paradise and to the 'damzelles' who splash there in light of descriptions of Eastern baths and bathing practices recorded in early modern travellers' accounts. The aesthetic represented in Acrasia's garden recalls Mughal art's ideal combination of the authentic and the ornamental. The narrator of Spenser's poem comments on the fine diffusion of boundaries between nature and artifice in describing the garden's fountain:

> And in the midst of all a fountaine stood
> Of richest substance, that on earth might bee,
> So pure and shiny, that the siluer flood
> Through euery channell running one might see;
> . . .
> Infinit streames continually did well
> Out of this fountaine, sweet and faire to see,
> The which into an ample lauer fell,
> And shortly grew to so great quantitie,
> That like a little lake it seemed to bee;
> Whose depth exceeded not three cubits hight,
> That through the waues one might the bottom see,
> All pau'd beneath with Iasper shining bright,
> That seemed the fountaine in that sea did sayle upright.
>
> (2. 12. 60. 1–62. 9)

The fountain's 'Jasper' ('a word of oriental origin' notes the *OED*, citing examples from Hebrew, Assyrian, Persian and Arabic), evokes the various 'marbers' that line the baths described in an account such as the French Nicholas Nicholay's 'Of the Bathes and manners of washing of the Turkes', in Book 2 of his *Nauigations, peregrinations and voyages, etc.* The 1585 English translation reads: 'the common bathes are beautified and set out with pillers in crustures tables and pauements of diuers marbers rare in colour and beautye . . . & in the midst is a faire fountaine of Marber, either of a natural spring or artificiall'.[29] 'A kind of precious stone' (Greek *iaswis*; Latin *iaspis*), rendering 'among the ancients . . . any bright-coloured chalcedony except carnelian, the most esteemed being of a green colour' (*OED*), 'jasper', when used as verb ('jaspered') comes to mean variegated, like a 'Black Marble'. Spenser's 'Iasper' fountain is, of course, the setting in the grounds of Acrasia's palace from which the '[t]wo naked damzelles' rise like the sun 'through the Christall waues', their blonde hair streaming water, who are momentarily oblivious in their delighted antics to the penetrating eyes of Guyon, the Palmer and the reader.

Nicholay makes ample mention of what he perceives as female homosexuality in his account of Turkish women's bathing habits. Comparing the Eastern women bathers to 'Sapho the Lesbia[n]' and noting their 'lasciuious voluptuousnes', Nicholay observes that the women

> do familiarly wash one another, wherby it co[m]eth to passe that amo[n]gst the wome[n] of Leua[nt], ther is very great amity proceeding only through the frequentatio[n] & resort to [the] bathes: yea & somtimes become so ferue[n]tly in loue the one of the other as if it were with men, in such sort that percieuing some maide[n] or woman of excelle[n]t beauty they wil not ceasse vntil they haue found means to bath with the[m], & to handle & grope them euery where at their pleasures so ful they are of luxuriousness & feminine wantonnes . . .[30]

While practices of female homosexuality, real or imagined, are less frequently noted, practices of sodomy are recorded widely by early modern travellers to the Levant. In his 1628 *Travels into Divers Parts of Asia and Afrique*, Thomas Herbert describes at the court of Shah Abas 'Ganimed Boyes in vests of gold', who with 'their curl'd haires dangling about their shoulders, rolling eyes, and vermillion cheeks . . . proferred the delight of Bacchus to such would relish it'.[31] In Acrasia's community of 'many faire Ladies' there is a suggestion of homoerotic attachment, especially in the narrator's description of the 'wanton merriments' of the fountain maidens (2. 12. 68. 7), and something similar is suggested in the description of the 'lasciuious boyes' of Acrasia's bower, who play with 'light licentious toyes', recalling the homosexual love of Islamic courtly art and culture as rendered in European travellers' accounts.

Acrasia's carefully wrought environs reproduce, in addition to the baths, the artistic fineness of the Middle Eastern gardens, which were arranged and cultivated to lead one through highly nuanced stages of sensual pleasure meant to evoke spiritual serenity and unity with the natural world. The narrator recounts

> Eftsoones they heard a most melodious sound,
> Of all that mote delight a daintie eare,

Such as at once might not on liuing ground,
Saue in this Paradise, be heard elswhere:
. . .
For all that pleasing is to liuing eare,
Was there consorted in one harmonee,
Birds, voyces, instruments, windes, waters, all agree.

(12. 70)

As before in the case of the fountain and its 'damzelles', again out of this setting of natural and artistic loveliness, the eroticized figures emerge, brought into focus by the narrator who directs our deeply gratifying experience of the natural setting this time to the vision of the 'Witch' pleasing herself with her lover, her breast bare but for the drops of water 'that like pure Orient perles adowne it trild'(12. 72. 2; 78. 5).

The gaze of Western travellers is further captured by the figure of the Eastern 'temple prostitute', of whom Barbosa, among others, gives an account. The Western ambivalence toward Oriental women is typified in Barbosa's admiration of their strength in carrying out the culture's prescriptions for their conduct, in the practices of *sati*, 'hook-swinging', and temple prostitution, for instance, and his repulsion at their 'bold . . . idolatry', which causes them to 'do such marvels for the love of their gods that it is a terrible thing'.[32] In his discussion of the Eastern women he encounters, Barbosa also provides an account of the courtesans who accompany the king's army. The women, Barbosa declares, 'are unmarried, great musicians, dancers and acrobats, and very quick and nimble at their performances'.[33] Jyotsna Singh notes in her critique of colonial narratives that the

native [Indian] woman is most typically caught [by British colonialists] in a binary opposition: as the sacrificial victim, the *sati* who must immolate herself, or as the *nautch* girl, the prostitute/dancer, often conflated with the sexualized figure in the *zenana*, the women's quarters, which Europeans often inaccurately represented as a harem.[34]

Margaret F. Rosenthal argues that the highly cultivated role of the sixteenth-century Venetian courtesan was inherited from the culture of the East, Venice being the gateway to the Orient through its trade.[35] The Italian courtesan also retains vestiges of the cultural influence of the *hetaira* of classical Greece, depicted on *oinochoe* (wine jugs) in jewels typical of the Near East or eastern Mediterranean, ornaments which Reeder notes 'clearly demonstrate [the *hetaira*'s] otherness'.[36]

The narrator of *The Faerie Queene* has moralized the sexuality of Acrasia and her community as indulgent in its excess, manipulative in its expression and destructive in its results. But this monstrous construction of female sexuality is shaded by Spenser's larger programme of assessing a spiritual (Protestant) purity against practices of idolatry in addition to those of Catholicism, such as those presented (from a Eurocentric viewpoint) by Eastern religions. Acrasia's sexuality, like that of her companions, becomes a palimpsest of cultural misrecognitions by Guyon, the Palmer and the narrator, as also by the reader and by Western knights like Mordant, Verdant and Grill, who become disorientated in Acrasia's highly sophisticated world. Spenser, partly implicated by reproducing and disseminating cultural stereotypes, also offers a critique of them, as it is the warriors' own disorientation which ultimately degrades, or 'brutalizes', these knights (however much it is projected outward), and not the practices themselves encountered in the world Guyon destroys to save them. In his allegorically effecting a moral conquest of the Orient in the Bower episode through Guyon's destruction of Acrasia's environs as the culmination of the journey in Book 2, Spenser contributes to England's attempts to lay claim to a privileged understanding of divine law, based on the superiority of Protestant Christian beliefs over all others, 'heathen' and 'idolatrous', a position then used to justify other forms of domination in the poem.

Notes

[1] Stephen Greenblatt, *Renaissance Self-Fashioning: From More to Shakespeare* (Chicago, 1980), p. 179.

[2] Ibid., p. 180.

[3] Ibid., p.80.

[4] Samuel Purchas (*Purchas his Pilgrimage* [London, 1614]) claims that 'The name of India . . . is applied to all farre-distant Countries', p. 451; Jose de Acosta, that 'Indies' refers to any 'countrie farre off' which is 'very rich and strange' in *Historia natural y de las Indias*, trans. E. G. (London, 1604), p. 47.

[5] Greenblatt, *Renaissance Self-Fashioning*, pp. 184–5. William Lithgow describes the 'Village of Eden' as 'the most fruitfull part of all Libanus, abounding

in all sorts of delicious fruits', *The Totall Discourse, of the Rare Aduentures, and painefull Peregrinations of long nineteene Yeares Trauayles, from Scotland, to the most Famous Kingdomes in Europe, Asia, and Affrica, etc.* (London, 1632), p. 194. He is critical of the 'silly people' who think the Garden of Eden was here, noting that there are, with this one, two other supposed locales for 'the earthly Paradice': at Damascus and in Mesopotamia (194–5). In placing Eden in the East, Lithgow follows most early modern geographers, exegetes and the map of the Geneva Bible (1560).

[6] Aristotle, 'Ethica Nicomachea', ed. Richard McKeon, *The Basic Works of Aristotle* (New York, 1941), pp. 980–1.

[7] Edward W. Said, *Orientalism* (New York, 1978).

[8] Ellen D. Reeder, *Pandora: Women in Classical Greece* (Baltimore, 1995); Margot Schmidt, 'Sorceresses' in Reeder, *Pandora*, pp. 57–62.

[9] William Wistar Comfort, 'The Saracens in Italian epic poetry', *Publications of the Modern Language Association* 59 (1944), 882–910. Michael Murrin asserts that 'Spenser follows this eastward drift [of the *chanson de geste* tradition] and locates faery in India', in *The Allegorical Tradition: Essays in its Rise and Decline* (Chicago and London, 1980), pp. 137–8.

[10] Sheila T. Cavanagh, *Wanton Eyes and Chaste Desires: Female Sexuality in* The Faerie Queene (Bloomington, 1994), p. 47.

[11] Ibid., p. 48.

[12] Ibid., p. 51.

[13] Ibid., p. 50.

[14] Norah M. Titley, *Persian Miniature Painting and its Influence on the Art of Turkey and India* (Austin, 1983), p. 95.

[15] Roy C. Craven, *A Concise History of Indian Art* (London, 1997), pp. 202–5; Anis Farooqi, 'Forward', *The Art of India and Persia* (New Delhi, 1979).

[16] 'The monster is the text's clitoris'; quoted in Tina Pippin, *Death and Desire: The Rhetoric of Gender in the Apocalypse of John* (Louisville, 1992), p. 85.

[17] Lithgow, *Totall Discourse*, pp. 219–20.

[18] Svetlana Loutchiskaja, 'L'Image des musulmans dans les chroniques des croisades', *Le Moyen Age: Revue d'histoire et de philologie* 3/4 (1999), 718.

[19] Gail Corrington Streete, *The Strange Woman: Power and Sex in the Bible* (Louisville, 1997), p. 5; Robert A. Bryan, 'Apostasy and the Fourth Beadman in *The Faerie Queene*', *English Language Notes* (December 1967), 87–91.

[20] Streete, *Strange Woman*, p. 5.

[21] Peter Stallybrass, 'Patriarchal territories: the body enclosed', in Margaret Ferguson, Maureen Quilligan and Nancy Vickers (eds), *Rewriting the Renaissance: The Discourse of Sexual Difference in Early Modern Europe* (Chicago, 1986), pp. 123–44.

[22] Mark Taylor, 'Of monsters and dances: masculinity, white supremacy, ecclesial practice', in Elisabeth Schüssler Fiorenza and Mary Shawn Copeland (eds), *Violence against Women* (London and Maryknoll, 1994), pp. 55–60; Streete, *Strange Woman*, p. 5.

[23] Ibid., p. 18.

[24] Ibid., p. 15.

[25] Philippa Berry, *Of Chastity and Power: Elizabethan Literature and the Unmarried Queen* (New York and London, 1989); Pamela Benson, 'Rule, Virginia: Protestant theories of female regiment in *The Faerie Queene*', *English Literary Renaissance* 15 (1985), 277–92; Maureen Quilligan, 'The comedy of female

authority in *The Faerie Queene'*, *English Literary Renaissance* 17 (1987), 156–71; Susanne Woods, 'Spenser and the problem of women's rule', *Huntington Language Quarterly* 4 (1985), 141–58; and Susan Frye, *Elizabeth I: The Competition for Representation* (New York, 1997). On women's rule and early modern European encounters of the 'Other', see Greenblatt, *Renaissance Self-Fashioning*, p. 181, and Ania Loomba, 'The great Indian vanishing trick – colonialism, property, and the family in *A Midsummer Night's Dream*', in *A Feminist Companion to Shakespeare*, ed. Dympna Callaghan (London, 2000), pp. 177–9.

[26] Fernao Lopez de Castanheda, *Historia do descobrimento e conquesta*, trans. Nicholas Lichefield (London, 1582), p. 34^r.

[27] Ibid., p. 34^v.

[28] *A Description of the Coasts of East Africa and Malabar in the Beginning of the Sixteenth Century, by Duarte Barbosa, a Portuguese*, trans. Henry E. J. Stanley from an early Spanish manuscript in the Barcelona Library (London, 1866), pp. 124, 126–67. There is also an edn of Barbosa from a trans. of a Portuguese text first published in Lisbon in 1812 and based on an early Portuguese MS, *The Book of Duarte Barbosa. An account of the countries bordering on the Indian Ocean and their inhabitants, written by Duarte Barbosa, and completed about the year 1518 AD*, trans. Mansel Longworth Dames (London, 1918)). In the sixteenth century, Barbosa's work was known through Ramusio's Italian version in *Navigationi et Viaggi* (Venice, 1563).

[29] Nicholas Nicholay, *The Nauigations, peregrinations and voyages, made into Turkie by Nicholas Nicholay Daulphinois, Lord of Arfeuile, Chambelaine and Geographer ordinaire to the King of Fraunce, etc.*, trans. T. Washington the younger (London, 1585), p. 58.

[30] Ibid., p. 60^r; Valerie Traub, 'The psychomorphology of the clitoris', *GLQ: A Journal of Gay and Lesbian Studies* 2 (1995), p. 87.

[31] Thomas Herbert, *Travels into Divers Parts of Asia and Afrique* (London, 1638), p. 169. See also Lithgow, 'The Turkes . . . discended of the Scythians or Tartars . . . are extreamely inclined to all sorts of lasciuious luxury; and generally adicted, besides all their sensuall and incestuous lusts, vnto Sodomy, which they account as daynty to digest all their other libidinous pleasures', p. 161 (mispaginated as p. 361).

[32] Barbosa, *An Account*, p. 220. Anthony Esolen applies ancient Semitic fertility rites and worship of the mother-goddess to a reading of 'economics' in Book 2 in 'Spenser's "Alma Venus": energy and economics in the Bower of Bliss', *English Literary Renaissance* 23 (1993), pp. 267–86.

[33] Barbosa, *An Account*, p. 212.

[34] Jyotsna G. Singh, *Colonial Narratives/Cultural Dialogues: 'Discoveries' of India in the Language of Colonialism* (London, 1996), p. 12.

[35] Margaret F. Rosenthal, *The Honest Courtesan: Veronica Franco, Citizen and Writer in Sixteenth-Century Venice* (Chicago, 1992).

[36] Reeder, *Pandora*, pp. 181–93.

13

Monstrous Tyrannical Appetites: '& what wonderfull monsters have there now lately ben borne in Englande'[1]

MARGARET HEALY

> Gradually . . . they [the Britons] went astray into the allurements of evil ways, colonnades and warm baths and elegant banquets. The Britons, who had had no experience of this, called it 'civilization', although it was a part of their enslavement. (AD 98. Cornelius Tacitus, *Agricola*, 21: 17)[2]

British anxieties about being enslaved to the 'evil ways' of Rome were not unique to the early modern period; nor was the curious but powerful imaginative and discursive association of 'elegant banquets' with tyranny. Tacitus' history of first-century Britain under the Roman general, Agricola, casts oblique aspersions at the morally degenerating effects of his fellow countrymen's notorious excesses (this was the century of Caligula and Nero) by putting compelling critiques of Roman luxury into the mouths of 'barbarian' Britons prior to their subjugation.[3] The feisty men of Mona (Anglesey) boast, for example, that they will resist the might of the Empire because they have their country, wives and parents to fight for, whereas their would-be vanquishers 'have nothing but greed and self-indulgence' (15: 12). However, and somewhat ironically, Tacitus records that the barbarous natives *were* eventually enslaved precisely because they learned 'to condone' and even to imitate the invaders' 'seductive vices', mistaking luxury for 'civilization' (16: 13, 21: 17). Tacitean history thus pithily and cynically emphasizes how the Britons were brought under control more through Roman pleasures than through force of arms, in the process raising interesting questions about the nature of civility. Undoubtedly, the vogue for Tacitus from the late sixteenth century played no small part in fuelling English fears about the iniquitous consequences of lavish feasts and specious hospitality, and their particular relation to loss of liberty; fears which are especially evident in seventeenth-century Puritan and Republican discourse.

Consider, for example, Master John Ball's rendition of a brief but highly significant episode from the life of the Protestant martyr, John Preston, who died in 1628.[4] The martyrologist's narrative describes a sort of interrogation by banquet – the epitome of ungodly consumption in the mid-1620s – conducted by the arch-villain of the piece, the king's favourite, the Satanic duke of Buckingham. Dr Preston's unorthodox positions on redemption and salvation were apparently giving cause for concern in high places and it was decided that he should be interrogated by his erstwhile patron, Buckingham, together with a panel of suspiciously Jesuitical-sounding 'subtil doctors'. At York House a 'sumptuous feast' was provided for the inquisitors' entertainment (512). The duke sat in the midst of the table among the doctors and it was proposed they should drink a health to the king. When Preston's turn came, he passed the glass to the next person having drunk very little. One of the doctors noticed this and Preston was chided for not drinking enough to pledge the health of the king. Unflinching in his temperance and resolve, he replied that:

> he had not willingly offended, but if it were an engine to court intemperence, and [to] ingage men unto greater quantities then themselves liked, it fell short of that modesty and freedome of the heathens . . . and was a sin in all, but in men of their degree and rank an abominable wickednesse. (512)

Ball describes the horrendous consequence for Preston of his brave and righteous rejoinder:

> The Duke misliked this incivility, and frowned on the Doctor that occasioned it . . . the duke had now seen the worth and way of Dr Preston, he had found that he could not winne him and make him his [so he would] wrack and sink him . . . he was resolved to break him if he could, yet in a civil Court way. (512)

There is far more to this narrative than a simple assertion of godly temperance: Preston's refusal of Buckingham's hospitality was a highly political move in the context of the 1620s, and it is the tangled relations between feasts, hospitality, civility, liberty and tyranny prior to and during the English Civil Wars that I wish to pursue here. My point of departure for reflecting on this topic was observing how the writings of the foremost Puritan–Republican poet of the mid-seventeenth century, John Milton, seem curiously preoccupied with food and its ill effects. Both *Comus* and *Paradise Regained*, for example, contain magnificent Satanic banquets from which the hungry virtuous must definitely – in the manner of Dr Preston – abstain; yet, beyond Eve's first bite at the forbidden apple, there is no biblical source for such temptation scenes.

In order to unravel the politics of gourmandizing excess in the mid-seventeenth century it is necessary to examine the cultural understanding of gluttony as it was evolving at least a century earlier. Reforming Protestantism had made much of the sins of appetite, as seen in the typical sixteenth-century Dances of Death. In 'The Daunce and Song of Death' (1569), for example, 'Sykenes Deathes minstrel' presides over the macabre dance in which representatives from all social groups are enlisted. In the upper left- and lower right-hand corners certain sins are singled out as particular harbingers of levelling sickness.[5] They both have to do with excessive consumption: in one vignette a usurer-merchant type is counting out his money; whilst in the other, food, drink and harlotry (construed as usury of the body in this period) are represented as particular heralds of disease and death. Protestant propaganda linked these sins of consumption obsessively with unreformed religion: monks and priests were notoriously depicted as gluttonous lechers in Protestant morality plays. Whilst the disease of Venus was closely associated with the venereal pox – syphilis – excessive consumption of food and drink had wide-ranging pathological consequences, according to contemporary medical paradigms. In *The Castel of Helth* (1539) Sir Thomas Elyot described the Englishman's passion for feasting every day on several different meats at the same meal. He lamented that such gluttony led to the prisoners of 'surfet' being tormented 'with catarrhes, fevers, goutes, pleurisies . . . and many other sycknesses, and fynally cruelly put to death by them, oftentymes in youth'.[6] Loss of liberty and death are closely associated here with lavish feasting and, as the sixteenth century proceeded, medical penmen added their voices one-by-one to an increasingly anxious chorus about the hazards of 'surfet'.

Thomas Cogan's regimen of 1584 rails:

> Now what a reproch is it, for man whome God hath created after his owne likenesse, and endued with reason, wherby he differeth from beasts, to be yet beastlike, to be moved by sense to serve his bellie, to follow his appetite contrarie to reason.[7]

Yet the constantly recurring metonymic relation between reason, bellies and beasts was not just empty rhetoric: it was underpinned by both Galenic and Paracelsian medical authority. Thomas Newton's translation of the Dutch physician Levinus Lemnius's medical regimen provides perhaps the fullest explanation of the physiological effects of over-consumption. Surfeiting leads to poor digestion and the production of 'superfluous', 'ill' humours, which in turn produce impure spirits and cause the 'brayne to be stuffed full of thicke fumes'. Reason is consequently dulled and the animal passions dominate, leading to 'lewd affections, and unbrydled motions' and ultimately to disordered, uncivil, even criminal behaviour.[8] Furthermore, the glutted body replete with ill humours is readily penetrated by a posse of evil influences ('bad angels', 'contagions') hovering perpetually around the soma waiting for a suitable opportunity for mischief.[9] Possession by the devil during a binge of eating and drinking was a real possibility in terms of such a medical paradigm.

But how did gluttony develop its more precise seventeenth-century political resonances to do with tyranny? I have alluded to the likely significance of the late sixteenth- and seventeenth-century vogue of Tacitus in this regard, but John Ponet's monstrous 'Child of Fulham' was undoubtedly another seminal influence on the Puritan–Republican mindset. Bishop John Ponet had fled to the Continent at the beginning of Queen Mary's reign. Settled in Strasbourg in 1554, he set about writing *A Shorte Treatise of Politic Power* designed to encourage rebellion against the Marian regime. It was published in Strasbourg in 1556, and again in 1639 and 1642 'to serve the turn of those times'.[10] Ponet's was the first of a line of Renaissance treatises on tyrannicide which includes works by John Knox, George Buchanan and John Milton, and its significance in shaping the corporeal pathologies of those accounts has been relatively neglected. In a chapter ominously entitled 'An Exhortacion or rather a warnyng to the Lordes and Commones of England', Ponet poses the question, 'And what wonderfull monstres have ther now lately ben borne in Englande?' (sig. K3ᵛ), and responds: 'A childe borne at Fulham by London even now this yeare, with a great head, evil shaped, the armes with bagges hanging out at the Elbowes and heles, and fete lame' (sig. K3ᵛ). The treatise proceeds to explain this monster's monstrous significance:

> And as the head of it is the greatest part, and greater than it ought to be, with to muche superfluitie of that it should not have, wherfore it must pull from the other membres to confort it, and lacke of that good proporcion it ought to have: so shall the governours and headdes of Englande sucke out the wealth and substaunce of the people (the politike body) and kepe it bare, so that it shall not be hable to help it self. (sig. K4ᵛ–5ʳ)

Here the nation's enormous head, full of humoral 'superfluitie' (waste), is consuming the common wealth and destroying the body. Ponet's *Treatise* is structured to link the swollen head with excessive eating and drinking on the part of those who have 'dronken of the hoore of Babilon's cuppe' (sig. E6ᵛ) – the Roman Catholic Antichrist – but more particularly with evil governors who flout the law and abuse their subjects by raising taxes and then consuming their ill-gotten profits on 'hoores, . . . banketting, unjust wars' (sig. G2ʳ).

Indeed, it is a 'lawe positive', Ponet asserts, that princes should use a 'meane kynde of diet' in order that they convert what they previously put to evil use 'to the relief of the povertie, or defense of their countrey' (sig. B5ʳ). Furthermore, Ponet's *Treatise* is unequivocal about the godly way to deal with such a swollen-headed tyrant who deludedly thinks he's a god, as the Pope thinks he's 'felowe to the God of Goddes' (sig. B3ʳ and 3ᵛ): 'Common wealthes and realmes may live, when the head is cut of, and may put on a newe head' (sig. D7ʳ). He is adamant that a prince cannot claim any 'absolute autoritie' (sig. C1ʳ) and maintains that natural law – accessible via 'mannes conscience'– testifies 'that it is naturall to cutte awaie an incurable membre, which (being suffred) wolde destroie the hole body' (sig. G6ᵛ).

Given the strong association of 'excess' of rulers with tyranny that we find in the humanist political treatises, it is not difficult to discern from the body images circulating around the Stuart kings and their officials in the 1620s and 1630s how far they were felt by some to have strayed down an ungodly path of government. Furthermore, they were self-proclaimed absolutists who considered themselves to be more than men, ruling by divine right: the court masques were entirely premised on this belief. Unwisely too, in the economic depressions of the 1620s and 1630s, in the midst of what one commentator described as 'great want and poverty' in the kingdom, their banqueting and masquing continued – indeed, even increased.[11]

The Stuart monarchs were notorious for their profligate hospitality. As soon as James ascended the English throne he doubled royal expenditure, lavishing enormous sums of money on his vast entourage of courtier friends and establishing extra country residences to entertain them. One contemporary described the Scottish influx tellingly as a horde of 'locusts [come to] devour this kingdome'.[12] The new king ordered extravagant banquets with a minimum of twenty-four courses, described like this by a contemporary observer:

> Dishes, as high as a tall man could well reach, [were] filled with the choycest and dearest viands sea or land could afford: And all this once seen . . . was in a manner throwne away, and fresh set on to the same height, having only this advantage of the other, that it was hot.[13]

We might pause to think here about the gap between the rhetoric of the court masques, which continually praise Stuart temperance, and the material reality of the excesses of court life. *Pleasure Reconciled to Virtue* of 1618, for example, opens with the surreal spectacle of a 'bouncing belly', a 'plump paunch' riding in triumph across the stage.[14] Comus is soon joined by an antimasque of men metamorphosed into 'monsters' by their excessive eating and drinking (78). As is usual in this art form, the antimasque is banished and replaced with an alternative, ideal vision. In this case a group of noble masquers led by Prince Charles emerge from Mount Atlas and, dancing in restrained and stately style, they enact measure, becoming the visual embodiment of temperance and the antithesis of 'effeminate' sensual pleasures enshrined in the bouncing belly of Comus and his rout (190). However, contemporary accounts suggest that the true vision was very different from the ideal. The king had a noted preference for the comic buffoonery of the antimasques over the stately vision of the masque proper, and grew particularly fed up with the slow, measured pace of *Pleasure Reconciled to Virtue*, eventually losing his temper and yelling, 'Why don't they dance? What did you make me come here for? The devil take all of you, dance!'[15] The dignity of the court collapsed completely at the end of that occasion when, as one ambassador reported, the king having left, 'like so many harpies the company fell on their prey', throwing the table containing the feast to the ground and shattering the glass platters.[16] It seems that masques could easily descend into chaotic orgies of consumption, with drunkenness playing a prominent part in the proceedings. Sir John Harington has left us a wonderful account of how a masque planned for the visiting king of Denmark in 1606 had turned into such a drunken debacle with the inebriated queen of Sheba – one of the figures in the masque – falling into the Danish monarch's lap, and the Virtues Hope and Faith both 'sick and spewing in the lower hall'.[17]

By the 1620s prominent English courtiers were vying with one another to determine who could produce the most lavish feasts but no one – it seems – could match the gourmandizing extravaganzas of the king's favourite, the duke of Buckingham. When he and Prince Charles returned from their abortive visit to Madrid to arrange a Spanish match for the prince (a project which had been extremely unpopular with English Protestants) reports circulated that Buckingham had hosted a feast at York House consisting of no fewer than 3,000 meat dishes.[18] This may well have been an exaggeration, but it was one that caught the public imagination. The notorious anti-Spanish play *A Game at Chess*, staged shortly after Charles's and Buckingham's return from Spain in 1623, made much of White House – English – gourmandizing proclivities and, through a range of subtle manœuvres in the fifth act, managed obliquely to imply that White House gourmandizers were outdoing even the feasting excesses of impious Roman tyrants. This tipped the script-writing into highly dangerous territory indeed, linking, as it did, gluttony with tyranny in the manner of Ponet's treatise on tyrannicide. However, the arch-tyrants of the piece emerge unequivocally as Black House, Spanish, 'gourmandizers' who are represented as voraciously consuming other nations to satisfy their Babylonian, Roman Catholic, absolutist ambitions (5. 3. 83–103).

Stuart feeding practices might not have been the subject of so much interest and concern if the body of the nation had been well fed. The common perception was, however, that while the head was using public money to gorge itself, the body was growing ever more slender, in the manner of Ponet's pitiful Child of Fulham. In the mid-1620s when Buckingham held his feast to outdo all feasts and when *A Game at Chess* was staged, England was emerging from a particularly deep and lengthy economic crisis which was associated with widespread suffering, a decline in the amount of circulating money, and a perceived decay of trade.[19] The country was glutted with woollen cloth it could not sell and workers were being laid off, causing widespread poverty and social unrest. A flurry of pamphlets diagnosing the nation's disease poured off the presses and commentators focused obsessively on 'the body of the trade' and her ingestion and waste.[20] As in the humoral bodily paradigm, a glutted economic body was perceived as disastrous; somehow England must find a way of selling more products than were imported. Voices in Parliament blamed East India trade for the acute shortage of circulating 'monies': gold and silver bullion was disappearing somewhere and East India trade seemed a likely culprit. The merchant representatives of the trading companies were quick to retaliate: both Thomas Mun and Edward Misselden, two highly respected merchant-economists, found the nature of the malady to be the nation's prodigality, its pride and excesses, and the subsequent massive importation of luxury foods and goods. Misselden's treatise concluded that the two extremes of poverty and prodigality in the kingdom were disastrous to the balance of trade. He lamented that while 'the poore sterve in the streets for want of labour: the prodigall excell in excesse, as if the world, as they doe, ran upon wheeles'.[21] Indeed, in the view of these trading tracts of the 1620s, the 'common wealth' was being consumed by the pride and excesses of certain prodigal types prone to luxurious consumption.

In the end, Parliament seemed to accept their verdict and the search was on for the gourmandizing culprits who were destroying the nation's health. They did not have far to look: just around the corner in York House someone commonly perceived as a particularly voracious consumer – the duke of Buckingham – was gorging his guests on a staggering 3,000 plates of meat. Furthermore, he was rumoured to have subjected at least one noted godly Protestant – Dr Preston – to inquisition by banquet. According to the martyrologist's account, Dr Preston's doom was sealed by his godly temperance, but the gourmandizing duke of Buckingham was shortly to be called to account for his Babylonian excesses. When he was impeached and charged with 'misemploying the king's revenue' in 1626, the discussions surrounding his liability were couched in particularly 'consuming' terms. He was considered more culpable because in the midst of '[w]eakness and consumption of the commonwealth he hath not been content alone to consume the public commonwealth treasure, which is the blood and nourishment of the state, but hath brought in others to help in this work of destruction'.[22] The suggestive 'others' is significant here: in fact, the contemporary discourse surrounding his corruption raises questions about who was most blameworthy, Buckingham or the king himself? Interestingly, Mun's trading pamphlet mentioned earlier, which had been in hot pursuit of prodigal bodies fuelling England's 'disease', had dwelt at length, in an unspecific way, on princely expenditure and abuses and had warned that '[a] Prince . . . is like the stomach in the body, which if it cease to digest and distribute to the other members, it doth no sooner corrupt them, but it destroyes itself' (*England's Treasure*, 70).

Mun's image of 'a Prince' as a greedy destructive paunch is particularly striking because it subverts the traditional view of a monarch as the head of the politic body governing with reason paramount: his anonymous prodigal prince is pure sensual appetite.[23] This is very much in keeping with the 1620s metaphorical landscape of excess in which some English bodies, including many highly placed 'paunches', were engaging in frenzies of consumption, while the commonwealth, denied the 'blood and nourishment' necessary for her survival, was languishing with 'weakness and consumption [wasting disease]'.[24] Food, money, land, health, bodies, justice and liberty circulated in metonymic relation to one another, and all were being 'eaten up' by the sensual excesses of iniquitous self-consuming Roman, Babylonian types. Indeed, representations of over-full excessive, and under-nourished declining bodies, pervade economic, political, legal, religious, medical and literary writings of the 1620s and 1630s. In the run-up to the Civil Wars, the poorly regimented imbalanced body is the site where the discourses of pathology intersect and merge, and where 'cures' are formulated, too.

  The politics of dietary regiment were explicated most fully in the writings of John Milton. Milton's 'reformed' masque, *Comus*, is, like *Paradise Lost* and *Paradise Regained*, and indeed the court masques, obsessed with food and feasting.[25] In all these texts consumption is a moral and political issue and whether their protagonists abstain from eating, consume in moderation or gorge themselves is immensely significant. *Comus*'s Lady, travelling to join her father, but lost in a 'drear wood' of 'perplexed paths' (37), tired and hungry, becomes embroiled in the clutches of 'swinish gluttony' personified, Milton's Comus, who conjures up a sumptuous banquet. As the young Lady, rejecting the feast points out (in language that recalls the insinuations of 'godly' Doctor Preston faced with Buckingham's banquet), only the 'good' can give 'good' things: who is offering the food, and why, is of crucial importance. Those with 'well-governed appetite', schooled in 'princely lore' (34) and accompanied by 'a strong siding champion Conscience' (211) – like Alice Bridgewater (the Lady) and her brothers – will be able to discern specious guides and reject bad hospitality.

  As Milton's masque instructs its audience, excessive eating and 'gorgeous feast[s]' (776) are evil and antipathetic to nature's 'sober laws' (765) because a principle of equity should govern consumption (767–72). As in Ponet, temperate consumption is a positive law with socio-economic implications. 'Lewdly pampered Luxury' – excess – leads to the hunger and suffering of the 'just man', and the preceding 'now' suggests a pressing immediate context. That context was the economic depression of the early 1630s. Milton wrote this masque to commemorate the installation of the earl of Bridgewater as Lord President of Wales at Ludlow Castle: a region particularly hit by high unemployment and poverty.[26]

  But kingship does exist in Milton's political model of dietary regiment, and his post-Restoration work, *Paradise Regained* (1670), provides the fullest explication of what kingship is – or perhaps, more accurately, of what it is not – through the vehicle of yet another Satanic banquet. In this epic we meet another traveller, this time none other than Jesus, wandering through the wilderness, absorbed in 'holy meditations' (1. 195. 189–90). The Son of God, forty days in the desert without food, and adamant that he is a man and will suffer as such, is soon accosted by the arch-consumer,

Satan, who has 'found . . . viewed . . . [and shockingly] tasted' him (2. 131). His first temptation is a sumptuous feast in 'regal mode' which, with its Ganymede types and ladies of the Hesperides (recalling the court masques) could easily be mistaken for a Stuart banquet. But Jesus' 'temperance invincible' (2. 408) is, of course, confirmed as he rejects Satan's 'regal' hospitality in no uncertain terms: 'thy pompous delicacies I contemn' (2. 390). Later, confronted with a tempting panoply of first-century Roman style luxury and riches, Jesus powerfully articulates an alternative 'regal diadem': inner governance is true kingship and, crucially, 'every wise and virtuous man' can attain this and 'is more a king' (2. 461–72). 'More a king than whom?' the text grooms us to ask: than the Stuart monarchs perhaps?

In 1642 Charles I had been accused of bringing in 'an arbitrary and tyrannical government'.[27] Shortly afterwards the Parliamentarian Philip Hunton posed the crucial question, 'Who shall be the judge of the excesses of the monarch?' and responded confidently:

> The superior law of reason and conscience must be judge, wherin every one must proceed with the utmost advice and impartiality. For if he err in judgement, he either resists God's ordinance or puts his hand to the subversion of the state.[28]

In the 1640s God's 'ordinance', accessible via reason and conscience in 'every wise and virtuous' regimented man, over-rode the king's and led to the justification for regicide. It seems that, in the imaginations of a significant number, Charles I had come to resemble a voracious paunch devouring the country's resources, acting unreasonably and threatening the nation's well-being. Anxieties about British re-enslavement to Roman, Babylonian 'evil ways' were undoubtedly highly operative too. Eventually, Ponet's cure was invoked, and the king's head was severed to save the health and liberty of the English commonwealth.

Notes

Parts of this essay are reproduced from *Fictions of Disease in Early Modern England: Bodies, Plagues and Politics* (Basingstoke, 2001).

[1] John Ponet, *A Shorte Treatise of Politic Power* (1556; Menston, 1970), sig. K3ᵛ. All references are to this edn.

[2] Cornelius Tacitus, *Agricola*, trans. A. R. Birley (Oxford, 1999), 21. 17. All references are to this edn.

[3] Tacitus had great respect for Julius Agricola himself, and praised his personal temperance.

[4] Thomas Ball, 'The life of Doctor Preston' (d. 1628), in *A Generall Martyrologie*, ed. Samuel Clarke (London, 1651), pp. 473–520. All references are to this edn. This episode is discussed in Alinda Summers, 'The banqueting scene in *Paradise Regained*: Milton's temptation to the anti-Puritan appetite', in William P. Shaw (ed.), *Praise Disjoined: Changing Patterns of Salvation in Seventeenth-Century English Literature* (New York, 1991), pp. 282–3.

[5] Anon., 'The Daunce and Song of Death', 1569, British Library, Huth 50 (49).

[6] Sir Thomas Elyot, *The Castel of Helth* (London, 1539), fo. 45^r.

[7] Thomas Cogan, *The Haven of Health* (London, 1584), fo. 3^v.

[8] Thomas Newton, *The Touchstone of Complexions* (London, 1576), fos. 19v, 10v.

[9] Ibid., fos. 21^v, 22^r.

[10] John Strype, cited in prefacing note to Scolar edn, unpaginated.

[11] Thomas Mun, *England's Treasure by Foreign Trade* (London, 1664), written 1622–3, p. 63.

[12] Francis Osborne, 'Traditional Memoirs of the Raigne of King James the First', in *The Secret History of the Court of James the First*, 2 vols, ed. Walter Scott (Edinburgh, 1811), I, pp. 150, 270. Cited in Albert H. Tricomi, *Anti-Court Drama in England, 1603–1642* (Charlottesville, 1989), p. 8.

[13] Osborne, *Memoirs*, I, p. 271, cited in Tricomi, *Anti-Court Drama*, p. 3.

[14] All references to Ben Jonson's masque are to *The Complete Masques*, ed. Stephen Orgel (New Haven and London, 1969), ll. 10, 26, 5.

[15] Cited ibid., p. 30.

[16] Cited in Patricia Fumerton, *Cultural Aesthetics: Renaissance Literature and the Practice of Social Ornament* (Chicago and London, 1991), p. 162.

[17] *The Letters and Epigrams of Sir John Harington*, ed. N. E. McLure (Philadelphia, 1930), pp. 119–20. See also Leah S. Marcus, *The Politics of Mirth* (Chicago and London, 1986), pp. 10–11.

[18] See Thomas Middleton, *A Game at Chess*, Revels edn, ed. T. Howard-Hill (Manchester, 1993), footnote on p. 180.

[19] On this crisis see particularly B. E. Supple, *Commercial Crisis and Change in England 1600–1642: A Study in the Instability of a Mercantile Economy* (Cambridge, 1959). Also esp. Edward Misselden, *The Circle of Commerce* (London, 1623), p. 3; and *Free Trade. Or, The Meanes to Make Trade Flourish* (London, 1622), pp. 7–10, 18, 28–9; Gerrard De Malynes, *A Treatise of the Canker of England's Common wealth* (London, 1601); William Sanderson, *A Treatise of the State Merchant* (London, 1629), fo. 227; Thomas Mun, *England's Treasure*, p. 34, and *A Discourse of Trade, From England unto the East-Indies, Answering to diverse Objections which are usually made against the same* (London, 1621), p. 41.

[20] See n.19.

[21] Misselden, *The Circle*, p. 132.

[22] John Pym, Hampshire Record Office: Jervoise MSS 07 Impeachment charges against the duke of Buckingham, as cited in Linda Levy Peck, *Court Patronage and Corruption in Early Modern England* (London, 1993), p. 192.

[23] On the centrality of the belly in this period see Michael Schoenfeldt, 'Fables of the belly in early modern England', in David Hillman and Carla Mazzio (eds), *The*

Body in Parts: Fantasies of Corporeality in Early Modern Europe (London, 1997), pp. 243–61.

[24] The quotations are from John Pym about the duke of Buckingham, see n. 22 above.

[25] John Milton, *Comus or A Masque Presented at Ludlow Castle* and *Paradise Regained*, in *Complete Shorter Poems*, ed. John Carey (London, 1971). All references are to this edn. See David Norbrook, 'The reformation of the Masque' in David Lindley (ed.), *The Court Masque* (Manchester, 1984), pp. 94–110. On the 'alimental vision' in *Paradise Lost*, see Michael Schoenfeldt, *Bodies and Selves in Early Modern England: Physiology and Inwardness in Spenser, Shakespeare, Herbert and Milton* (Cambridge, 1999).

[26] On the stagnation in the west in the 1630s see Supple, *Commercial Crisis*, pp. 120–5.

[27] Quoted in Conrad Russell, *The Causes of the English Civil War* (Oxford, 1990), p. 131.

[28] Philip Hunton, *A Treatise of Monarchy* (1643), in *Divine Right and Democracy*, ed. David Wootton (Harmondsworth, 1986), p. 188.

III

Consuming Genders, Races, Nations

14

Reading Between and Beyond the Lines

∽

ANDREW HADFIELD

Just as national identities are never static phenomena, nor are they stable or uncontested. The nation always consists of a series of groups, each competing for the right to speak for its inhabitants and so express its proper form. The public sphere, however it is envisaged, is invariably a space characterized by noisy argument. As Homi Bhabha has observed, the establishment of any national identity always involves an attempt to unite contradictory desires and conceptions of reality: 'The scraps, patches, and rags of daily life must be repeatedly turned into the signs of a national culture, while the very act of the narrative performance interpellates a growing circle of national subjects'.[1] On the one hand a conservative impulse wishes to preserve the nation in terms of its contemporary existence as represented by a series of commonly observable features: the pound, the eisteddfod, fish and chips, rugby, Shakespeare's plays and so on. On the other, nations change through the course of time, absorbing new inhabitants (asylum-seekers, economic migrants, ethnic minorities), losing some who emigrate or die out, developing new social forms and institutions while others recede in importance or cease to exist altogether (heavy industry, domestic servants, the number of women in employment). These changes obviously transform the nature of national identity so that the reality of the nation is invariably at odds with its self-representation.

The nation is often represented as a woman: Britain as Britannia, Ireland as Cathleen Ní Houlihan, the newly discovered continent of America as a naked, reclining woman with open arms, welcoming the virile conquistadors, as in Jan van der Straet's famous engraving of 'America' (*c*.1600).[2] The effect of the 'motherland' is to cast its citizens as male and efface women as '(m)others'. Equally significant, in the Middle Ages and Renaissance as today, are attempts to exclude different races from the assumed core identity of the nation. Jews were frequently cast as alien peoples throughout Europe, even when they made up a substantial portion of a nation's populace and helped establish the character and form of important cities.[3] Although there were only a small number of Africans in England at the end of the sixteenth century, Elizabeth I clearly saw them as a threat to racial purity and the erosion of English identity. In 1596 she sent out an order with one Edward Banes to remove ten 'blackamoors' out of the country, 'of which kind of people there are already here too many', and arranged an exchange of eighty-nine English prisoners from Spain and Portugal with an equal number of 'blackamoors'. Elizabeth also urged her subjects to get rid of Moorish servants so that they could be 'served by their own countrymen'. In 1601 she reiterated her position, demanding that 'the great number of niggers and blackamoors which (as she is informed) are crept into this realm . . . who are fostered and relieved here to the great annoyance of her own liege people, that want the relief which those people consume'.[4] And, as the researches of Nabil Matar have demonstrated, the story of the extensive English contact with the Ottoman Empire in the six-teenth and seventeenth centuries, the Turks and the peoples of North Africa, has been ignored and effaced.[5] This is primarily because subsequent English historians have failed to understand that the likelihood of Englishmen turning Turk was far greater than the possibility of Turks becoming English, even though the assertions of contemporary writers tried to paint a picture of inevitable Christianization. A stubborn policing of national boundaries and pride in a pure identity often hides a more complex reality.

However, the history of the nation as a concept is not simply blighted by spatial and ethnic forgetting, but also involves temporal exclusion. In the most influential historical account of the nation in recent years, Benedict Anderson argues that the history of the nation did not really begin until the late Renaissance, with the rise of printing. The circulation of books and journals in the increas-ingly standardized form of the vernacular inaugurated by printing enabled groups of people who read the same material to become 'imagined communities', sharing goals and ideals, even if they had no real connection with the countrymen and women they claimed as compatriots. Before this happened, according to Anderson, a Latinate culture dominated and enabled a ruling, dynastic elite to control the populace at large within a 'traditional' framework of governmental and ecclesiastical power.[6] For Anderson, the age of nationalism was the age of the novel and the newspaper. Medieval people did not, he argues, have a real concept of the nation – or, rather, any they did have was over-ridden by their sense of belonging to a larger Christian community.

In making this argument, Anderson is simply following the prevailing wisdom of other scholars of the nation.[7] The same assumption was also made by Jürgen Habermas when he formulated his influential argument of the development of the public sphere. Using similar evidence to Anderson, Habermas argued that 'a realm of our social life in which something approaching public opinion can be informed' developed in eighteenth-century Europe out of the establishment of institutions such as Parliament, newspapers and coffee houses.[8] In making the 'public sphere' a post-Enlightenment phenomenon Habermas effectively caricatures the Middle Ages and the Renaissance as homogeneous periods in which the rule of monarchs was accepted and went unchallenged by articulate citizens.[9]

The essays in this section of the volume all mount a serious challenge to such patriarchal, ethnocentric assumptions and partial readings of history. Ruth Evans argues that, although historians have often assumed that medieval, clerical culture was fundamentally homogeneous, it was nothing of the sort. Commentators have read many texts as products of a pervasive ideology denigrating women and equating them with demons as polluters of men when such works were, in fact, often challenging these very assumptions. Our misreading of a fragmented and contestatory culture as a unified one ultimately stems from a belief that arguments about the rights of citizens, the status and role of women, and the development of a secular culture able to throw off the dominance of the Church, are essentially 'modern'. As the editors have also suggested in their introduction to this volume, the mythological representation of the Middle Ages as alien in time and mentality is one to be challenged, as is the ahistorical assumption that people who lived a long time ago must *always* have behaved and thought differently from us 'moderns'.

Evans shows that in a variety of fourteenth-century texts – Chaucer's *Wife of Bath's Tale*, the vernacular romance *Sir Orfeo*, the Latin prose narrative *De Origine Gigantum* (which narrates the mythical foundation of the island of Albion (Britain) by Albina and her sisters) and the late fifteenth-century York pageant *Joseph's Trouble about Mary* – the misogynistic representation of women by an official clerical hierarchy is mocked, challenged or destabilized. While a clerical culture sought to separate the corporeal and the ethereal, *De Origine* showed that this was impossible within the demands of the narrative realism expected in vernacular romance, a form that clearly influenced this Latin text. The result is that the sexuality of both women and demons was rendered problematic, indicating the crisis at the heart of the genealogy of the nation, which had to rely for self-definition on what it wished to exclude, that is, women and other 'aliens'. A similar – but not identical – problem is integral to the plot of *The Wife of Bath's Tale*. In her suggestion that friars have replaced demons as the main threat to women enjoying free access to the country at large, Chaucer's Alysoun openly mocks clerics. However, Evans argues further, Chaucer also suggests by means of this tale that friars actually make expedient use of the myth of dangerous incubi in order to cover up their own sexual crimes and abuse of women. Along the same lines, but perhaps more problematic still, the York play, *Joseph's Trouble about Mary*, hints that sexual identity may not, in fact, be natural at all, but relies on a repeated performance or re-enactment of cultural narratives concerning sexuality for its own credibility, a clear challenge to notions of stable hierarchy. If men can imitate angels successfully, then surely it is possible for one gender to imitate the other? All four texts, as Evans's argument reveals, demonstrate that public culture, social and sexual politics were actively debated in late medieval England and that few writers were prepared to accept an 'official' version of society without intellectual challenge.

In the second essay in this section Sue Niebrzydowski shows that, despite the openings in medieval culture pointed out by Evans, racial and sexual boundaries were often policed in order to preserve the purity of the nation. Niebrzydowski's subject is Chaucer's *The Man of Law's Tale*, specifically the mothers it represents. She shows how the text contrasts a series of mothers, deliberately portraying a black Muslim mother as 'particularly monstrous and *other* because in order to preserve her Muslim faith, she puts her own needs before those of her son, even resorting to his murder'. As Nabil Matar has shown, Muslims were seen as dangerous enemies, members of a powerful 'anti-Christian empire', and so were admired and feared as well as dismissed as savage and barbarous.[10] The need to produce hostile representations of Muslims and the Islamic faith was motivated by a fear of powerful rivals rather than a sense of condescending superiority to inferior people, hence the vitriolic force of many depictions of people and culture. The Sowdanesse is represented as the opposite of the good Christian mother as embodied by Custance, standing in effect as a figure of the 'anti-mother'. Such a representation serves, therefore, as a template not only for the policing of gender practices but also as a delimitation of the boundaries between the 'civilized' and the 'uncivilized' in the wider context of race. As Niebrzydowski suggests of the Sowdanesse, 'her body and behaviour serve as the site in which Western anxieties about *woman* and *race* are played out'.

While Evans shows how some aspects of medieval culture were more keen to include marginal and alienated figures than we often recognize, Niebrzydowski reminds us that elsewhere a racist Christian Eurocentrism made every effort to exclude peoples and creatures who failed to measure up to the norm of racial and cultural whiteness. When a woman from within the boundaries of the home culture does transgress the rules of motherhood as spectacularly as the Sowdanesse, she is carefully excluded in different ways in order to preserve the myth of unity. Donegild, dowager queen of Northumberland, another monstrous mother who does all she can to prevent Custance marrying her son, Alla, is represented as a pagan fairy from a land remote in space (Northumberland) and time. While the Sowdanesse constitutes a real threat to Christian values, Donegild is represented as a mythical figure, irrelevant to the contemporary concerns of late fourteenth-century England.

In an essay that can usefully be read alongside Evans's, Sujata Iyengar compares and contrasts a series of translations of Heliodorus' Greek romance, *Aithiopika* (*c*.230–275 CE), a key influence on the development of prose fiction in Elizabethan England. Iyengar shows how the romance reverses the 'racial and aesthetic assumptions' of Hellenistic and early modern European culture, challenging the equation of 'whiteness with transparent meaning, blackness with opaque mystery'. The essay illustrates the extent to which dominant sixteenth-century cultural representations were, like those of the fourteenth century, being hotly contested. Iyengar argues that the novel may have enjoyed its popularity specifically because it challenged accepted modes of reading the body, 'in particular . . . ways of reading racial and sexual difference'. The novel tells the story of Chariclea, the white daughter of the black King Hydaspes and Queen Persina of Ethiopia. In doing so it enables the translators to interrogate the ways in which race was conceived and constructed in the early modern period, to decide whether race – and, in particular, skin pigmentation – was a category established by geographical location, as influential thinkers such as Jean Bodin claimed, or whether it was inherited and – crucially – whether race could change over time, and if so how?[11] A useful comparison can be made with John Fletcher's *The Island Princess* (1621), which also has a white-skinned princess, Quisara, born of black parents, whose aristocratic status offsets her colour.[12] In *Aithiopika*, Persina gazes at a religious image of Andromeda when she conceives Chariclea, causing the child to resemble the goddess rather than her husband. Translators of the text, as Iyengar demonstrates, interpret the act of generation in differing ways, showing how it illustrates the power of art to influence human affairs, reveals the fluid and unstable nature of racial categories, and suggests the ways in which other constituents of identity, notably gender, can also be transgressed. Their versions reveal the lively and controversial nature of early modern debates about racial and sexual identity.

Taking up this theme, Kirstie Gulick Rosenfield explores the relationship between witchcraft and narrative as forms of persuasion and considers how these forms intersect with issues of power. While Brabantio is ostensibly wrong to label Othello's power over Desdemona as witchcraft, the play suggests that he is right to feel that narratives – such as the travel stories that Othello uses to woo Desdemona – are forms of magic. If narrative can construct identity, then, like an audience's experience in the theatre, different narratives can transform, redefine, undermine and ultimately consume other identities. In essence, narrative cannot be contained and always exceeds the intentions of the speaker, causing different narratives to compete for attention and for the status of 'truthful' discourse. The result is that narratives are always contested, which is exactly what happens in *Othello* after Iago has produced the 'monstrous birth' that precipitates the tragedy (although his plan would not work if Othello's narrative of constructing his identity was not already contested).

As Rosenfield points out, 'narrative is witchcraft because it causes monstrous generation, the crime of birthing traditionally associated with midwives and witches'. While seeming to be misogynistic, this recurrent image can also be read as revealing what happens when men not only control the production of stories and histories, but also try to appropriate the means of biological reproduction (at least, symbolically). Shakespeare, like Chaucer and the anonymous author of *De Origine Gigantum*, deliberately exposes some of the more pernicious effects of patriarchy and offers them up for critique. Monstrosity, of course, is not the preserve of women, but of those discourses which define them as such. Thus, it is not the union of Othello and Desdemona that will produce monsters; instead, monsters are the sterile and destructive offspring of Iago's envy and frustrated desire, as well as of the racist and sexist culture to which he wholeheartedly belongs. Just as the women in the play seek balanced and equal sexual union, so are they also truth-tellers. A potent example is the oral narrative passed down through the generations, as demonstrated by the handkerchief story. Such narratives appear to be superstitious but really warn of impending disaster and preserve the real story of women's fidelity, even though the tellers of such tales are usually labelled as witches and banished from society. Othello misreads the importance of this story and cannot see that the real problem is his credulousness rather than Desdemona's supposed infidelity. Just as Macbeth misreads the prophecies of the witches as signs of his safety rather than impending destruction, so does Othello misread the charm of the handkerchief as a sign of women's infidelity rather than for its ability to reveal the truth.

According to Rosenfield, *Othello* is a complex fable dealing with the process of narration and the relationship between narrative, identity and truth, showing how questions of race, gender and witchcraft are fundamental issues of human society and story-telling. Desdemona is destroyed because she dares to challenge the authority of the father and chooses an exogamous marriage which, if consummated, will undoubtedly lead to miscegenation, the ultimate race/gender crime. This 'monstrous birth' is aborted by the one Iago produces, as patriarchal authority takes its savage revenge.

However, what the essays collected in this section of the book demonstrate is that cultural authority cannot be taken for granted and read as monolithic. Whilst *Othello* tells the story of the apparent impossibility of miscegenation, it does so only to expose the forces ranged against those who would label 'transgression' as a 'monstrous birth', turning the language of patriarchy against itself. The essays of Ruth Evans, Sue Niebrzydowski, Sujata Iyengar and Kirstie Gulick Rosenfield all demonstrate that writers in the Middle Ages and Renaissance were often as keen to revise and reverse traditional assumptions of racial, national and masculine dominance, as they were to produce narratives upholding the status quo. As ever, we should not take cultural narratives at face value, but need to read between and beyond their lines, in order to unearth the multiple discourses which they continue to consume and contest.[13]

Notes

[1] Homi K. Bhabha, 'DissemiNation: time, narrative, and the margins of the modern nation', in Homi K. Bhabha (ed.), *Nation and Narration* (London, 1990), pp. 291–322 (297).

[2] For analysis, see Peter Hulme, *Colonial Encounters: Europe and the Native Caribbean, 1492–1797* (London, 1986), pp. xii–xiii, 1–3.

[3] See David Katz, *The Jews in the History of England, 1485–1850* (Oxford, 1994), introduction; James Shapiro, *Shakespeare and the Jews* (New York, 1996), introduction.

[4] Cited in Julia Briggs, *This Stage-Play World: Texts and Contexts, 1580–1625* (2nd edn, Oxford, 1997), pp. 95–6.

[5] Nabil Matar, *Islam in Britain, 1558–1685* (Cambridge, 1998); *Turks, Moors and Englishmen in the Age of Discovery* (New York, 1999). See also Lisa Jardine, *Worldly Goods: A New History of the Renaissance* (London, 1996).

[6] Benedict Anderson, *Imagined Communities: Reflections on the Origins and Spread of Nationalism* (London, 1983), chs 2–3.

[7] See, for example, Ernest Gellner, *Nations and Nationalism* (Oxford, 1983); E. J. Hobsbawm, *Nations and Nationalism since 1780: Programme, Myth, Reality* (Cambridge, 1990).

[8] Jürgen Habermas, 'The public sphere', *New German Critique* 3 (1974), 49–55.

[9] For comment, see Andrew Hadfield, *Literature, Politics and National Identity: Reformation to Renaissance* (Cambridge, 1994), pp. 5–7; David Zaret, *Origins of Democratic Culture; Printing, Petitions, and the Public Sphere in Early-Modern*

England (Princeton, NJ, 2000).

¹⁰ Matar, *Islam in Britain*, p. 190; *Turks, Moors and Englishmen*, p. 12.

¹¹ For discussion, see Margaret T. Hogden, *Early Anthropology in the Sixteenth and Seventeenth Centuries* (Philadelphia, 1964); Margo Hendricks and Patricia Parker (eds), *Women, 'Race' and Writing in the Early Modern Period* (London, 1994); Kim F. Hall, *Things of Darkness: Economies of Race and Gender in Early Modern England* (Ithaca, NY, 1995).

¹² For discussion see Andrew Hadfield, *Literature, Travel and Colonial Writing in the English Renaissance, 1545–1625* (Oxford, 1998), pp. 254–64; Michael Neill, *Putting History to the Question: Power, Politics, and Society in English Renaissance Drama* (Ithaca, NY, 2000), ch. 12.

¹³ See Annabel Patterson, *Reading between the Lines* (London, 1993).

15

The Devil in Disguise: Perverse Female Origins of the Nation

ॐ

RUTH EVANS

Tertullian famously reminded women of their collective historical role as entry point for the polluting forces of the demonic. 'You are the gateway of the devil,' he pronounced with his customary reticence, 'you are the one who unseals the curse of that tree, and you are the first one to turn your back on the divine law.'[1] Western Christendom's view of women as the weakest link between the natural and the supernatural world is a medieval commonplace. It informs the spiriting away of Queen Heurodis by the king of faery in the Middle English romance *Sir Orfeo*, the Wife of Bath's observation that incubi once laid in wait for innocent women in 'every bussh or under every tree' (III.879) and Joseph's sardonic suggestion in the York Corpus Christi Play that Mary must have been impregnated by a (bad) angel. But the incubus motif also occurs in medieval historiography, where it fixes and maintains not only sexual difference but also the borders of the nation and its proper governance.[2] In the hugely popular legend of Albina, a disgraced and exiled band of sisters found 'Albion' and then copulate with invisible demons, giving birth to a race of giants. This all-girl foundation-narrative invents an outlandish prehistory for Brutus' founding of Britain, one that serves to differentiate the true, manly nation from the perverse, female one.

This essay traces the chain of associations that links women's fragile and disturbing sexuality with the supernatural and with originary myths. Although I will be concerned primarily with the ways in which the textual manifestations of this concatenation challenge misogynist presumptions, the question of women's implication with origins suggests a much larger argument, which this short essay cannot fully address: if women make trouble for the nation, they also trouble the notion of a pure origin. And the question of origins is an especially pressing one for Western culture today. In philosophy, psychoanalysis, literature, genetics and phylogenetics we are rethinking our profoundest connections with ourselves, with others and with the past. The content of the medieval Albina legend has become synonymous with its historical fate, for it concerns what we also seek for in it: ways of disturbing the past, as well as of finding a connection with it. It provokes a rethinking of the past in which our medieval origins appear less settled than we had imagined.

But first we need to attend to the historical meanings behind the juxtaposition of women and demons. Dyan Elliott claims that this association reveals the clerical fear of women's contagious impurity:

> The deep logic at work [in medieval ecclesiastic culture] can be reduced to a very basic principle: men, who were strongly self-identified with the powers of reason and the will, feared what became of themselves when they slept. But these same men, who were relatively sanguine, even comforted, by the thought of a sleeping woman (or so fairy tales would have us believe), were extremely nervous about women's waking activities. And so female pollutions, foregrounded as conscious and deliberate, ultimately presage the carnal woman's vulnerability to the incubus.[3]

Elliott describes the work of ideology not logic. It is ideology that reverses the pattern of gendered waking and sleeping by representing *women* as asleep when the devil enters. Celibate men were horrified by their wet dreams. But women, who menstruated, were known to be both polluted and polluting. So, blame the sleeping woman for admitting the devil: that way the clergy could sleep on, untroubled.

But these clerical origins, powerfully explanatory as they are, do not tell us everything about the deployment of the incubus motif in medieval vernacular texts. In the Albina legend, for example, women's alliance with demons is complex and divided. This legend is a *langue* with many and various *paroles*, told and retold in all three major literary languages of medieval England (Anglo-

Norman, English, Latin) from the early fourteenth to the sixteenth centuries.[4] These retellings range from the early fourteenth-century *Thopas*-like English metrical version in the Auchinleck manuscript (MS Edinburgh, Advocates 19. 2. 1)[5] to the numerous variants in Anglo-Norman, Latin and English, in prose and verse, that are appended to the popular *Brut* chronicle.[6] There are also three medieval Welsh retellings.[7] Another English version appears in Thomas of Castleford's *Chronicle of England* (c.1327), and in the prologue to John Hardyng's fifteenth-century *Chronicle*, of which there are sixteenth-century editions.[8] The earliest version, a short poem known by the title *Des Grantz Geanz*, was composed in Anglo-Norman in the first quarter of the fourteenth century and then translated into Latin prose (1338–40).[9] It is to this Latin text, known in most of its sixteen surviving manuscripts as *De Origine Gigantum*, that I shall refer. Existing only in unstable variants, the legend exemplifies the proliferation and heterogeneity that characterizes what Bernard Cerquiglini teasingly calls the 'essential plurality' of medieval textuality: its *variance*.[10] And variance is one name for what violates the notion of a pure origin.

In the legend, Albina and her sisters, daughters of the king of either Greece or Syria (there are two different traditions) plot to kill their husbands if they are not granted sovereignty over them. Betrayed by the youngest daughter, they are cast adrift in a boat to die. Making landfall on an uninhabited island, they found the kingdom of Albion. In a parody of the Fall, the sisters defile the paradisial land they have colonized by over-indulging in its plentiful food. As a result, they become inflamed with sexual desire. Demon-incubi happily oblige (as they would), and the women conceive and give birth to a monstrous progeny of giants, who then reproduce incestuously and rule the land for the next few hundred years. Quite what *nation* is here imagined is never made clear, but 'Albion' is the precursor of the land that was later, according to a tradition which was given the stamp of authority by Geoffrey of Monmouth's mighty *Historia Regum Britannie*, dubbed 'Britain' by the noble Trojan patriarch, Brutus.[11] In Geoffrey's account Brutus arrives to mop up the giants and to get the (perverted) course of 'British' history back on a proper, civilized track.

Why was this such a wildly popular story? And why the need to install this kind of prehistory? On the one hand, the various translations, retranslations and generic transformations of the

Albina legend position these texts within the powerful ideological structure of *translatio imperii et studii*, the myth of the transfer of learning and power from Greece to Rome, and thence to Europe, as part of a project of colonial conquest and expansion.[12] And on the other, many of the vernacular retellings answer to a burgeoning lay middle-class taste for lurid and romantic adventure. The story satisfyingly fills in some gaps in Geoffrey's eminent and upmarket *Historia* by offering a genealogy for the giants whom Brutus has to exterminate and an explanation of why the land is called Albion. And it responds to the need for a 'national' origin-myth that elaborates on the Old Testament stories of the peopling of the prehistoric world by giants: Genesis 6: 2–4, for example, offers an account of how the sons of God, often construed as fallen angels, bred with the daughters of men and engendered a race of giants.

But a full understanding of the protonationalist uses of the Albina legend must await analysis of all of its retellings. Because the Anglo-Norman and English versions have already received some attention, I will be focusing here on the barely discussed Latin prose version, the *De Origine Gigantum*, produced in Glastonbury in the early 1330s and roughly contemporaneous with *Sir Orfeo*, with which it has some links.[13] In an unusual reversal of the traditional medieval source/target language expectations, the *De Origine* is a *Latin* translation *from* the Anglo-Norman. It represents an attempt to reclericalize this particular tradition of popular historiography, romance and the supernatural by rewriting it as 'serious' history. Like several of the earliest vernacular retellings, the *De Origine* is co-opted on behalf of nationalist interests, namely the Scottish question. Appearing within twenty years of the Declaration of Arbroath (1320), it is followed in the earliest manuscript (Longleat, Marquis of Bath 39) by four pieces relating to Scottish claims to independence.[14] The Albina myth supplies a parallel to the legend of Scota who was reinterpreted in the early fourteenth century, at a time of considerable political conflict between the English and the Scottish, as the eponymous founder of Scotland (not Ireland, as she was originally identified).

The text's presentation of women's dangerous sexuality, their polluting contact with incubi and their unleashing of monsters, crucially transmits an understanding of political foundations that is inseparable from questions of sexual difference. But to read the *De Origine* alongside Middle English vernacular romances and

popular drama in which the incubus motif also appears is to
glimpse a rather different cultural narrative: namely the prehistory
of the witch. According to Dyan Elliott, the clerical fantasy
of women and demons as agents of defilement runs a course in
which demons become progressively disembodied and women
concomitantly assume the primary role of embodiment of sin.
This shift makes the materialization (and demonization) of the
witch in the early modern period, in Elliott's words, 'virtually
irresistible' (164). As demons cease to be bodies, so women assume
sinfulness.

The *De Origine,* however, does not entirely bear out this
narrative. Commentators, including Cassian (d. 435), denied that
incubi could have sexual intercourse with human women, but this
text does not agree. Having satisfied their hunger, Albina and her
sisters leave themselves open to demonic invasion:

> Cumque talibus refocillate cibariis uires recuperarent amissas et
> nutribilium esu dapum grosse essent et crasse ceperunt calore accendi
> uenereo et titillacione carnis urgeri. Quod demones incubi
> perpendentes assumptis hominum sibi formis cum mixtura feminei
> seminis oppresserunt easdem et euanuerunt continuo. Nec femine uiros
> uiderunt sed tantummodo uirile opus senserunt. (96–103)

> And when, revived with such fare, they had recovered their lost
> strength, having eaten a nutritious repast, they were fat and coarsely
> they began to be inflamed with sexual desire and felt an urge for the
> titillation of the flesh. For demon incubi, seeing their advantage and
> having assumed the shape of men, raped the women, intermingling
> their seed with the women's seed, and immediately vanished into thin
> air. The women did not see men but nevertheless they felt a man's work.
> (105–11)

In one sense, this passage reaffirms traditional clerical views. It
links women's appetitive nature to their sexual incontinence. It
alludes to the familiar 'two-seed' theory, namely that women as
well as men produce a seed necessary to generation, a theory
invoked here because the text links conception with the women's
immoderate and whorish pleasure.[15] Also in play are the categories
of pollution and purity that are constructed by the prohibitions of
Leviticus 18: 22–5, 27, in which the Lord warns the people of Israel
of the dangers of sexual liaison across borders:

With a man you will not mix in coitus as with a woman because it is an abomination. You will not copulate with any beast: nor will you be defiled with it. A woman will not lie with a draught-animal, nor will she copulate with it: because it is an enormity. Do not pollute yourselves in any of these things with which all the [other] nations were defiled, whom I will cast out before your sight. And by which things the land was polluted: whose enormities I will punish so that [the land] may vomit forth its inhabitants . . . For all those cursed things the inhabitants of the land who were before you did, and they polluted it.

The demonic offspring of Albina and her sisters represent the Levitical 'other nations', those who precede the Chosen People (Brutus and his ilk): in the words of the twelfth-century *Glossa Ordinaria*, 'Demons: who on account of their multitude are called all the nations.' Elliott argues that the gloss is anachronistic because, despite its alignment of demonic activity with same-sex intercourse and bestiality, by the later Middle Ages demons were losing their bodies: as corporeality becomes newly valued in the later Middle Ages, so demons become disembodied. But in the *De Origine* the incubi are *not* entirely disembodied. They take on the bodies of men in order to have sex. The text struggles with the contradiction: the previously disembodied and invisible incubi assume the bodies of men and yet remain invisible to the women, who can only *feel* them having sex with them: 'They felt a man's work.' The Latin text has *uirile opus senserunt* (103). This may be partly explained by Honorius Augustodiensis (d. after 1140), who argues for the shape-shifting abilities of demons in their dealings with humans:

> Just as humans are able to colour their bodies, namely to whiten or darken them or cover them with clothes, so demons are able to transfigure their bodies into various forms – either to show splendid [bodies] for deceiving or hideous ones for terrifying.[16]

But despite the unnaturalness of the proceedings in the *De Origine*, the demons take the shape of men, not devils (and *not* women), and the sex they engage in is normatively heterosexual. This may bear out Elliott's point that disembodied demons in the later Middle Ages are 'ironically deployed as gatekeepers of sexual morality' (128). The Anglo-Norman source-text is ambiguous, for

though the demons are invisible, the women 'soulement senteient /
Come feme deit homme faire / Kant se entremettent de tiel affaire'
(430–2: they only felt / as a woman should do to a man? *or* what a
man should do to a woman? / when they [the women? the incubi?]
begin such a business). The clash between the clerical imperative of
demonic disembodiment and the demand for narrative realism
means that for sex to take place there must be bodies. If the
women's sexuality is problematic, then so is that of the demons.

In *Sir Orfeo*, a vernacular romance composed very close in date
to the earliest versions of the Albina myth (and also appearing in
Auchinleck, together with one Middle English Albina version),
Orfeo's wife, Heurodis, is whisked away to the Otherworld by the
'king o fairi' (283) for sleeping under an 'ympe-tre' – a grafted tree
– itself an 'unnatural' object that metonymically suggests
Heurodis' feminine vulnerability to the supernatural.[17] The poem
plays with the notions of pollution that link a medieval fantasy of
woman with a fantasy of the demonic: Heurodis rubs her hands
and feet, scratches her face until it bleeds, and tears her dress, in a
mimicry of the bodily dismemberment that the Faery-King
threatens to visit on her if she does not go with him to the
Otherworld: 'Whar þou be, þou worst y-fet, / & to-tore þine limes
al, / þat noþing help þe no schal' (170–2). But the king of the fairies
is no sexually predatory incubus. Nor is the poem concerned with
the anxious notions of sexual purity that characterize so many
clerical discussions of both women and demons. In part this is
because the successful resolution of Orfeo's quest to get Heurodis
back requires that she be a courtly and unpolluted prize worth
retrieving, so that she can enable the poem's deployment of the
traditional medieval analogy between proper marriage and proper
kingship. And while the fairy world is sometimes represented as
sinister it is not completely 'other' to the kingdom of England. The
king of the fairies is just as splendidly regal as Orfeo, his court just
as courtly. The poem simply does not fit the clerical polarities,
despite the fact that the compiler or patron of one of the manuscripts in which it appears – the London-produced Auchinleck –
seems to have been interested in monstrous women and demonic
alterity, for the manuscript, as I have noted, also includes a Middle
English translation of the Albina legend. And the explication –
only in the Auchinleck version – that Orfeo's city Thrace is in fact
Winchester suggests a comic attempt to claim for Winchester the

same kind of classical heritage that was claimed for London – as Troynovant – in Geoffrey's Brutus legend. *Sir Orfeo* shares an interest with the *De Origine* in vernacular historiography. Its themes of the lost wife and the lost kingdom mark its political concerns with the recovery of the past, but it is also concerned with the dynamic processes of temporal change: while the fairy world is frozen, Heurodis and Orfeo participate in the flux of time.[18]

In Chaucer's *Wife of Bath's Tale* (*c*.1392–5), however, the association between women and the demonic is treated ironically.[19] According to Alysoun of Bath, in 'th'olde dayes of the Kyng Arthour' the land was filled with 'fayerye' and elves. But now the holy friars have chased out these supernatural beings with their 'grete charitee and prayeres' (III.865) and their sheer physical numbers ('As thikke as motes in the sone-beem', II.869): now women can walk abroad with impunity, meeting only the friar, who – God forbid – will do no more than behave disrespectfully towards them:

> For there as wont to walken was an elf
> There walketh now the lymytour hymself
> . . . Women may go saufly up an down.
> In every bussh or under every tree
> Ther is noon oother incubus but he,
> And he ne wol doon hem but dishonour.
>   (3. 873–81)

So threat is replaced by reassurance. But the comic double-take here involves of course the ironic analogy between the incubus and the friar, an analogy secured through the carefully strategic grammar of '*noon* other incubus *but* he'. This construction produces not the *displacement* of the incubus by the friar but rather their strong identification. It is an analogy that also makes a telling proto-feminist point about the clerical origins of the association between women and the demonic. For Alysoun of Bath's sly reference to the friar in incubus-drag reveals not only why women might have to fear friars but also why there is a need to cover up male sexual violence towards women.

Although the Wife is never explicit about the sexual threat to women represented by the 'fayeryes', she is explicit about the threat represented by 'lymytours': dishonour, the euphemistic cover-up for rape that is also an allusion to the social consequences of rape, namely the public shame that makes women, like the daughter of Symkyn the miller in *The Reeve's Tale*, spoiled goods in the eyes of those men who want to preserve their market value. *The Reeve's Tale* is explicit about the *clerical* desires invested in the preservation of the daughter Malyne's virgin status: it is her grandfather, 'the person of the toun', who intends to make her 'his heir' and to 'bistowe hire hye / Into some worthy blood of auncetrye' (I.3977–82). Her father Symkyn's outrage when he learns that Aleyn the clerk has slept with her makes plain the sense in which the Wife uses the term 'dishonour': ' "Who dorste be so boold to disparage / My doghter, that is come of swich lynage?" ' (I.4271–2). Having a *clerk* undo *clerical* privilege contributes a further level of irony. For it is precisely in the interests of friars to claim to have ritually cleansed the land of faery-incubi, allowing themselves a free rein for sexual conquest. If ecclesiastic culture simultaneously creates the incubus and the woman as agents of pollution to ward off fear of their own sexual impurity, then anti-fraternal satire speaks of what is repressed within clerical culture: namely violence towards women. The Wife's allusion to the friar-incubus displacement constitutes a preamble to her tale of male sexual violence towards women and female retribution.[20]

The immediate context for the Wife's allusion suggests that she is taking a side-swipe at the Friar for his criticism of her performance ('This is a long preamble of a tale!', III.831). But her reference also works to reveal a broader structure of displacement within clerical culture, continuing the critiques of Jankyn's *Book of Wikked Wyves* that she made in her *Prologue*. Just as her *Prologue* makes a telling point about how clerks misrepresent the fantasy of woman which they themselves have created as the 'truth' about women, so she begins her tale by revealing what is at stake for the clergy in their anxious imagining of women's diabolic pleasures: the repression of their bodily desires. Although the tale she tells – a romance – is not as obviously clerical as her prologue, the structure of displacement is still strongly at work in it: in the various displacements of the Midas story, and in the displacements that make the hag's own supernatural status not simply a reinforcement of the clerical association but a form of reversal that disrupts the very terms it inhabits. For the hag is able to use her own supernatural status to teach the knight a lesson about proper behaviour, a lesson that may be also aimed at the pilgrim-Friar. Against Elliott's claim that demons became pro-gressively disembodied in the course of the later Middle Ages (164), Chaucer's hag brings the body right back in, making her very status as body – 'foul and old' (III.1213) – the means for revealing just how much the clerical association of women and the supernatural is about the preservation of normative standards of corporeal whole-ness and perfection.

The figure of the incubus surfaces in other vernacular texts, including the late fifteenth-century York pageant, *Joseph's Trouble about Mary*. This pageant articulates for its audience the anxieties generated by the paradox of the virgin birth and the lurking possibility of Mary's adultery, engaging with ritualized notions of purity and pollution. Joseph's anxious interrogation of Mary about the father of her child emphasizes these concerns: ten times he asks her variations on the question 'Whose ist Marie?' (l. 103). At one point one of Mary's maidens protests to Joseph that no adultery has taken place: 'here come no man in þere wanes / . . . Saue an aungell ilke a day anes / With bodily foode hir fedde has he' (ll. 123–6). To which Joseph sarcastically replies:

> Þanne se I wele youre menyng is
> Þe aungell has made hir with childe.
> Nay, som man in aungellis liknesse
> With somkyn gawde has hir begiled,
> And þat trow I.
>
> (ll. 134–8)[21]

As Elliott points out, Augustine addresses the question of angels sleeping with women (128–35) in his attempt to distinguish between the bodies of demons and those of angels. The pageant can be seen as grappling with the questions discussed earlier, since the 'man in aungellis liknesse' suggests a popular version of the disembodied demon. According to the *Malleus Maleficarum* (1487), the phrase 'because of the angels' in 1 Corinthians 9, which warns that a woman 'ought to have a covering on her head, because of the angels', is believed by 'many Catholics' to refer to incubi.[22] This is reinforced by the logic of typology at work in the York Play, insofar as Mary is an antitype of Eve and the Annunciation a type of reversal of the Fall, a typology often secured through the traditional word-play on Eva/*Ave*. Moreover, late medieval culture was intensely preoccupied with the relationship between human sexuality and the Fall: a number of clerical writers, for example, claimed that an angel, disguised in Adam's body, was forced to have sex with Eve.[23] Joseph's comic riposte, however, with its reference to disguise – the potential adulterer is dressed in 'aungellis liknesse'– could also be read as satirizing debates over the embodiment of angels and demons. It invites the audience to read the theological niceties of such debates (and their misogynist impulses) otherwise: what is at stake is not the ontological corporeality of angels and demons but the bizarre corporeality of *both* as a kind of *performance*. If men can 'pass' as angels, then perhaps sexual difference is also a performance? Although the pageant relies for its comedy on clerical and misogynist associations between women and the supernatural, it also profoundly destabilizes those associations.

Just as Mary and Joseph play out anxieties within the (holy) family, the meetings between women and the supernatural in medieval foundation stories are also to do with family, and with the relation between family and nation. The woman–demon coupling looks at first like an inversion of the usual narratives of genealogically patterned chronicles in the high Middle Ages. According to Gabrielle Spiegel, examples of such chronicles in thirteenth-century France were concerned to represent lineage as 'primarily a representation of the transmission of lands, ignoring the remaining members of the biological family [younger sons; women] not included in the patrimonial legacy'. They were '[w]ritten above all to exalt a line and legitimize [the family's] power', displaying 'the noble family's intention to affirm and extend its place in political life'.[24] But the actions of Albina and her sisters are not simply an inversion of these genealogical narratives. Rather, the text offers a more ambivalent inscription of their role. To pursue Spiegel's point, one might argue that if the project of genealogical chronicles is to suggest 'the human process of procreation and filiation as a metaphor for historical change', then both *Des Grantz Geanz* and the *De Origine* foreground the role of procreation and *female* filiation, putting women centre-stage in the process of historical change.[25] That this is represented in terms of a monstrous coupling should not detract from the narrative's very real attention to the women's participation in processes of 'legitimate' social order. Johnson observes that, in the longer Anglo-Norman version, certain of the women's (and indeed of the giants') actions could also be represented as a series of mimicries and repetitions of the rituals by which social, political and cultural power is affirmed in the patriarchal societies from which the women are exiled and by which the community they found is eventually conquered. (32)

Freud observes in his case history of the Rat-Man that the way in which an individual constructs a story about his or her identity involves 'a complicated process of remodelling analogous in every way to the process by which a nation constructs legends about its early history'.[26] Where the Middle Ages located the question of origins in the nation and its foundations, we now locate them in the self. That women's sexuality is at the centre of late medieval vernacular origin-myths may suggest that we look to these texts not only for the prehistories of the witch and the nation, but for ways in which they open up a (feminist) future. More work needs to be done on how medieval originary stories explore, at the phylo-genetic level, the relationship between recollection and reconstruction which is also at the heart of the Freudian ontogenetic project, reminding us that both psychoanalysis and historiography make sexual difference central to the cultural transformations of the present and the future. The feminine will be what troubles both the question of origins and the question of the Middle Ages.

Notes

[1] Tertullian, *The Appearance of Women*, quoted in Alcuin Blamires with Karen Pratt and C. W. Marx, *Woman Defamed and Woman Defended: An Anthology of Medieval Texts* (Oxford, 1992), p. 51.

[2] Jeffrey Jerome Cohen, 'Monstrous origin: body, nation, family', in *Of Giants: Sex, Monsters, and the Middle Ages* (Minneapolis and London, 1999), pp. 29–61. On the validity of the premodern 'nation' see Andrew Hadfield, 'National and international knowledge: the limits of the histories of nations', in Neil Rhodes and Jonathan Sawday (eds), *The Renaissance Computer: Knowledge Technology in the First Age of Print* (London and New York, 2000), pp. 106–19.

[3] Dyan Elliott, *Fallen Bodies: Pollution, Sexuality, and Demonology in the Middle Ages* (Philadelphia, 1999), p. 58.

[4] On the extraordinarily polyglot nature of later medieval England, see Jocelyn Wogan-Browne, Nicholas Watson, Andrew Taylor and Ruth Evans (eds), *The Idea of the Vernacular: An Anthology of Middle English Literary Theory, 1280–1520* (University Park, PA and Exeter, 1999), pp. 331–4.

⁵ *An Anonymous Short English Metrical Chronicle*, ed. Ewald Zettl, EETS os 196 (London, 1935), pp. 46–55.

⁶ Lesley Johnson, 'Return to Albion', *Arthurian Literature* 13 (1995), 19–40 (21); for edns, see *The Brut, or The Chronicles of England*, ed. F. W. D. Brie, EETS os 131 (London, 1906, repr. 1960).

⁷ See B. Roberts, 'Ystori'r Llong Foel', *Bulletin of the Board of Celtic Studies* 18 (1958), 337–62.

⁸ *Castleford's Chronicle or the Boke of Brut*, ed. Caroline D. Eckhardt, EETS os 305 (Oxford, 1996); *The Chronicle of John Harding*, ed. H. Ellis (London, 1812), p. 26.

⁹ See Georgine E. Brereton (ed.), *Des Grantz Geanz: An Anglo-Norman Poem* (Oxford, 1937); for the Latin text, see James P. Carley and Julia Crick 'Constructing Albion's past: an annotated edition of *De Origine Gigantum*', *Arthurian Literature* 13 (1995), 41–114; for its trans. see Ruth Evans (trans.), 'Gigantic origins: an annotated translation of *De Origine Gigantum*', *Arthurian Literature* 16 (1998), 197–211 (repr. in James P. Carley (ed.), *Glastonbury Abbey and the Arthurian Tradition*, Arthurian Studies 42 (Woodbridge and Rochester, NY, 2001), pp. 417–32). All subsequent references will be to these edns, with line numbers in parentheses in the text.

¹⁰ Bernard Cerquiglini, *In Praise of the Variant: A Critical History of Philology*, trans. Betsy Wing (Baltimore and London, 1999), p. 27.

¹¹ *The Historia Regum Britannie of Geoffrey of Monmouth*, ed. Neil Wright (Cambridge, 1984), pp. 21–2; I, 16–18.

¹² See Wogan-Browne et al., *Idea of the Vernacular*, pp. 317–19; 367–70; and Richard Waswo, 'Our ancestors, the Trojans: inventing cultural identity in the Middle Ages', *Exemplaria* 7 (1995), 269–90 (272–3).

¹³ Johnson, 'Return to Albion', discusses the Anglo-Norman version; Cohen, 'Monstrous origin', the Middle English.

¹⁴ Carley and Crick, 'Constructing Albion's past', p. 70. On the link between *Des Grantz Geanz* and the politics of Scottish independence, see Johnson, 'Return to Albion', p. 25. John Hardyng used the Albina legend to defend *England's* right to rule over Scotland: Cohen, 'Monstrous origin', n. 31.

¹⁵ Joan Cadden, *Meanings of Sex Difference in the Middle Ages: Medicine, Science, and Culture* (Cambridge, 1993), pp. 52–3, 62, 93–7, 200–1: on the link between female seed and female pleasure, see pp. 93–7.

¹⁶ Elliott, *Fallen Bodies*, p. 129.

¹⁷ A. J. Bliss (ed.), *Sir Orfeo*, 2nd edn (Oxford, 1966). All quotations are taken from the Auchinleck version in this edn, with line numbers given parenthetically in the text.

¹⁸ On the past in *Sir Orfeo*, see Felicity Riddy, 'The uses of the past in *Sir Orfeo*', *Yearbook of English Studies*, ed. G. K. Hunter and C. J. Rawson, 6 (1976), 5–15.

¹⁹ *The Riverside Chaucer*, ed. Larry D. Benson, 3rd edn (Oxford, 1988).

²⁰ On rape in late medieval law and in Chaucer's tale, see Corinne J. Saunders, 'Woman displaced: rape and romance in Chaucer's *Wife of Bath's Tale*', *Arthurian Literature* 13 (1995), 115–31.

²¹ *Joseph's Trouble about Mary*, in *The York Plays*, ed. Richard Beadle (London, 1982), p. 120.

²² 'Blessed Isidore, in the last chapter of his 8th Book, says: Satyrs are they who are called Pans in Greek and Incubi in Latin. And they are called Incubi from their practice of overlaying, that is debauching. For they often lust lecherously after

women, and copulate with them; and the Gauls name them Dusii, because they are diligent in this beastliness . . . As to that of St. Paul in I. Corinthians xi, A woman ought to have a covering on her head, because of the angels, many Catholics believe that "because of the angels" refers to Incubi': Jacobus Sprenger and Heinrich Kramer, *Malleus Maleficarum*, trans. Montague Summers (London, 1928), Book I.

²³ See Elliott, *Fallen Bodies*, p. 143.

²⁴ Gabrielle M. Spiegel, 'History, historicism, and the social logic of the text in the Middle Ages', *Speculum* 65 (1990), 59–86 (78–9); Evans, 'Gigantic origins', p. 210.

²⁵ Johnson suggests that the Anglo-Norman text exhibits a similar process, with Albina expressing 'a desire to make her mark on historical time (to enter men's time, in effect)', 'Return to Albion', p. 31.

²⁶ *The Standard Edition of the Complete Psychological Works of Sigmund Freud*, ed. James Strachey et al., 24 vols (London, 1953–74), X, p. 206, n. 1.

16

Monstrous (M)othering: The Representation of the Sowdanesse in *Chaucer's* Man of Law's Tale

ക

SUE NIEBRZYDOWSKI

In medieval culture, as indeed within our own, successful mothering is a key facet of the construction of the female body, for on it depends not only the physical and social wellbeing of the child but also the continuation of society itself. Chaucer's *Man of Law's Tale*[1] is peopled with mothers and has motherhood at its heart. A sequence of mothers pass through the text: Custance's mother, a Muslim Sowdanesse, Donegild (the mother of Custance's husband, King Alla) and finally Custance herself who becomes the mother of Maurice, the issue of her marriage to King Alla. This essay explores and interrogates the Sowdanesse's representation as a mother in light of those medieval discourses that historically and politically objectify her – Christian attitudes towards mothering, and responses to women of colour as refracted through natural histories, travel writing, bestiaries and cultural memories of the Crusades. As the perpetrator of the murder of her son and ruler the Sowdanesse is to be viewed, we are instructed by the Man of Law, as the monstrous (m)other with a consuming appetite for power, with whom the Christian Custance's mothering of the Emperor Maurice is to be compared and contrasted.

Whilst discussions of mothering are few,[2] those which survive suggest that during the later Middle Ages mothering becomes an interest of the Church and is recognized as an occupation that merits both appreciation and instruction. Clarissa Atkinson notes that between the thirteenth and fifteenth centuries there is a new appreciation of marriage, family and motherhood which offers up an alternative route towards female sanctity.[3] Late medieval hagiography reflects this, for example, in the popularity of the lives of two notable, married, female saints who were mothers, Elizabeth of Hungary and Bridget of Sweden,[4] and, of course, in the emphasis on the mothering of Mary. In her portrayal as *Mater Dolorosa* and the *Pietà*, Mary as mother broods over the secular arts and her successful mothering is celebrated in late medieval England by the feast of her Purification, known as Candlemas Day.[5] In the long text of her *Revelations of Divine Love*, Julian the anchoress of Norwich, very possibly a wife and mother herself before she became enclosed, describes God as a mother figure.[6] In her vision of how and why God is like a mother, Julian defines the best properties of human mothering thus:

> The moders service is nerest, redyest and sekirest, for it is most of trueth . . . The moder may leyn the child tenderly to her brest . . . To the properte of moderhede longyth kinde love, wisdam and knowing, and it is good . . . The kynde, loveand moder that wote and knowith the nede of hir child, she kepith it ful tenderly as the kind and condition of moderhede will. And as it wexith in age she chongith hir werking but not hir love. And whan it is waxen of more age, she suffrid that it be bristinid in brekyng downe of vices to makyn the child to receivyn vertues and graces.[7]

The best mother is one who not only loves, nurtures and permits her child's chastising for its spiritual good, but also whose love never changes and who puts the needs of her child *first*.

Julian of Norwich is unusual in her recording of her attitudes towards motherhood in her text. Atkinson's observation that 'mothers did not write about motherhood, but their lives and experiences were profoundly affected by the work of those who did'[8] remains the case for the majority of medieval women. Medieval discussion of mothering is based upon a long tradition of male-authored texts. St Paul makes it clear in the First Epistle to Timothy that the primary function of married women is motherhood, in order to populate the world with Christians (1 Timothy 2: 14). St Augustine perpetuates this belief when he writes that woman was created by God to be man's helper 'for the sake of bearing children'.[9] While early Christianity defined the purpose of motherhood, the Middle Ages engaged also with the nature of mothering and the maternal bond. Silvana Vecchio has remarked on the importance of motherly love during the Middle Ages, arguing that 'maternal love was not considered a duty: it was taken for granted . . . A mother's love was compassionate and given to sacrifice'.[10] Instructive examples of maternal love are to be found in sermons, such as the loving mother who warms her child's hands over burning rushes in winter or another who cares for her child in sickness by lighting a candle and praying for his health, promising a vow should he recover.[11]

During the Middle Ages, child-rearing was seen as specifically woman's work that entailed skills to be learned. Such teaching was often disseminated from the pulpit. A mother's responsibility for children's safety and discipline were key topics that were brought to parishioners' attention regularly. In a canon of the Council of Canterbury (1236), for example, priests are ordered to exhort mothers, *every Sunday*, not to sleep in the same bed with their infants because they might accidentally smother them; also infants were not to be left near fire or water without a guardian.[12] Concern about 'overlaying' (suffocating the baby when in bed with an adult) persisted as it features in John Mirk's *Instructions for Parish Priests*, a Middle English translation of an earlier Latin work carried out in around 1400.[13]

Whilst few works that instruct in 'proper mothering' have survived, those that do demonstrate that during the Middle Ages it was considered the mother's responsibility to protect the child, promote its good health and instil in it proper obedience to its parents. Underpinning this was the assumption that mothers held their children in some affection. This affective, selfless maternal behaviour is certainly exhibited by Custance who offers care and comfort to her baby son on their enforced banishment from their home:

> 'Pees, litel sone, I wol do thee noon harm.'
> With that hir coverchief of hir heed she breyde,
> And over his litel eyen she it leyde,
> And in hir arm she lulleth it ful faste.
>
> (ll.834–9)

Custance's Christianity is framed by her devotion to its key mother figures. She prays to Saint Anne, the mother of Mary (l. 641) and then to the *Mater Dolorosa* herself at the point when, as the mother of a child about to be falsely and maliciously banished from his heritage, she most needs pity for her child's plight (l. 853). In contrast to the maternal behaviour exhibited by the Christian Custance, the mothering of the Sowdanesse is constructed as particularly monstrous and *other* because in order to preserve her Muslim faith, she puts her own needs before those of her son, even resorting to his murder. She destroys and disrupts the emerging paradigm for motherhood as devised in the West, and her body and behaviour serve as the site in which Western anxieties about *woman* and *race* are played out.

The primary source for *The Man of Law's Tale* is Nicholas Trevet's *Anglo-Norman Chronicle*, written around 1334 and the source for yet another version of the story in John Gower's *Confessio Amantis*, written around 1390.[14] It is probable that Chaucer made some use of Gower's version but Chaucer's characterization of the Sowdanesse and her mothering is far more developed than either of his sources and its vicious attack on the Sowdanesse is a feature unique to Chaucer. The dominant narrative in the tale is that of the hagiography of the heroine, Custance, the daughter of the emperor of Rome. Custance is a missionary bride sailing from the Latin West to the Islamic East to marry the Sowdanesse's son, the Sowdan of Syria, who chooses to renounce Islam so that, according to ecclesiastical law, the marriage may take place.

Foregrounded in Chaucer's characterization of the Sowdanesse is her religion and also her race. By the time that Chaucer was writing, *Sowdanesse* (variant spelling *soudanesse*) is understood to mean the female form of *sowdan* – the 'sultan' who was the supreme ruler of a Muslim state such as Persia, Egypt and Syria.[15] Muslims are frequently designated *Saracens* in this period. This term suggests not only an understanding of one who practises the Muslim faith but also persons who could be different in skin colour from white Europeans: blue (blue-black), yellow (very light skin) or as black as Moors.[16] Contact between white Europeans and darker-skinned Saracens had taken place since the Crusades. The religious prejudice towards the Muslim faith that underpinned these ventures helped to initiate a construction of racism founded upon asserting a sense of white, Christian superiority over and separateness from those who were Muslim in faith and who had non-white skin. Such attitudes are in direct contrast to what Dorothee Metlitzki notes as taking place on a rational level: 'in science and philosophy, the assimilation of Arabic material proceeded deliberately and systematically because it was the work of individual scholars who recognised the Arabs as mediators of Greek philosophy and science'.[17] Such religious prejudice was supported, however, by the cultural construction of the 'fantastic *other*', that is, of the representation of the bodies of people of colour as having a physiology that is often bizarre, threatening and different from that of Europeans. The 'fantastic *other*' features in the work of Pliny the Elder (23–79 CE), is prevalent throughout the Middle Ages as illustrated in the travel writings of John Mandeville, and continues well into the sixteenth century in the writing of the Renaissance diplomat and spy Richard Hakluyt (1551/2–1616).[18]

In his *Natural History*, Pliny talks about how the outermost districts of Ethiopia produce such human monstrosities as tribes of people without noses, those who have no upper lip and others without tongues.[19] During the Middle Ages, the description of other races began to appear in travel writing that owed a great debt to Pliny. Widespread in medieval encyclopaedias and travel texts is a definition of the white European through contrast with the dark-skinned *other*, whose 'fantastic' biological and social alterity is exposed and found wanting through comparison with its white counterpart. John Mandeville's travel writing, circulating throughout the fifteenth century, tells fabulous tales of women with remarkable characteristics from Turkey, Arabia, Egypt, Libya, India and, like the Sowdanesse, from Syria. Mandeville describes the Amazons who will allow no man to govern that land, women with jewels in their eyes who can kill with an angry look, young brides with snakes within them which fatally sting their husbands on their penises during sexual intercourse and wives who celebrate the deaths of their children.[20] In each case, white, European physiognomy and custom is the 'norm' against which the dark-skinned body's deviance is displayed through its difference, both biological (jewels for eyes, lethal looks, lethal vagina) and cultural (women who deny patriarchal rule, who take joy in the death of offspring).

Initially the Sowdanesse is portrayed as hostile religious 'other' through her refusal to expel Muhammad's law from her heart. In this respect, she is an antitype of another woman of colour, the queen of Sheba,[21] who renounces her paganism to embrace Christianity. The queen of Sheba appears in the Bible in 1 Kings 10–13 and 2 Chronicles 9: 1–12, where she comes in search of King Solomon's wisdom. Subject to a wealth of allegorical interpretation, Origen (*c.*185–254), who influenced later tradition down to the Middle Ages, presents her as the image of the lovely black pagan whose faith could be her salvation. Such a reading is echoed by Isidore of Seville (*c.*570–636) who saw the queen as representative of those who came from paganism to Christianity of their own volition.[22] In contrast to the queen of Sheba, the Sowdanesse will not renounce her Muslim faith and, to emphasize its evil, Chaucer portrays Islam as an idolatrous religion.

Much of the disapprobation expressed towards the Sowdanesse, however, is gendered and directed against her unwomanly body and non-maternal behaviours. Called 'the mooder of the Sowdan' (l. 323), which emphasizes that she is a both a Muslim and a mother, the Sowdanesse is introduced after Custance has agreed to go 'unto the Barbre naciuon' and pronounced that 'wommen are born to thraldom and penance / and to been under mannes governance' (ll. 286–7). Unlike Custance, who accepts what patriarchy has mapped out for her and accedes to her powerlessness in a patriarchal world, the Sowdanesse is proactive in her fate. She would rather die than be in thrall to Christianity through renouncing Islam, a condition that has to be met if her son is to marry Custance, and further, she has an appetite for autonomy and power that is conspicuously absent from Custance's characterization. To avoid her forced conversion and most especially to seize power for herself, the Sowdanesse behaves in a very unmaternal manner. She plots to murder her son at a feast, a particularly monstrous act as it perverts that most maternal of behaviours: the sustaining of life through the giving of food.

The non-maternal body of the Sowdanesse is signalled by epithets that present the monstrous perversion of her womb. Being labelled a 'well of vices' (l. 323) indicates that her body (perhaps a vaginal image is intended in 'well') spawns vices rather than offspring. The degeneration of her maternal potential continues as she is called 'roote of iniquitee' (l. 358). As such, the Sowdanesse is the antitype of St Anne, whose liturgical titles include *Radix Sancta* (Holy Root), signifying her status as grandmother and genetrix of the most holy dynasty.[23] In contrast, the Sowdanesse as 'root' produces only sin.

That which lies at the heart of successful mothering, her gender, is also attacked. She is called 'virago' (l. 359), a term that Jill Mann suggests has overtones of 'mannishness'.[24] According to Joan Cadden, medieval medical texts defined 'virago' as a woman who had manly virtues or, after Isidore of Seville, that she had particular strength and does men's jobs, or most prominently in the late Middle Ages, that she remained a virgin and held the virtues of incorruptibility and the ability to resist feminine passion.[25] These uses of 'virago' could, however, be applied positively as she is also always believed to be 'unambiguously on the female side of the anatomical spectrum'.[26] It is clear from the Man of Law's admonition 'O feyned womman' (l. 362), that the Sowdanesse's 'mannishness' is of a very different kind: she is not true to her gender and the epithet is not applied positively. Susan Schibanoff has commented that the Sowdanesse's ultimate danger is that she would like to be a man.[27] Indeed, in calling her a second Semiramis (l. 359) Chaucer signals her associations with another mannish woman of colour, a militant queen of ancient Syria or Assyria in around 800 BCE, who was routinely accused of 'sexual promiscuity of the grossest and most vivid kind'.[28] This included committing incest with her son and passing as a man in order that she might prevent her son from ruling and retain the kingdom for herself.[29] The intended parallel with the Sowdanesse's political ambition to 'al the contree lede' (l. 434) is unmistakable. In her behaviour as a virago and a second Semiramis, the Sowdanesse is shown to deny her biological role of mother, and to attempt to pervert patriarchal rule by taking over the kingdom.

The Sowdanesse's monstrous (m)othering is emphasized through her comparison with creatures that are monstrous in their combination of the human and the bestial, in their reproductive potential and in their care of their young. In addition, her racial 'otherness' is further signalled through her comparison with these unnatural beasts. The Man of Law describes her as a serpent or the devil hiding in a woman's form when he addresses her as 'O serpent under femynynytee, / Lik to the serpent depe in helle ybound!' (ll. 360–1). This image is informed by the theological tradition of portraying the devil who tempted Eve as a snake with a woman's head,[30] and its use suggests the contrast between the apparent normality of her upper half and the repulsiveness and monstrosity of the lower, where the Sowdanesse's organs of generation lie.

Having been called a serpent, the Sowdanesse is next referred to as a scorpion (l. 404). The scorpion was considered grotesque within the animal kingdom because it violated boundaries and transgressed limits through being a strange union of reptile and insect.[31] Medieval bestiaries usually contain descriptions of the scorpion, an exotic creature that was considered unmaternal because, according to Pliny's *Natural History* on which much of the bestiaries' details are based, the scorpion is said to brood eleven at a time and kill all but one of her offspring. The thirteenth-century *Ancrene Wisse* states that the scorpion, like the serpent with which the Sowdanesse has just been compared, demonstrates the same monstrous fusion of human and beast:

Scorpiun is a cunnes wurm. Þe haueð neb as me seið sumdeal ilich wummon & neddre is bihinden. Makeð fei er semblant. & fikeð mid te heaueð & stingeð mid te teile.

The scorpion is a kind of serpent. It has a face so I have said, rather like a woman's and its hind parts are those of a serpent. It makes a semblance of fairness, practises deceitful flattery with its head and stings with its tail.[32]

Not only does she kill her offspring as does the scorpion but the Sowdanesse also displays precisely the same duplicity – fair face, foul intent – of which the *Ancrene Wisse* warns: she deceives via her facial expression. The Sowdanesse hides her real intent by greeting her son with a kiss (l. 386) and when she first meets Custance, the Sowdanesse feigns maternal joy and, 'receyveth hire with also glad a cheere / As any mooder myghte hir doghter deere' (ll. 396–7). The Man of Law warns that, for all her flattery, the Sowdanesse 'caste under this ful mortally to stynge' (l. 406). By calling her a scorpion, the Sowdanesse's lack of maternal feeling is emphasized together with her duplicity, and the murderous dis-patching of her son can be seen to be true to her bestial nature.

By the close of the section in which she features, the Sowdanesse is presented as being beyond motherhood, that is, as post-meno-pausal. At the treacherous feast the Sowdanesse is described as old. Prior to this, her plotting and riding out dressed 'riche and gay' (l. 395) in order to meet her son and welcome Custance give the impression of a relatively young and active woman. It is only having successfully orchestrated the stabbing and cutting to pieces of all at the feast that her old age is emphasized. She is called 'olde' (ll. 414, 432) and 'cursed krone' (l. 432). It is as if her rejection of her motherhood, as realized through her murder of her son, finally becomes written on her body.

The implication of the insults thrown at her is that the Sowdanesse is a counterfeit and antipathetic Muslim (m)other, as opposed to the Christian Custance who represents the maternal ideal. In the eyes of Western patriarchy the Sowdanesse's sins are multiple. She rejects Christianity and the role and lot of Western women which is one of 'thraldom and penance' as expounded by Custance. She perverts the Western ideal of motherhood, is mannish and betrays her maternal body and reproductive potential since her womb has become the nest of every vice. She counterfeits the maternal affection of a mother; she lies to her son about renouncing her religion so that his wedding can take place and deceives him with a kiss (l. 386). Her complete betrayal of the maternal bond lies in her murder of her son in order that she can satisfy her appetite for power.

Donegild, the dowager queen of Northumberland and a second mother (and mother-in-law) in the tale, also chooses action over suffering.[33] She too is accused of being 'mannysh' (l. 782). Like the Sowdanesse, Donegild refuses to give up her religion (here pagan) to convert to Christianity and does not approve of Custance as a fit wife for her son, Alla. Donegild is 'ful of tirannye' (l. 696) and malice, resorts to accusations about the paternity of Custance and Alla's child, suggesting that Custance 'delivered was / Of so horrible a feendly creature / That in the castle noon so hardy was / That any while dorste ther endure' (ll. 750–3) and succeeds in engineering Custance and Maurice's banishment from Northumberland. Like the Sowdanesse, Donegild places her own interests before those of her son but, unlike her Muslim counterpart, this white queen mother does not resort to the murder of her own child, thus signalling how much more wicked and treacherous a Muslim (m)*other* can be. This is not the only difference between the two mothers; the Sowdanesse is more monstrous in her perversion of the maternal bond and in her apparent ability to defy Western patriarchy's attempt to curb and contain her.

Donegild inhabits Northumberland, which is presented as a land from which most Christians have fled and which is largely pagan.

In the presentation of this section of his tale it is as if the Man of Law has slipped into a different time-frame, contemporary neither with the rest of his story nor with his and Chaucer's own world, and has shifted from hagiography into the genre of fairy tale. The effect is to transmute Donegild from a medieval queen dowager and mother of the ruling monarch, a role of equivalent status to that played by the Sowdanesse, to 'a wicked embodiment of folk-lore motif' as noted by Glory Dharmaraj.[34] Donegild's evil does not threaten the medieval world in the same way as does that of the Sowdanesse who, along with her son, has a footing in contemporary reality and operates in the medieval world of realpolitik of Syrian merchants trading their spices, silks and cloth of gold in Rome. To paraphrase Metlitzki, the Sowdanesse is a concrete and powerful embodiment of a profoundly alien and terrifying *real* enemy that actually threatened Christian survival.[35] Donegild is dealt with in true fairy-tale fashion with her execution on the order of her son, thus nullifying the threat she represents and punishing her for her non-maternal behaviours. In contrast, at the close of the tale and, as it were, back in the 'medieval world', the emperor of Rome sends his senator to take revenge on the Syrians and 'brennen, sleen and brynge hem to meschance / ful many a day' (ll. 960–5). Here the Man of Law breaks off and we are never sure whether the Sowdanesse has been punished and killed or, as is rendered possible by the lacuna in her story, if she continues to live on in Syria, remaining the ever-present and unconquerable threat to the West of the non-white Eastern *other*.

Notes

[1] Geoffrey Chaucer, 'Man of Law's Tale', *The Riverside Chaucer*, ed. Larry D. Benson (Oxford, 1988), pp. 89–104.

[2] Shulamith Shahar notes the few references to woman as mother in contemporary medieval sources in *The Fourth Estate: A History of Women in the Middle Ages*, trans. Chaya Galai (London, 1983, repr. 1984), p. 98.

[3] Clarissa Atkinson, *The Oldest Vocation: Christian Motherhood in the Middle Ages* (Ithaca, NY, and London, 1991), p. 144. For a detailed discussion of the topos of the maternal martyr in the Middle Ages see Barbara Newman, *From Virile Woman to Woman Christ: Studies on Medieval Religion and Literature* (Philadelphia, 1995), pp. 76–107.

[4] The lives of these women as married women, mothers and saints is explored by Marc Glasser, 'Marriage in medieval hagiography', *Studies in Medieval and Renaissance History* 4 (os 14) (1981), 3–34.

206 *Sue Niebrzydowski*

[5] Gail McMurray Gibson, 'Blessing from sun and moon: churching and women's theater', in Barbara A. Hanawalt and David Wallace (eds), *Bodies and Disciplines: Intersections of Literature and History in Fifteenth-Century England*, Medieval Cultures 9 (Minneapolis and London, 1996), pp. 139–54 (141).

[6] Marion Glasscoe (ed.), *Julian of Norwich's A Revelation of Love* (Exeter, 1976, repr. 1986, 1989, 1993). The possibility that Julian had been a wife and mother is suggested in both Alexandra Barratt (ed.), *Women's Writing in Middle English* (London, 1992), p. 108, and Elizabeth Spearing (trans.), *Julian of Norwich: Revelations of Divine Love* (London, 1998), p. x. This is a possibility first argued by Benedicta Ward in 'Julian the Solitary', in Ken Leech and Benedicta Ward (eds), *Julian Reconsidered* (Oxford, 1988), pp. 11–35.

[7] Julian of Norwich, *Revelation*, pp. 73–4.

[8] Atkinson, *The Oldest Vocation*, p. 26.

[9] St Augustine, *De Genesi Ad Litteram*, 401–16, as trans. in Alcuin Blamires (ed.), *Woman Defamed and Woman Defended: An Anthology of Medieval Texts* (Oxford, 1992), p. 79.

[10] Silvana Vecchio 'The good wife' in Christiane Klapisch-Zuber (ed.), *A History of Women:* ii. *Silences of the Middle Ages* (Cambridge, MA, and London, 1992), p. 123.

[11] Gerald R. Owst, *Literature and Pulpit in Medieval England* (Oxford, 1961), pp. 34, 35.

[12] Renate Blumenfeld-Kosinski, *Not of Woman Born: Representations of Caesarean Birth in Medieval and Renaissance Culture* (Ithaca, NY, and London, 1990), p. 13.

[13] T. Erbe (ed.), *Mirk's Festial: A Collection of Homilies by Johannes Mirkus (John Mirk), Part I*, EETS 96 (London, 1905), p. 5, l. 156.

[14] Both Trevet's and Gower's versions can be found in W. F. Bryan and Germaine Dempster (eds), *Sources and Analogues of Chaucer's Canterbury Tales* (Chicago, 1941), pp. 165–83.

[15] As quoted under the entries for *soudan* and *soudanesse* in *Middle English Dictionary*, ed. H. Kurath and S. Kuhn, 11 vols, part S.11, Soth–Speche (Ann Arbor, 1989).

[16] See under the entry for *saracen* in *Middle English Dictionary*, vol. S–Slyrke (Ann Arbor, 1986). In the *Sultan of Babylon*, written *c.*1400, the 300,000 Saracens who fell in battle are described as 'some bloo, some yolowe, some as blak as more' (l. 1005), in Alan Lupack (ed.), *Three Middle English Romances* (Kalamazoo, MI, 1990), p. 34.

[17] Dorothee Metlitzki, *The Matter of Araby in Medieval England* (New Haven and London, 1977), p. 249.

[18] H. Rackham (trans.), *Pliny: Natural History with an English Translation*, 10 vols (London, 1961), 6. 35, II, pp. 184–96. For Mandeville, see Malcolm Letts (ed.), *Mandeville's Travels: Texts and Translations* (London, 1953), 2 vols; Richard Hakluyt (ed.), *The Principal Navigations Voyages Traffiques and Discoveries of the English Nation* (Glasgow, 1903) 12 vols.

[19] Rackham, *Pliny*, 6. 35, II, pp. 476–85.

[20] Oxford, Bodleian MS Rawlinson D. 99, as printed in *Mandeville's Travels*, ed. Letts, II, pp. 419–68.

[21] The belief of Josephus, a Jewish historian writing in the first century CE, that the queen of Sheba ruled over Egypt and Ethiopia is identified in Marina Warner, *From the Beast to the Blonde: On Fairy Tales and their Tellers* (London, 1990), p. 106.

[22] Jacques Devisse, *The Image of the Black in Western Art*, 3 vols (Lausanne, 1979), II, p. 129. Jerome believed that Ethiopians were black because they were born of the devil and because of their ignorance of God: once metaphorically 'slain' by the word of God they will become, again metaphorically, white and pure. See Devisse, *Image of the Black*, I, p. 17 where he translates the relevant section of Jerome, *In Zachariam*, 2. 9.

[23] Warner, *Beast to the Blonde*, p. 88.

[24] Jill Mann, *Feminist Readings: Chaucer* (Hemel Hempstead, 1991), p. 130.

[25] Joan Cadden, *Meanings of Sex Difference in the Middle Ages: Medicine, Science and Culture* (Cambridge, 1993), pp. 205–6.

[26] Ibid., p. 205.

[27] Susan Schibanoff, 'Worlds apart: orientalism, antifeminism, and heresy in Chaucer's *Man of Law's Tale*', *Exemplaria* 8/1 (Spring, 1996), 56–86 (85).

[28] Joyce Tyldesley, *Hatchepsut: The Female Pharaoh* (Harmondsworth, 1998), p. 191.

[29] Schibanoff, 'Worlds apart', pp. 85–6.

[30] The tradition was transmitted during the Middle Ages by Petrus Comestor in his *Historia scholastica libri Genesis*, ch. 21, PL 198: 1072, as quoted in Benson, *The Riverside Chaucer*, p. 869, nn. 360–1.

[31] David Williams, *Deformed Discourse: The Function of the Monster in Mediaeval Thought and Literature* (Exeter, 1996), p. 179.

[32] J. R. R. Tolkien (ed.), *The English Text of the Ancrene Riwle: Ancrene Wisse edited from MS Corpus Christi College, Cambridge 402*, EETS 249 (Oxford, 1962), p. 107.

[33] Mann, *Feminist Readings*, p. 130.

[34] Glory Dharmaraj, 'Multicultural subjectivity in reading Chaucer's *Man of Law's Tale*', *Medieval Feminist Newsletter* 16 (Fall 1993), 4–8, 6.

[35] Metlitzki, *The Matter of Araby*, p. 197.

17

An Ethiopian History: Reading Race and Skin Colour in Early Modern Versions of Heliodorus' Aithiopika

ॐ

SUJATA IYENGAR

Heliodorus' *Aithiopika* narrates the difficulty of reading the body, in particular, that of its heroine, Chariclea, born white to the dark-skinned King Hydaspes and Queen Persina of Ethiopia because her mother gazed upon a religious icon (a picture of Andromeda) during conception.[1] Secretly exposed at birth by Persina, raised by a succession of foster-fathers, during the course of the romance Chariclea falls in love with a young Thessalian, Theagenes, and eventually returns to Ethiopia, where Hydaspes fails to recognize her and attempts to sacrifice the lovers to the gods. In a dramatic recognition-scene, oral, written, painted and bodily evidence finally convinces Hydaspes that this fair-skinned Greek girl is indeed his daughter. The romance concludes with the lovers' marriage and the abolition of all human sacrifice in Ethiopia.

Hellenistic and early modern European culture associated pallor with transparent meaning, blackness with opaque mystery. As Peter Fryer and others have documented, during the seventeenth century the black presence in Britain changed in character, increasing in size and moving from occasional domestic service, entertainment and sex-work in London at the turn of the sixteenth century to widespread domestic slavery in Britain and the Americas by the turn of the next. The ancient English association of manual labour with dark or 'sun-burned' skin (because outdoor workers became tanned or 'tawny' from exposure to the sun's rays) gradually came to be linked to 'race', freshly understood to correspond to visible ethnic difference (to, say, the skin of imported African workers, whose blackness now marked their destiny as well as their origin). In 1656 Isaac La Péyrère's *Praedomitiae* suggested that human beings might belong to different species, an argument further developed by François Bernier into a system of racial classification in 1687.[2] Similarly, anatomists' discoveries challenged the old one-sex model (which imagined male and female existing on a single bodily continuum, and which treated gender as a mutable category) and redefined gender as a bodily characteristic that was now interpreted as fixed or essential.[3] The *Aithiopika*, however, completely overturns these racial, sexual and aesthetic expectations. As Daniel Selden observes in an article about the *Aithiopika*'s influence on African–American literature: '[t]he valence of the skin colours familiar from America stands dia-metrically reversed . . . the aristocracy is black, and . . . the white body . . . shows up as aberrant . . . cast out and ultimately sub-jected through battering and enslavement to control.'[4] Likewise, O. A. W. Dilke comments that this romance spectacularizes a whiteness found wanting by black royalty, so that Chariclea's exposure reflects 'not only the fear of an accusation of adultery but the desire to get rid of a child held at her birth to be unworthy of such a great royal family'.[5]

Some argue that any supposed blackening or Ethiopianizing of Chariclea and Theagenes represents rather a blanching or Hellen-ization of the Ethiopians (symbolized by the latter's ultimate abolition of human sacrifice, seemingly as a direct result of encountering Hellenized Chariclea and Greek-born Theagenes). As Arthur Heiserman observes, the novel counters this implication by satirizing the superstition of 'Delphian Apollo', epitomized by Chariclea's 'foolish' Greek foster-father Charicles.[6] I would add that Chariclea, moreover, pleads not against the custom of human sacrifice in itself but that she, as a royal daughter, should not be its victim. The motion against human sacrifice comes from the thoroughly Ethiopian Sisimithres, Chariclea's first foster-father, who is 'black as [he] could be',[7] and who, with his fellow Gymnosophists ('naked sages'), urges both the king and the Ethiopian people that religious murder, whether human or animal, is 'barbaric . . . nor do we believe that is pleasing to the divinity'.[8] The Gymnosophists were traditionally based in India, but

Heliodorus draws upon Philostratus' account of a group of Ethiopian sages who brought Gymnosophist teachings back to Ethiopia[9] to emphasize not a Greek but an Oriental tradition of respect for human and animal life. Sisimithres later convinces the king that class, caste and colour should have no bearing on justice.

Perhaps one of the reasons for this story's popularity in the early modern era (certainly, I would argue, a compelling reason for its renewed popularity in our own) is its challenge to bodily hermeneutics and, in particular, to ways of reading racial and sexual difference. Thomas Underdowne's prose translation, *Æthiopian Historie* (1569), Jacques Amyot's prose translation, *Histoire Aethiopique* (1559), William Lisle's verse adaptation, *The Faire Ethiopian* (1631), John Gough's stage-play, *The Strange Discovery* (1640) and an anonymous Caroline manuscript drama, *The White Ethiopian*, render Chariclea's whiteness visible to varying degrees.[10] Three moments of racial reading stand out particularly within the *Aithiopika*: the oracle informing Theagenes and Chariclea of their Ethiopian destiny, Persina's explanatory letter to Chariclea and Chariclea's birthmark, the final proof of her Ethiopian and royal heritage. Early modern writers transform these colour-coded crossings and conversions according to emergent understandings of race.[11]

The mysterious Delphic oracle prophesies the lovers' journey 'to the black land of the sun' where they will earn '[a] crown of white on brows of black'.[12] According to Selden, the final Greek line translates literally as 'a white crown shall be affixed on blackening brows',[13] employing the present participle, *melainomenon*, μελαινομενον (blackening) to indicate 'at the very least the recognition of the indeterminacy of race'.[14] Chariclea and Theagenes begin the romance as white Greeks and finish it as black Ethiopians, darkening through the illuminating story.

Renaissance texts vary in their recognition of this oracular and racial ambiguity. Underdowne's oracle predicts travel to a '[c]ountrie scortche, / with Phebus blasinge beames', where they '[w]hite Miters shall obtaine'.[15] Through the 'white Miters', Underdowne links the sun-worshippers in Ethiopia to another Ethiopian realm, the mythical medieval kingdom ruled by the Christian Prester John. Underdowne also refers specifically to the

Greek myth of Phaethon, Phoebus' unruly son whose ill-conceived chariot-ride in the sun-god's vehicle burned the Ethiopians 'blacke and swart' when he swooped dangerously close to the earth.[16] The prophecy here connects Ethiopian religious practices with those of the Christian Church while simultaneously retaining Heliodorus' references to the cult of the Sun. Stephen Greenblatt finds this divine double consciousness typical of early modern under-standings of religious rituals (in particular, those involving human sacrifice or wounding), arguing that European observers gazed upon self-mutilated foreigners (or at least, upon foreigners whom *they perceived* as human sacrifices) in simultaneous horror and recognition: wounds were signs of the Other's difference but also letters of the universal language of the divine.[17] Underdowne retroactively Christianizes the Ethiopians so that Theagenes and Chariclea serve as religious rather than political leaders.

Jacques Amyot imagines that fairness conceals fundamentally dark skin, that 'their lovely crowns' are 'both enclosed with white' ('leurs beaux chefz tous deux de blanche enceincte'),[18] as if their blackness hides beneath their white headdresses, like an infant struggling to be born (the pun on *enceinte* meaning 'enclosed' and also 'pregnant' is present even in early modern French). William Lisle, on the other hand, imagines blackness and religious differences crowning or covering the lovers' paleness when 'their tanned temples [are] crowned with Turban white'.[19] The pale Chariclea and Theagenes have become tanned or made tawny by the sun (again, like Chariclea's mythical Ethiopian ancestors, burned black by Phaethon's fatal charge), in an ethnic crossing that converts coronets or crowns, signs of English royalty, into the exotic Eastern 'Turban' that shines whitely in contrast to their newly darkened brows.

The Caroline manuscript play *The White Ethiopian* perhaps comes closest to Heliodorus' ambiguous register. After travelling to Ethiopia, 'where downright rayes / Make yᵉ earth smoake by parching dayes', the lovers' reward comprises '[w]hite garlands on the blacker ground',[20] a comparative racial category in a dramatization that, as we shall see, foregrounds the story's references to negritude and pallor. These Ethiopians are twice blackened, once by Phaethon and once more by the oracle. The sun's rays parallel the white garlands, just as the 'blacker ground' figures both the lovers' bodies and the scorched equatorial earth.

The mysterious oracle is partly explained by the hieroglyphic letter written by Persina, left with her exposed child and deciphered by the canny priest Calasiris. It describes the Ethiopians' descent from the Sun and from Perseus and Andromeda, whose images adorn the royal bedchamber where Chariclea was conceived. Initially shocked by Chariclea's 'skin of gleaming white, something quite foreign to Ethiopians', Persina quickly understands

> the reason: during your father's intimacy with me the painting had presented me with the image of Andromeda . . . depicted stark naked, for Perseus was in the very act of releasing her from the rocks, and had unfortunately shaped the embryo to her exact likeness.[21]

Persina alludes to a theory attributing the colour of a child to its mother's impressions or thoughts at the time of conception (compare the folk-belief that a baby's strawberry-mark indicates that its mother experienced a fright during pregnancy). Gazing upon Andromeda's fair, naked body during the act of love, Persina conceives a child resembling not herself or her husband, but the picture. She worries that she will be accused of adultery, that nobody will believe her fantastic explanation. And in fact, Hydaspes' angry incredulity in the final scene lasts an embarrassingly long time: Terence Cave argues in *Recognitions* that Hydaspes' scepticism, even when faced with letters, tokens and the picture, proves the inadequacy of empirical proof.[22] 'It is required / You do awake your faith', says Shakespeare's Paulina in another unlikely recognition-scene;[23] later, Coleridge would identify this kind of 'faith' as essentially literary, 'the willing suspension of disbelief'. Heiserman cogently observes that Heliodorus' heroine seems to be providing readers with a self-consciously literary display of '[f]our of Aristotle's five sorts of recognition scenes' as documented in the *Poetics*: tokens (bodily, decorative and written); self-revelation; stagey contrivance; and finally inference, in order to illustrate a sustained parallel between artistic and divine creation and power.[24] Presented with artistic and literary evidence – the picture of Andromeda, the testimony of Sisimithres, Persina's letter – Hydaspes must awaken his faith. Life imitates art, or, as Calasiris puts it, '[a]rt can break nature', a *sententia* so apt for this novel that Underdowne found it worthy of marginal signposting.[25]

Andromeda Naked. From Johannes Florianus's 1615 Dutch translation of Ovid's *Metamorphoses* (Sig. 16ᵛ). It is reproduced by kind permission of the Huntington Library, San Marino, California

The accident of Chariclea's birth and her miraculous restoration additionally demonstrate the power of art or literature to create, break down and restore categories of classification: black/white, Ethiopian/foreign, chaste/adulterous. Even though Persina is not guilty of physical infidelity, her same-sex fantasy (or at least, her interest in art!) competes with her affection for her husband: in Underdowne's translation, the colour of her child demonstrates the fluidity of race, nationality and the direction of sexual desire. Note her confused or omitted pronouns, and the elision of time: 'because I looked upon the picture of Andromeda naked, while my husbande had to doo with me (for then [when] he [Perseus] first broughte her from the rocke, [I] had by mishappe ingendred presently a thing like to her)'.[26] Persina identifies herself with Andromeda, naked, shackled and passive, Hydaspes with Perseus, armed, mobile and active. She describes lovemaking as 'my husbande had to doo with me' twice within two pages, a phrase suggesting that her true interest hangs on the walls, in the 'picture of Andromeda naked'. The final phrase reverses the subjectivity of the child and the picture: the embryo is a 'thing' engendered, while an object that resembles a living creature, the picture, earns the pronoun 'her'.

If Underdowne emphasizes art's power over nature, then the author of *The White Ethiopian* turns the materials of literary production into living signs of revelation. Having revised his adaptation (originally composed in a mixture of blank verse and couplets) into regular couplets, he intensified the play's references to blackness. The original *White Ethiopian* superscribes Persina as 'Queen of Ethiopia' in her letter, but the revised version adds,

> Compelled by the most severest law
> Of keeping reputation makes my inke
> Blacker then is my skin or eyes that winke',[27]

an interpolation that associates blackness with secrecy and darkness but also, paradoxically, with literary discovery. This dramatization interests itself in comparative degrees of blackness and fairness, and the role of the sun and sun-worship in creating blackness (through tanning, and through the original fall of Phaethon) and illuminating it. Persina conceives when 'the King was warmed . . . in a summer roome', as if the sun had impregnated her, like Spenser's Chrysogonee, and when Persina writes, 'The sunne so black a crime had seldom seen', [28] she spots the full irony of her situation: the white child threatens to *blacken* Persina's reputation for a crime that is not adulterously *black* at all.

Just as race and desire prove ambiguous, comparative, so Heliodorus' *Aithiopika* additionally links the process of racial crossing with the sexing of Chariclea. Chariclea's white body misleads observers, a false witness to her race and origin, but truthfully testifies to her gender. For Chariclea, female hetero-sexual love is the love that dare not speak its name; her insistence on maintaining her virginity leads her adoptive and biological fathers to pathologize her because, they claim, she will not acknowledge sexual desire for men and 'realize that she was born a woman',[29] or 'know her sex'.[30] 'Sex' to us means both sexual differ-ence and sexual intercourse; for Chariclea's fathers, sexual inter-course, or the desire for it, *defines* sexual difference. Since Chariclea steadfastly refuses to confess her love for Theagenes, her bodily responses become a substitute for the words she will not utter. It is only having fallen in love, and agreed, at least theoretically, to surrender her pathological virginity, that she begins her racial crossing, and this surrender is never uttered outright by Chariclea (as Selden, Egger and others observe) but narrated for her, first by Calasiris and finally by Persina. Approached directly by Calasiris and urged to confess her feelings for Theagenes, Chariclea still cannot talk; Calasiris must pronounce, 'Theagenes has captured your heart at first sight'.[31] Similarly, at the very end of the romance, threatened by torture, Chariclea cannot speak her love, but confesses it to Persina behind the scenes; only when Persina tells Hydaspes and the assembled crowd that Chariclea and Theagenes are affianced is Theagenes saved from ritual sacrifice and Chariclea cleared of the imputation of insanity.

Although Chariclea's words are constrained, her body is eloquent. When she first sees Theagenes at the temple, she blushes at the sight of him, and blanches as her love takes root. Her somatic response to Calasiris' interrogation is to kiss his hand, weeping,[32] and to break into 'rivers of perspiration'.[33] For an Elizabethan and seventeenth-century audience, blushing is racially coded, a mark of pale beauty, sexual desire and shame. Early modern moral philosophers and anti-cosmetic pamphleteers argued that a blush that could not be seen was a blush that did not exist, that shame and morality could not exist without blushes, and that therefore black and dark-skinned peoples, who did not visibly redden, did not experience shame. Thomas Wright writes in *The Passions of the Mind in Generall* that the fair-skinned inhabitants of northern climes enjoy a 'natural inclination to virtue and honesty' because of their 'very blushing', in contrast to 'certain brazen faces, who never change'.[34] Shakespeare's black-skinned Moor, Aaron, calls white 'a treacherous hue, that will betray with blushing / The close enacts and counsels of the heart'.[35]

Heliodorus, in contrast, offers readers various ways of reading the body – blushing, bodily fluids and marks – that are independent of skin colour, like Chariclea's tears of lovesickness, or her copious sweat when Calasiris discovers her secret love and reveals her Ethiopian heritage, or her revelatory birthmark in the final recognition scene. Heliodorus additionally makes blackness compatible with blushing. Chariclea continues to redden even after she crosses racial lines and the white garland sits upon her black/blackening/blacker brow when Hydaspes asks her to describe her relationship with Theagenes.[36] Likewise, Hydaspes' nephew and chosen match for Chariclea (a parallel to the groom chosen by Charicles, who is also a nephew) blushes deeply enough that 'even in his black skin he could not conceal the blush that suffused his countenance'.[37]

Amyot and Underdowne faithfully translate Chariclea's blushes, palings, weepings and transudations. At their first meeting, Theagenes and Chariclea displayed 'five hundred countenances . . . in shorte time, and the changinge of all kinde of coloure',[38] 'in infinite varieties' ('en infinie sortes').[39] When Calasiris first attends the languishing Chariclea, 'her colour was gonne out of her face, and the heate therof, was quenched with teares, as if it had ben with water'.[40] By the time Calasiris finishes speaking, Chariclea's bodily reaction is more pronounced, the heat restored to her body: 'in a great swette',[41] 'the sweat ran down her whole body' ('la sueur luy couloit par tout le corps').[42] *The White Ethiopian* transfers the 'teares' to the servants watching over the lovesick Chariclea and to her grieving father,[43] but later includes Chariclea's colourful and watery responses to Calasiris simultaneously, so that its heroine issues 'a lake of sweat' 'with many a blush'.[44]

William Lisle and John Gough, however, alter the spiritual character and corporeal manifestation of Chariclea's love. In Gough's play, Theagenes and Chariclea, in an elaborate (and unplayable) stage-direction, 'blush'd and then became pale again' at first sight, and then blush no more; [45] Chariclea demonstrates her lovesickness not by changing colour but by lying on her bed.[46] Gough replaces her excessive reluctance to utter her love by making her state baldly, 'I love Theagenes'.[47] Her later blushes and perspiration in the Greek story appear instead as colour on the cheeks of her embarrassed mother, whose angry husband enquires:

> What meaneth this, Persina, that thy blood
> Thus comes and goes, and that thy countenance
> Weaves such an alteration?[48]

Crimson cheeks here are signs of sexual shame, associated with 'alteration' and the threat of female fickleness, adultery or deceit ('weaving'). Once Chariclea has confessed her love for Theagenes, she is free from shame and thus from blushing.

Lisle's Chariclea, in contrast, speaks innocently through repeated blushing, her cheeks stained with 'sudden blushing die'[49] at the revelation of her love; the copious sweat marking her discovery in earlier tellings of the story becomes a fungible flow that could be decorous, valuable, feminine tears: 'Her colour's gone, her all-delighting grace / With pearly show'r allayed'.[50] Like Shakespeare's Aaron, Hydaspes sees the ability to change colour by blushing as evidence of insurmountable racial difference: Chariclea's 'color, now so peregrine', he says, proves that she 'can be none of mine'.[51] Lisle's king and queen emphasize their blackness and their fundamental difference from Chariclea by describing themselves not as rulers of 'Ethiopia' but as king and queen of 'Blackmoreland',[52] a metonym that avoids the Christian associations of 'Ethiopia', as do the 'tanned Turbans' of Lisle's oracle, and links Africa to an Islamic rather than a Christian tradition. They see themselves as a 'Blackmore paire' in contrast to this child 'so beautiful and faire', a rhyming couplet and hidden pun that intensifies their negritude (they are *more black* than Chariclea, and, as rulers of 'Black-more' land, live among *more blacks*, in a scorching climate that makes them yet *more black* with every day that passes).

The lengthy and tense recognition-scene is only the culmination of a series of challenges to Chariclea's fugitive identity, which remains subject to confirmation and reconfirmation throughout the novel, through code-names, passwords and physical tokens.[53] Chariclea's token is her ring, but Theagenes' is a scar on his knee obtained pursuing a boar, like Odysseus' scar confirming Eurykleia's suspicion that her former nursling has returned. In fact Chariclea never has to assure Theagenes' identity this way; she recognizes him instantly. Ironically, neither code-names nor physical tokens convince Theagenes and Hydaspes: both depend upon bodily attributes. Theagenes recognizes 'the brilliance of her eyes'[54] and the most compelling physical proof of Chariclea's identity, the true confirmation of her 'parentage and descent',[55] proves to be the 'sign of her race': her birthmark.[56]

A stippled 'ring of ebony staining the ivory of her arm',[57] the birthmark recalls in its shape the magic ring *Pantarbe* that Persina hides with her baby, and the Sun, the Ethiopian deity. Hilton proposes that it presents Chariclea as two-toned and therefore divine, like the Goddess Isis; on the other hand, I would suggest, Chariclea's pied beauty makes her human in its imperfection (think of Nathaniel Hawthorne's short story *The Birthmark*, where the little red hand upon the otherwise-perfect face of the protagonist's wife proves to be the only grip holding an angel upon earth, or of classical and seventeenth-century fashions recommending artificial beauty spots to evade the evil eye). It also distinguishes her from the 'picture of Andromeda naked', the religious icon which she so strongly resembles. Amyot's translation is close to many modern versions, imagining 'a black mark, which was like a small piece of perfectly smooth ebony, staining her white arm shining like ivory' ('un sein noir, qui estoit comme une petite pièce d'Hébène toute ronde, tachant son bras blanc et poly comme l'voire').[58] The participial phrase dangles slightly in both Amyot's sentence and my own, allowing Chariclea's arm to glow like ivory in contrast to the mark even as the dark mole gleams like ivory in contrast to the arm. Underdowne conveys the mole's mottling but little else, adding a confusing reference to elephants: 'Cariclia uncovered her lefte arme, and aboute it there was in a manner a mole, muche like to the strakes, that Elephantes have'.[59] His Latin source reads: 'Nudavit illis Chariclia sinistram, et erate quasi ebenus quaedam, in circuitu brachium tanquam elephantem maculans'.[60] 'Chariclea exposed her left arm, and there was something there like ebony, in a circle around her arm, spotting the ivory' (my translation). Presumably Underdowne misunderstood *elephantem maculans* to mean 'spotted elephant', although *elephantem* agrees with *brachium* ('arm') and is clearly a metonym for 'ivory'.

Underdowne's error conjures an image of the ring *surrounding* Chariclea's arm ('aboute it'), humanizes her with the down-to-earth word 'mole' and vividly picks up on the striking stripes or stains on Chariclea's arm. The birthmark is a kind of royal seal, like a ring; Amyot turns it into a jewel, and Chariclea into another artefact (transforming her back into a picture, or a deity) by smoothing the rough stripes on the stippled birthmark. Hilton argues that the mole's dappled surface not only allies Chariclea's mark with Odysseus' streaky scar but also evokes, because of Sisimithres' reference to 'race' (*genos*), an inherited 'mottled skin or melanoma'.[61] What proves Chariclea's Ethiopian identity is not the mark's uniform obscurity, or a perceived similarity to the dark skin of her people, but its idiosyncratic streakiness, its difference from her own skin and from most Ethiopians'. Sisimithres seems to be emphasizing the predominance of race (understood as *genos*) as rank and kinship to a royal race, rather than as skin colour and national identity.

In Lisle's text, however, pallor makes rank visible more literally. His blushing Chariclea displays her whiteness even through her birthmark, which is not black but 'blue . . . / like azure ring / On polish't lu'rie'.[62] The references to blue and azure associate Chariclea with 'blue blood' or royalty – another early modern way of displaying whiteness. The 'azure ring' is a royal seal, but one which demonstrates her absolute difference from her parents, the 'Blackemore paire'. Chariclea cannot be touched or stained with even the slightest hint of blackness and Lisle distinguishes his white heroine from her black parents even after her birth has been proven and explained, whereas Gough allows Chariclea to wash her Ethiopian father white and make her mother blush (differently put, to *change colour*).

Thus, Chariclea's increasing pallor in these translations corresponds to new and fluctuating ways of understanding race and gender in the early modern period. Where Underdowne faithfully avers along with Heliodorus that 'art can breake nature', or even that nature itself can produce, through the magic of maternal impression, a child who does not resemble its parents and whose sex and race are indeterminate for most of the story, Lisle and Gough strive to diminish the radical ambiguity of Heliodorus' novel and to stabilize Chariclea's sex and race through her heredity rather than through her actions, asserting her social rank and forcing it to match her skin tone by retroactively blanching her parents. Perhaps, then, this provided the only early modern solution available for what was becoming a troubling paradox in early modern England – the conjunction of royalty, blackness and power.

Notes

I thank the Huntington Library and the University of Georgia Research Foundation for financial support, Darlene Ciraulo for research assistance, and Margo Hendricks, Mary Nyquist, Wes Williams, Nancy Felson and Andrew Hadfield and the editors for responses.

[1] Heliodorus' *Aithiopika* is usually dated between 230 and 275 CE, although J. R. Morgan puts it as late as the fourth century CE ('Introduction', in Sir Walter Lamb (trans.), *Ethiopian Story* (London, 1997), pp. xvii–xviii). The standard Greek text appears in R. M. Rattenbury and T. W. Lumb (eds), *Héliodore: Les Ethiopiques*, 3 vols, (Paris, 1935). Unless otherwise indicated, the modern trans. used is J. R. Morgan's, which appears as 'An Ethiopian story', in B. P. Reardon (ed.), *Collected Ancient Greek Novels* (Berkeley, CA, 1989), pp. 349–588.

[2] Peter Fryer, *Staying Power: The History of Black People in Britain* (London, 1984), p. 144.

[3] Thomas Laqueur, *Making Sex: Body and Gender from the Greeks to Freud* (Cambridge, MA, 1990).

[4] Daniel L. Selden 'Aithiopika and Ethiopianism', in Richard Hunter (ed.), *Studies in Heliodorus*, Cambridge Philological Society. Supplemental 21 (Cambridge, 1998), p. 208.

[5] O. A. W. Dilke, 'Heliodorus and the colour problem', *La Parola del Passato* 193 (1980), p. 268.

[6] Arthur Heiserman, *The Novel before the Novel: Essays and Discussions about the Beginnings of Prose Fiction in the West* (Chicago, 1977), p. 192.

[7] Morgan, *Story*, p. 403.

[8] Ibid., p. 565.

[9] Dilke, 'Colour', p. 267.

[10] Thomas Underdowne (trans.), *An Æthiopian Historie* (London, 1569), Huntington Library copy; William Lisle, *The Faire Ethiopian* (London, 1631), microfilm; British Library, Harley Manuscript 7313, 'The White Ethiopian'; Jacques Amyot (trans.), *Histoire Aethiopique* (Paris, 1559), Huntington Library copy; John Gough, *The Strange Discovery*, (London, 1640), microfilm. Other copies consulted include the British Library copy of Amyot's *Histoire* (Lyons, 1579) and the British Library copy of Gough's *Strange Discovery* (London, 1640). Arthur Duncan Matthews edited *The White Ethiopian* (unpublished Ph.D. dissertation, University of Florida, 1951), but his edn reproduces the author's revisions, not the unrevised irregular couplets.

[11] Peter Erickson identifies two 'waves' of racially inflected Renaissance literary criticism ('The moment of race in Renaissance Studies', *Shakespeare Studies* 26 (1998), 27–36). The 'first-wave' work of Eldred Jones's *Othello's Countrymen* (London, 1965) and G. K. Hunter's 'Othello and colour prejudice', *Proceedings of the British Academy* 53 (London, 1968), discussed the significance of dark-skinned characters in Renaissance drama. In the early 1990s, however, a new wave of critics considered the gendered, colonial and class conditions producing Renaissance discourses about race: see Ania Loomba, *Gender, Race, Renaissance Drama* (Manchester, 1989); Margot Hendricks and Patricia Parker (eds), *Women, 'Race' and Writing in the Early Modern Period* (London, 1994); Kim F. Hall, *Things of Darkness* (Ithaca, NY, 1995).

[12] Morgan, *Story*, p. 409.

[13] Selden, 'Ethiopianism', p. 182.

[14] John Hilton, 'An Ethiopian paradox: Heliodorus, Aithiopika 4. 8', in Richard Hunter (ed.), *Studies in Heliodorus* (Cambridge, 1998), p. 89.

[15] Underdowne, *Historie*, K2.

[16] Arthur Golding (trans.), *The XV Bookes of P. Ovidius Naso, entytuled Metemorphosis* (London, 1575), Vol. II, fo. 20, microfilm.

[17] Stephen Greenblatt, 'Mutilation and meaning', in David Hillman and Carla Mazzio (eds), *The Body in Parts: Fantasies of Corporeality in Early Modern Europe* (New York and London, 1997), pp. 221–41.

[18] Amyot, *Histoire*, Fᵛ. All trans. from Amyot are my own unless otherwise noted. The British Library edition (Lyons, 1579) gives 'leurs beaux tempes' to 'deux de blanche enceinte', 'their lovely *temples*', in a pun (or perhaps eye-skip error) that picks up the *temple* where they met and Chariclea's vocation as priestess.

[19] Lisle, *Faire*, G4.

20 'The White Ethiopian', fo. 36.

21 Morgan, *Story*, pp. 432–3.

22 Terence Cave, *Recognitions* (Oxford, 1988).

23 William Shakespeare, *The Winter's Tale*, in G. Blakemore Evans et al. (eds), *The Riverside Shakespeare* (Boston, 1973), 5. 3, ll. 93–4.

24 Heiserman, *Novel*, p. 198; Aristotle, *Poetics*, ed. Stephen Halliwell (Cambridge, MA, 1995), p. 16.

25 Underdowne, *Historie*, M3.

26 Underdowne, *Historie*, O.

27 'The White Ethiopian', fo. 48ᵛ.

28 Ibid., fo. 49.

29 Heliodorus, *An Ethiopian Romance*, trans. and intro. Moses Hadas (Philadelphia, 1999), p. 63.

30 'The White Ethiopian', fo. 34.

31 Morgan, *Story*, p. 435.

32 Ibid., p. 434.

33 Ibid., p. 435.

34 Thomas Wright, *The Passions of the Mind in Generall*, ed. William Webster Newbold (New York and London, 1986), p. 82.

35 William Shakespeare, *Titus Andronicus*, ed. Jonathan Bate (London, 1995), 4. 2, ll. 119–20.

36 Morgan, *Story*, p. 572.

37 Ibid., p. 575.

38 Underdowne, *Historie*, Lᵛ.

39 Amyot, *Histoire*, F5.

40 Underdowne, *Historie*, M1ᵛ.

41 Ibid., O2ᵛ.

42 Amyot, *Histoire*, Hiii.

43 'The White Ethiopian', fo. 42ᵛ.

44 Ibid., fo. 51ᵛ.

45 Gough, *Discovery*, Act 2, scene 7, E1ᵛ.

46 Ibid., Act 2, scene 10, E3ᵛ.

47 Ibid., Act 3, scene 6, G3.

48 Ibid., Act 5, scene 6, L4ᵛ.

49 Lisle, *Faire*, K2ᵛ.

50 Ibid., H4.

51 Ibid., Z2.

52 Ibid., I4.

53 Morgan, *Story*, p. 449.

54 Ibid., p. 494.

55 Ibid., p. 569.

56 Hilton, 'Paradox', p. 89.

57 Morgan, *Story*, p. 569.

58 Amyot, *Histoire*, T6ᵛ.

59 Underdowne, *Historie*, Mm2ᵛ.

60 Stanislaw Warschewiczki, *Heliodori Aethiopicae Historiae* (Basle, 1552), Huntington Library copy, Z3.

61 Hilton, 'Paradox', p. 89.

62 Lisle, *Faire*, Z2ᵛ.

18

Monstrous Generation: Witchcraft and Generation in Othello

KIRSTIE GULICK ROSENFIELD

In response to Brabantio's accusation that Othello has bewitched his daughter to unnatural deeds and rebellion, Othello tells a story of telling a story. He relates to his judges how he wooed Desdemona with his life adventures, weaving a tale that she begged to hear, episode upon episode. Pieces of this original narrative slip into his narrative of romance, and the audience, along with the military tribunal, is wooed as Desdemona was wooed; he fascinates us with his storytelling. 'This only', claims Othello, 'is the witchcraft I have used' (1. 3. 171).[1] Othello denies that he practises witchcraft, but his words invoke the converse of this denial: he has used witchcraft because the everyday practice of telling tales is a form of sorcery.[2] He abuses the world not with an art that is prohibited, but with one that is licensed and conventional to the world in which he moves. 'I think this tale would win my daughter too', confesses the Duke (1. 3. 173). But narrative witchcraft is not just a product of Othello's romantic stories: the text of *Othello* defines all narratives as witchcraft, and often they prove evil. Narratives, we learn, are witchcraft because they have transformative power like that of the sorceress. Consumed through the ear rather than through the mouth, narratives are witchcraft because they abuse the mind as spells abuse. They cause monstrous generation which parallels the type of demonic union also documented by Ruth Evans in this volume, and disrupt conventional notions of masculine authority, just as the witch does.

Besides defining narrative as witchcraft, the text of *Othello* also suggests that narrative constructs identity, but that the production and consumption of alternative narratives can threaten that identity. Narrative consumption results in 'monstrous generation' – a term that traditionally diagnosed witchcraft because popular belief assigned birth abnormalities to sexual activities with witches and demons. Monstrous generation also links witchcraft and demonism to racial monstrosity and excessive sexual appetite, but *Othello* uncouples these links by rewriting witchcraft as a metaphor for the narrative construction of cultural identities. These discussions come together if we think about cultural narrative as a form of witchcraft which reconstructs identities and defines otherness (and which thus determines who gets defined as a witch). This essay will argue that narrative, like the performance that physicalizes it, practices a witchcraft that is uncontainable, but that Shakespeare legitimizes the practice for the theatre through creative metaphor.

Othello initiates the definition of narrative as witchcraft with his claim that his stories were the only witchcraft he used on Desdemona. Desdemona's father, Brabantio, tells us that Othello is 'an abuser of the world, a practicer / Of arts inhibited and out of warrant' (1. 2. 79–80). If Othello is 'an abuser of the world', he is an abuser of the word as well. By his own confession, his words bewitch. In Renaissance witchcraft tracts, the words of a spell are its source of transformative or abusive potency. Witchcraft is the power to make something into something that it is not, in the absence of a physical cause. Iago shows us that narrative has such a power: he makes Othello a green-eyed monster, Desdemona a whore and his own wife a shrew simply by telling tales of them as such. A narrative can thus work the same as witchcraft as an agency of transformation, but such transformations in *Othello* are only possible because they reiterate a larger cultural narrative in which to be black is to be monstrous, and to be female is to be whorish or shrewish. Iago bewitches by telling lies which are made truths by conventional fictions.

As the stories of *Othello* unfold, however, we comprehend that narratives designed to contain and control are, in fact, uncontainable. Opposing narratives within the text highlight conflicts between written and oral history, between old wives' tales and patriarchal narrative, between the generation of stories and the generation of monsters. That is, narrative authority is always contested. Of course, Shakespeare creates narratives, and by staging them he physically creates things that are not what they are, participating himself in 'textual' or 'performative' witchcraft. In this way he reappropriates witchcraft, inscribing his art with the representational power of women's words and the generational power of women's bodies. At the same time the text of *Othello* suggests that cultural narratives are themselves more insidious and damaging forms of witchcraft. As both Ruth Evans and Bettina Bildhauer also identify in this volume, such narratives can abuse our ears and generate monstrous births while cultivating the kind of superstitions that result in traditional witch-beliefs and persecution. In other words, there is a difference between creative narratives as forms of prophetic witchcraft, and cultural narratives of absolutism, which *are* demonic witchcraft.

Brabantio originally accuses Othello of using magical potions to cast spells because he is convinced that his daughter could be with the Moor only as a result of foul deeds. Chaste and pure, Desdemona could have participated in an evil union only if an external source of evil had stolen away her reason. He accuses Othello of witchcraft because the state is not legally bound to return Desdemona. He knows, as does Othello, that Othello's 'services . . . / Shall out-tongue [Brabantio's] complaints' (1. 2. 18–9). Othello's greater authority, however, can be offset by proof that he used illegal potions or devilish assistance to abduct Desdemona:

> She is abused, stol'n from me and corrupted
> By spells and medicines bought of mountebanks;
> For nature so preposterously to err,
> Being not deficient, blind, or lame of sense,
> Sans witchcraft could not.
>
> (1. 3. 62–6)

The key to his argument is that the inversion of nature involved in miscegenation is a parallel to the inversion of nature caused by witchcraft; Desdemona could never love Othello's blackness unless he practised demonism. To Brabantio this is not a case of love-bewitching, but rather a serious crime.

Othello naively claims words to be his only crime. But, as the text makes clear, words are as potent as any potion imagined by Brabantio. Narratives construct identity, and the abuse of this construction is itself witchcraft of words. If narratives have the power to transform the romantic lover, they can transform other listeners equally. Othello proves this point in his verbal seduction of the military tribunal in which he provides a narrative of a narration. Patricia Parker argues that the use of narrative in *Othello* substitutes for what the eye does not or cannot see.[3] Othello must narrate his wooing of Desdemona because no one witnessed it. He fills the 'grave ears' (1. 3. 126) rather than the eyes of the court with the same 'discourse' that Desdemona 'with a greedy ear / Devour[ed]' (1. 3. 151–2). Desdemona envisions Othello's earlier adventures and the tribunal witnesses their courtship by hearing those stories retold. In its legal formulation, witchcraft was a crime disclosed only in the telling. Spells are invisible, and sorcery's words have efficacy without physical causation. In Othello's case, both the crime and its proof are narratives, and both have verbal efficacy: Desdemona falls in love, and the court acquits by consuming his stories. Counter to his claim of innocence, Othello's narratives are indeed a form of bewitchment.

As recent criticism has frequently noted, *Othello* centres on narrative 'fashioning' of subjectivity.[4] The plot is told and retold as each character's past and present is constructed through storytelling. Stephen Greenblatt, for example, argues that Othello is self-fashioned by narrative, first by his own and then by internalizing Iago's. Both parallel the ideological narratives constructed by Renaissance culture, particularly those of orthodox Christian attitudes toward sexuality. Othello's identity, he writes: 'depends upon a constant performance, as we have seen, of his story, a loss of his own origins, an embrace and perpetual reiteration of the norms of another culture'.[5] Karen Newman counters that Othello's stories represent a rehearsal, not a loss, of his origins: Othello reiterates his origins through tales of slavery, monstrous races and the witchcraft genealogy of the handkerchief. In telling these stories he bewitches, even as he espouses Venetian values and culture.[6]

It is Iago who reiterates the ideological narratives of his culture. His stories, relying on conventional stereotypes of 'race' and gender, mutate Othello's story. Othello learns to speak of himself from Iago's ideological point of view, and thus loses himself to a third-person narrative that exiles him from his own history. Othello becomes a victim of narrative witchcraft when that narrative proves more potent than his own. In other words, the transformative power of narrative cannot be controlled fully, and alternative narratives have contesting power. According to Greenblatt: 'Iago knows that an identity that has been fashioned as a story can be unfashioned, refashioned, inscribed anew in a different narrative: it is the fate of stories to be consumed or, as we say more politely, interpreted.'[7]

As witchcraft, Iago's narratives transform the self into something other, abusing the body and mind as potions and spells do. The meanings of 'abuse' multiply in the text as part of the nexus of witchcraft, narrative and identity. From the outset, Iago confesses his intent 'to abuse Othello's ear' (1. 3. 396) with false report. Othello was an 'abuser of the world' who 'abused' Desdemona's 'delicate youth with drugs or minerals' (1. 2. 79, 75). Brabantio speaks of the abuses of witchcraft, and early modern witchcraft tracts referred to the 'misuses', 'perversions' or 'adulterations' practised by witches. But along with these meanings, in the sixteenth century abuse had the rhetorical definition of 'the improper use of words'. It conveyed the sense of misrepresentation and wronging with words. Iago is guilty of these linguistic manipulations, carrying out the crime Othello was originally charged with by abusing all those around him. He hints that Desdemona's 'delicate tenderness will find itself abused' (2. 1. 233–4), while he instructs Roderigo to 'abuse' Cassio 'to the Moor' (2. 1. 307), and Bianca must defend herself against the title of strumpet with which Iago has 'abused' her (5. 1. 125). While Othello's abusive words bewitch love, Iago's more powerful word games practise an abusive form of witchcraft that unravels self-narratives and creates alternative plots. The linguistic variations of 'abuse' – as improper language and as sorcery – amalgamate in Iago's plotting as he concocts witchcraft with words.

In *Othello*, as I have suggested, narrative is witchcraft because it causes monstrous generation, the crime of birthing traditionally associated with midwives and witches. Iago's witchcraft with words is a symptom of his desire to have the ultimate transformative power – that of generation – and the text draws parallels between birthing of narratives and birthing of monsters. Iago searches for a method by which to abuse Othello's ear and latches on to the story of infidelity: 'I hav't. It is engendered. Hell and night / Must bring this monstrous birth to the world's light' (1. 2. 44–5). He engenders an idea which, once told, gestates within Othello, while Iago plays midwife to its birth. So the abused ear becomes a vessel for verbal impregnation. Abuse takes on a sexual dimension that is reinforced by other usages in the text of *Othello*: Desdemona speaks of adultery by asking Emilia if 'there be women [who] do abuse their husbands / In such gross kind?' (4. 3. 64), and Iago confesses that it is his nature to 'spy into abuses' (3. 3. 160). Abuse, then, is the deception of husbands, and implies illicit sexual activity of the type Iago suspects and spies into. Othello comes to desire his aural encounters with his ancient and begs Iago not to 'mak'st his [Othello's] ear / A stranger to thy [Iago's] thoughts' (3. 3. 155–7). Othello longs to consume Iago's stories with his ear, although ear abuse carries with it the implication of rape by Iago's tongue. In Act 3, scene 1, a musician and a clown pun on the connection between tails and tales: the 'tail' of a wind instrument becomes the suggestion of a penis but is reinterpreted as a narrative tale. Iago's tales, then, are the penis that penetrates Othello's ear and result in a monstrous pregnancy of jealousy. According to Emilia, jealousy 'is a monster / Begot upon itself, born on itself' (3. 4. 162–3). Othello conceives and labours with the 'green-eyed monster', and 'strong conceptions' (5. 2. 57). Abuse is now the witchcraft of male–male insemination which results in monstrous generation, as well as sorcery with words and physical transformation.

Iago's 'engendering' and Othello's 'conception' suggest the possibility of female-less generation through the male mind. The term 'pregnant' in early modern England could refer to wits as well as to wombs, while the dual uses of 'conception', 'issue' and 'delivery' connect birthing with male speech and thought.[8] 'Wit', which Iago describes as his methodology for abusing Othello, was slang for genitalia, thus relating to tail/tale as an inseminating subject. Iago imagines his fertile mind impregnating his enemies and breeding plots. He is consumed by the desire for procreative potency; not only does he fantasize inseminating Othello and providing issue for Roderigo, but he pictures himself pregnant as well. The image of the pregnant male is frequently invoked by early modern poets to describe the difficult process of giving birth to the work of art.[9] The narrative Iago delivers, however, is a 'lame and impotent conclusion', according to Desdemona (2. 1. 161). Iago fantasizes that he is mother, father and midwife to the plots and narratives he gestates, a fantasy which demands complete control

over the reproductive process. The monstrous results of his pregnancy summon images of the witch and her sexual liaisons with
the devil which were believed to produce deformed infants. Thus
narrative – which is the foetus of male births – is again connected
to witchcraft. Iago becomes the demon poet, inseminating ears
with words and gestating plots that result in impotence and death,
and which stand in for true generation.

Iago uses the popular beliefs narrated by cultural authority –
those of demonic witchcraft, racial monstrosity and female
consumption – to reconstruct the subjectivity of his victims. But in
Othello, narrative creation itself is always potentially demonic. If
narrative can transform and abuse, it can generate monsters as well
as art. The clever poet, like Iago, can usurp cultural narratives of
authority. The pregnant poet and Iago empower themselves with
metaphors of generation. Yet they also have the power to use those
same metaphors to disempower and demonize. Iago tells us stories
of Othello's procreative potential that make Othello a demon. As
we have seen, birth defects were regularly attributed to witchcraft
and the results of demonic or excessive sexuality were the same:
monsters were born to wicked women and unnatural unions.
Blackness was also a symptom of the monstrous. In the
Elizabethan imagination black skin was the consequence of Noah's
son Cham's adulterate disobedience to his father. *Malleus
Maleficarum* describes Cham as the first witch, whose evil brought
blackness upon his descendants.[10] Original adulteration, then,
resulted in original monstrosity. Othello's 'monstrous birth' is a
predictable result of both his alleged witchcraft and his blackness.
The union between Othello and Desdemona will be an unnatural
union equal to that of adultery and will produce only monsters.[11]
Iago plays on this fear, invoking images of bestial sexuality:
'tupping rams' (1. 1. 91), 'horses' (1. 1. 115), and 'the beast with
two backs' (1. 1. 119), while insisting that Othello's seed will bring
forth 'neighing nephews' (1. 1. 115), and 'monsters' (1. 3. 405).

Monstrous births, however, we know to be a result of Iago's
gestations; remember that he will bring the monstrous birth of
Desdemona's infidelity and Othello's jealousy 'into this world's
light' (1. 2. 45). Othello's jealousy is due to Iago, but so is the image
of Othello as a black fiend. Iago generates monsters – that is, the
devilish Othello and the unfaithful Desdemona – with his cultural
narrative of demonized blackness and miscegenation. He simply

delivers the popular beliefs that allow Othello's 'white colleagues [to] describe miscegenation in the same terms they use for adultery – as a monstrous union potentially productive of "gross issue" '.[12]

These are also the terms used for witchcraft and liaisons with the devil. Reginald Scot describes the 'ouglie divell', which frightens children into obedience, as 'having hornes on his head, fier in his mouth, and a taile in his breech, eies like a bason, fanges like a dog, clawes like a beare, *a skin like a Niger*, and a voice roring like a lion'.[13] Othello is a devil because of his skin and he is a beast because he is a devil. Iago clearly paints him in such a light, invoking the anxiety about patriarchal lineage that both blackness and demonism inspire:

> Even now, now, very now, an old black ram
> Is tupping your white ewe. Arise, arise!
> Awake the snorting citizens with the bell,
> Or else the devil will make a grandsire of you.
>
> (1. 1. 90–3)

Later he describes Desdemona's necessary revulsion at the choice she has made, 'What delight shall she have to look upon the devil?' (2. 1. 227), and insists that because of Othello's hideousness 'her delicate tenderness will find itself abused' (2. 1. 234). Again we see Iago transforming with narratives, gestating altered and monstrous selves by reiterating popular cultural beliefs.

Iago then engages with a cultural narrative of female desire which Othello internalizes. He paints Desdemona as a witch for her unnatural union with Othello and associates her desire for Othello's blackness with an uncontrolled appetite. He again calls upon conventional belief which personified prohibited desires and excessive lust in the form of black men or strange animals, images which associated such desires with the devil.[14] Joseph Klaits has argued that the same belief system that assigned black men a reputation for sexual potency consistently linked women to Satan and to sex: the most subjugated groups in early modern society were identified with moral licentiousness and thus with an evil that must be controlled.[15] Thus when Othello begins to turn the description of devil on Desdemona, labelling her a 'fair devil' (3. 3. 494), a 'sweaty devil' (3. 4. 42) and 'O devil, devil' (4. 1. 247), we see him succumb to a cultural condemnation of his blackness and her sexual desire. We also hear echoes of the accusation that witches 'distract the minds of men, driving them to madness, insane hatred and inordinate lusts'.[16] Othello blames his own distraction, madness and lust on Desdemona's perverse desires. He transposes his evil on to her, just as Iago transposes his demonism on to Othello. Desdemona's desire, as we have seen, is constructed from the outset as a result of Othello's narrative witchcraft. In other words we see the narrative construction of women as desiring, lustful demons as a means of maintaining control over their bodies.

The text of *Othello* suggests that cultural narratives are ideological mechanisms of absolutism. The play demonstrates several attempts to contain the threat of female desire by inscribing women within written narratives. Desdemona's body, initially described as a poet's writing, is rewritten in a narrative of infidelity. The poet (and the text) write her as an object to be desired. Her purity is preserved with the permanence of ink. Initially, Othello privately reads Desdemona's body, but we know from Cassio's speech (2. 1. 64–7) that her description is open to all, leading Othello to inscribe her body with a new narrative of Iago's creation. She becomes the poet's 'fair paper' upon which the word 'whore' is written (4. 2. 69–70). The paragon of fame that 'excel[led] blazoning pens' is a foul paper in her rewriting, her body now not just an object of narration, but an object upon which narration can be copied. Male narratives are written down to prevent their transformation, but even the permanence of ink on paper cannot prevent recopying. This editing transforms her body from contained and controllable to sexually leaky and, ultimately, to no body at all, that is, a corpse on her marital bed. Her dead body represents another monstrous birth of their narratives, her transformation a witchcraft of reinterpretation and rewriting.

If narratives can be manipulated through rewriting, then contesting narratives are always available, threatening absolutism with their own magical power. The witchcraft of male narratives can change a woman from virgin to whore or from living to dead, but the cultural narratives that inscribe women are themselves leaky. They are threatened by contesting narratives, just as Iago's narratives of deception are contested by the action of the play. Inscribed narratives in *Othello* are contrasted with oral stories, prophetic utterances and tales told by women which undermine the boundaries of gender and the narratives of control uttered by voices of authority. For example, Othello tells an old wives' tale of witches with his story of the handkerchief. He describes to Desdemona the Egyptian 'charmer' who wove 'magic' into the web of the handkerchief he gives her (3. 4. 59, 71). His mother used it as a charm to bewitch her husband's 'eye'. In the story, the loss of the handkerchief will symbolize the loss of a husband's love, but for Othello it becomes a symbol of Desdemona's infidelity and therefore its loss betokens the loss of his manhood.[17] His narrative, one of matriarchal lineage and of stories his mother told, predicts his own unmanning. Told by women, old wives' tales are related to shrewishness and to witchcraft and thus to the disruption of masculine order. Othello also tells a tale told to him by his mother which was told to her by an Egyptian witch. The oral story, like the handkerchief, is a mode of women's communication and history. Both the Egyptian storyteller and the weaver of the handkerchief were women of prophecy; the former could 'almost read / The thoughts of people' (3. 4. 59–60) and the latter 'sewed the work' in 'prophetic fury' (3. 4. 74). These narratives, passed orally from woman to woman, both contain and contest the patriarchal stories woven around women's fidelity.

The handkerchief's association with female narratives, female blood and sorcery also connects it to concerns with the female imagination and its potential for evil in popular belief. It seems that women too can gestate with their imaginations. The danger is that they might produce deformed or monstrous infants instead of the narratives or poems delivered from the male mind.[18] Women's narratives threaten the authority of those produced and institutionalized by men. The difficulty is that 'when a woman thinks alone, she thinks evil', so ensuring the safe production of male infants is always threatened by women's open imagination.[19] A woman's tongue is equally detrimental to the safe production of male infants; the open mouth is a parallel to open genitalia. The speaking woman thus is a symbol of female degradation and lust. She is also a threat to gender definitions, encroaching on the male territory of speech and thought. Her tongue becomes the symbol of her masculinity: telling tales gives her a male tail, and the female tongue becomes a usurped penis. It is no wonder then, that the shrew and the witch were often indistinguishable in contemporary accusations. Both undermined a rigid social order that depended on gender difference to define itself. Open mouth and open genitals were an open cauldron of change. The criminalization of the shrew and the witch attempted to contain the disorder they represented, and to silence the stories they might tell.

The characters in *Othello* reiterate these cultural narratives about women's tongues and imaginations just as they retell narratives of blackness, inscribing both Othello and Desdemona as witches. Desdemona's crime is that her imagination has led her to miscegenation, to speak in public and to undermine her father's authority by taking responsibility for her own desires. In doing so she replaces herself as a visual object, or one that is observed by the eye, with a subject to be heard by the ear. Her speech defines her as a shrew or witch, in opposition to the prevailing narratives of masculine authority which inscribe women as silent. Iago creates a similar mythology around his own wife. Emilia does not utter a word before he has labelled her a shrewish scold and simultaneously accused her of promiscuity. She says only two lines in her entire first appearance – and those are to deny Iago's charges that she speaks too much – but simply by 'thinking' she violates his code for her honour. He interprets her for all of those who listen to him as a woman who imagines evil and who gives too much of her lips, both verbally and sexually, and his interpretation presides over her silence. Suggestion is enough for Iago to generate a monstrous narrative of infidelity and shrewishness for his wife too.

As Emilia dies, however, her words become a divine truth, re-narrating Desdemona's body and her own previously condemned thoughts. Her narrative is essential in revealing what has really happened in the play. Iago, whose words generate the monstrous births of narrative witchcraft, is finally clearly associated with the demonic. The devil who has conjured and abused so effectively with words now chooses silence: 'From this time forth I never will speak word' (5. 2. 312). The play concludes with a 'bloody period' (5. 2. 367); the period at the end of a sentence signifying the end of a text and the end of a tale also marks the end of violent abuse and the endpoint or abortion of a pregnancy. Iago's fantasy of male narrative impregnation does not produce creative birth, therefore; rather, it gestates violence and ends with a bloodied bed of death. His narratives transformed and abused, pouring the witchcraft of words into the receptive ear as he stopped up the mouth of truth.

Othello, however, is itself a creation from the words of its author. The play is a performance to be displayed before our eyes and poured into our ears. If narrative is witchcraft, then Shakespeare writes himself into that craft. This is an odd alignment, when we consider the horrors perpetrated by narrative in a text that concludes that 'all that is spoke is marred' (5. 2. 368). Indeed, the play purposefully debunks a notion that narrative is a form of male generation, arguing instead that this is a fantasy of monstrous and violent proportion. Witchcraft, too, is tied to images of monstrous pregnancies and sterility in popular belief and legal definitions. The male fear of the witch is the fear of his loss of procreative power. In equating generation with narrative and witchcraft, Shakespeare suggests that the loss of generative ability is equivalent to the loss of narrative power. The threat of witchcraft is the potential loss of the ability to tell patriarchal stories. Such stories, however, are themselves abusive witchcraft because they perpetuate cultural fictions of race and gender as truths; they transform a person into someone or something else. Cultural narratives are methods of control, but, as *Othello* makes clear, those narratives are uncontainable in their retelling and in their interpretation. The narratives of patriarchy are thus contested by their association with witchcraft and by the privileging of female stories and oral tales.

Notes

[1] All quotations and line numbers are taken from *The Complete Works of William Shakespeare*, ed. David Bevington, 4th edn (New York, 1992).

[2] Witchcraft was used both literally, as the practice of 'magic or sorcery' and, from the end of the sixteenth century, figuratively: 'Power or influence like that of a magician as exercised by beauty or eloquence; *spec.* bewitching or fascinating attraction or charm', *Shorter Oxford English Dictionary*.

[3] Patricia Parker, 'Fantasies of "race" and "gender": Africa, *Othello* and bringing to light', in Margo Hendricks and Patricia Parker (eds), *Women, 'Race' and Writing in the Early Modern Period* (London and New York, 1994), p. 90.

[4] For a list of examples see Alan Sinfield, *Faultlines: Cultural Materialism and the Politics of Dissident Reading* (Berkeley, CA, 1992), p. 29, n. 2.

[5] Stephen Greenblatt, *Renaissance Self-Fashioning: From More to Shakespeare* (Chicago, 1980), p. 245.

[6] Karen Newman, *Fashioning Femininity* (Chicago, 1991), p. 83.

[7] Greenblatt, *Renaissance Self-Fashioning*, p. 238.

[8] Katharine Eisaman Maus, *Inwardness and Theatre in the English Renaissance* (Chicago and London, 1995), p. 197.

[9] Elizabeth Harvey discusses several examples of the pregnant poet in *Ventriloquized Voices: Feminist Theory and English Renaissance Texts* (London and New York, 1992), pp. 76–115.

[10] Heinrich Kramer and James Sprenger, *Malleus Maleficarum* (1486), trans. Montague Summers (New York, 1948), p. 15.

[11] Michael Neill, 'Unproper beds: race, adultery, and the hideous in *Othello*', *Shakespeare Quarterly* 40 (1989), 408–9.

[12] Maus, *Inwardness and Theatre*, p. 122

[13] Reginald Scot, *The Discoverie of Witchcraft* (London, 1584), ed. Montague Summers (London, 1972), p. 86; my emphasis.

[14] Keith Thomas, *Religion and the Decline of Magic* (Harmondsworth, 1971), p. 475.

[15] Joseph Klaits, *Servants of Satan* (Bloomington, IN, 1985), p. 76.

[16] Kramer and Sprenger, *Malleus Maleficarum*, p. 14.

[17] For a detailed discussion on the symbolism of the handkerchief and its connection to Desdemona's loss of virginity see Lynda E. Boose, 'Othello's handkerchief: "the recognizance and pledge of love"', *English Literary Renaissance* 5 (1975), 360–75.

[18] As Sujata Iyengar also identifies in her essay in this volume, popular belief stressed an effect of the female imagination on birth. This is reflected in Renaissance reproductive writings, for example: 'The imagination of the Mother operates most forcibly in the Conception of the child. How much better then were it for women to lead *contented* lives, that so their imaginations may be pure and clear, that so their conception may be well formed.' Nicholas Culpeper, *A Directory for Midwives* (London, 1671), p. 94.

[19] Kramer and Sprenger, *Malleus Maleficarum*, p. 43.

Select Bibliography

❧

Aers, David, and L. Staley (eds), *Powers of the Holy: Religion, Politics and Gender in Late Medieval English Culture* (University Park: Pennsylvania State University Press, 1996).

Andersen, Jørgen, *The Witch on the Wall: Medieval Erotic Sculptures in the British Isles* (London: George Allen & Unwin, 1977).

Anderson, Benedict, *Imagined Communities: Reflections on the Origins and Spread of Nationalism* (London: Verso, 1983).

Archibald, Elizabeth, 'Sex and power in Thebes and Babylon: Oedipus and Semiramis in classical and medieval texts', in Gernot Wieland (ed.), *Classical Antiquity and the Middle Ages* (Kalamazoo, MI: Medieval Institute Publications, forthcoming).

Atkinson, Clarissa, *The Oldest Vocation: Christian Motherhood in the Middle Ages* (Ithaca, NY, and London: Cornell University Press, 1991).

Bahktin, Mikhail, *Rabelais and his World*, trans. Hélène Iswolsky (Cambridge, MA: MIT Press, 1968).

Barr, Helen (ed.), *The Piers Plowman Tradition* (London: Everyman, 1993).

Barratt, Alexandra, ' "In the lowest part of our need": Julian and medieval gynaecological writing', in Sandra McEntire (ed.), *Julian of Norwich: A Book of Essays* (New York and London: Garland, 1998), pp. 240–56.

Bartlett, Ann Clark, *Male Authors, Female Readers: Representation and Subjectivity in Middle English Devotional Literature* (New York and London: Cornell University Press, 1995).

Beckwith, Sarah, *Christ's Body: Identity, Culture and Society in Late Medieval Writings* (London: Routledge, 1993).

Benson, Pamela, 'Rule, Virginia: Protestant theories of female regiment in *The Faerie Queene*', *English Literary Renaissance* 15 (1985), 277–92.

Berry, Philippa, *Of Chastity and Power: Elizabethan Literature and the Unmarried Queen* (New York and London: Routledge, 1989).

Betteridge, Thomas, 'Anne Askewe, John Bale, and Protestant history', *Journal of Medieval and Early Modern Studies* 27 (1997), 265–84.

Bhabha, Homi K. (ed.), *Nation and Narration* (London: Routledge, 1990).

Biddick, Kathleen, 'Genders, bodies and borders: technologies of the visible', *Speculum* 68 (1993), 389–418.

Bothwell, J., P. J. P. Goldberg and W. M. Ormrod (eds), *The Problem of Labour in Fourteenth-Century England* (Woodbridge, 2000).

Brooks, Chris, and Andrew Saint (eds), *The Victorian Church: Architecture and Society* (Manchester, 1995).

Bullón-Fernández, María, *Fathers and Daughters in Gower's* Confessio Amantis: *Authority, Family, State, and Writing* (Cambridge: D. S. Brewer, 2000).

Butler, Judith, *Bodies that Matter: On the Discursive Limits of 'Sex'* (New York: Routledge, 1993).

——, *Gender Trouble: Feminism and the Subversion of Identity* (London and New York: Routledge, 1990).

Bynum, Caroline Walker, *Fragmentation and Redemption: Essays on Gender and the Human Body in Medieval Religion* (New York: Zone Books, 1991).

——, *Holy Feast and Holy Fast: The Religious Significance of Food to Medieval Women* (Berkeley, Los Angeles and London: University of California Press, 1987).

——, *Jesus as Mother: Studies in the Spirituality of the High Middle Ages* (Berkeley, Los Angeles, London: University of California Press, 1982).

Cadden, Joan, *Meanings of Sex Difference in the Middle Ages: Medicine, Science and Culture*, Cambridge History of Medicine (Cambridge: Cambridge University Press, 1993).

Campbell, Mary Baine, *The Witness and the Other World: Exotic European Travel Writing 400–1600* (Ithaca, NY: Cornell University Press, 1988).

Cavanagh, Sheila T., *Wanton Eyes and Chaste Desires: Female Sexuality in* The Faerie Queene (Bloomington: Indiana University Press, 1994).

Cave, Terence, *Recognitions* (Oxford: Clarendon, 1988).

Cerquiglini, Bernard, *In Praise of the Variant: A Critical History of Philology*, trans. Betsy Wing (Baltimore and London: Johns Hopkins Press, 1999).

Cixous, Hélène, 'Sorties', in *The Hélène Cixous Reader*, ed. Susan Sellers (London: Routledge, 1994), pp. 37–46.

Cohen, Jeffrey Jerome, *Of Giants: Sex, Monsters, and the Middle Ages* (Minneapolis and London: University of Minnesota Press, 1999).

—— and B. Wheeler (eds), *Becoming Male in the Middle Ages* (New York: Garland, 1997).

Cohn, Norman, *Europe's Inner Demons: The Demonization of Christians in Medieval Christendom* (London: Pimlico, 1993 [1975]).

Copjec, Joan, 'Vampires, breast-feeding, and anxiety', *October* 58 (1991), 24–43.

de Lauretis, Teresa, 'Desire in narrative', in *Alice Doesn't: Feminism, Semiotics, Cinema* (London: Macmillan, 1984), pp. 103–57.

——, 'Eccentric subjects: feminist theory and historical consciousness', *Feminist Studies* 16 (1990), 115–50.

Deutsch, Helen, and Felicity Nussbaum (eds), *'Defects': Engendering the Modern Body*, (Ann Arbor: University of Michigan Press, 2000).

Devisse, Jacques, *The Image of the Black in Western Art*, 3 vols (Lausanne: Hanspeter Schmidt, 1979).

Dharmaraj, Glory, 'Multicultural subjectivity in reading Chaucer's *Man of Law's Tale*', *Medieval Feminist Newsletter* 16 (Fall 1993), 4–8.

Dilke, O. A. W., 'Heliodorus and the colour problem', *La Parola del Passato* 193 (1980), 264–71.

Dolar, Mladen, ' "I shall be with you on your wedding-night": Lacan and the Uncanny', *October* 58 (1991), 5–23.

Donavin, Georgiana, *Incest Narratives and the Structure of John Gower's Confessio Amantis* (Victoria, BC: University of Victoria Press, 1993).

Donegan, Jane B., *Women and Men Midwives: Medicine, Morality and Misogyny in Early America* (London: Greenwood Press, 1978).

Douglas, Mary, *Pollution and Danger* (London, Boston and Henley: Routledge & Kegan Paul, 1969).

Edmunds, Lowell (ed.), *Oedipus: A Folklore Casebook* (New York and London: Garland, 1983).

Edwards, Robert R., and Vickie Ziegler (eds), *Matrons and Marginal Women in Medieval Society* (Woodbridge: Boydell Press, 1995).

Elliott, Dyan, *Fallen Bodies: Pollution, Sexuality, and Demonology in the Middle Ages* (Philadelphia: University of Pennsylvania Press, 1999).

Erickson, Peter, 'The moment of race in Renaissance Studies', *Shakespeare Studies* 26 (1998), 27–36.

Ferguson, Margaret W., Maureen Quilligan, and Nancy Vickers (eds), *Rewriting the Renaissance: The Discourse of Sexual Difference in Early Modern Europe* (Chicago and London: University of Chicago Press, 1986).

Fissell, Mary, 'Gender and generation: representing reproduction in early modern England', *Gender and History* 7/3 (1995), 433–41.

Fletcher, Anthony, 'Manhood, the male body, courtship and the household in early modern England', *History* 84 (1999), 419–36.

Foucault, Michel, *Discipline and Punish: The Birth of the Prison*, trans. Alan Sheridan (New York: Vintage, 1979).

——, 'Nietzsche, genealogy, history', in *Language, Counter-Memory, Practice: Selected Essays and Interviews by Michel Foucault*, ed. Donald F. Bouchard, trans. Donald F. Bouchard and Sherry Simon (Ithaca, NY: Cornell University Press, 1977), pp. 139–64.

——, *The Final Foucault*, ed. J. Bernauer and D. Rasmussen (Cambridge, MA: MIT Press, 1994).

——, *The History of Sexuality*, vol. 1 (Harmondsworth: Penguin, 1990).

Frantzen, Allen J., 'When women aren't enough', *Speculum* (1993), 445–71.

Freud, Sigmund, *The Standard Edition of the Complete Psychological Works of Sigmund Freud*, ed. James Strachey et al., 24 vols (London: Hogarth Press and the Institute of Psycho-Analysis, 1953–74).

Fryer, Peter, *Staying Power: The History of Black People in Britain* (London: Pluto Press, 1984).

Gellner, Ernest, *Nations and Nationalism* (Oxford: Blackwell, 1983).

Gilbert, Ruth, *Early Modern Hermaphrodites: Sex and Other Stories* (London: Palgrave, 2002).

Gilchrist, Roberta, *Gender and Material Culture: The Archaeology of Religious Women* (London and New York: Routledge, 1994).

Goldberg, Jeremy P., *Women, Work, and Life Cycle in a Medieval Economy: Women in York and Yorkshire, c.1300–1520* (Oxford: Oxford University Press, 1992).

Green, Miranda, *Symbol and Image in Celtic Religious Art* (London: Routledge, 1989).

Green, Monica H., *Women's Healthcare in the Medieval West: Texts and Contexts* (Aldershot, Burlington, Singapore and Sydney: Ashgate, 2000).

Greenblatt, Stephen, *Marvelous Possessions: The Wonder of the New World* (Oxford: Clarendon, 1988).

——, *Renaissance Self-Fashioning: From More to Shakespeare* (Chicago: University of Chicago Press, 1980).

Hadfield, Andrew, *Literature, Politics and National Identity: Reformation to Renaissance* (Cambridge: Cambridge University Press, 1994).

——, *Literature, Travel and Colonial Writing in the English Renaissance, 1545–1625* (Oxford: Clarendon, 1998).

Hall, Kim F., *Things of Darkness: Economies of Race and Gender in Early Modern England* (Ithaca, NY: Cornell University Press, 1995).

Hanawalt, Barbara, and David Wallace (eds), *Bodies and Disciplines: Intersections of Literature and History in Fifteenth-Century England*, Medieval Cultures 9 (Minneapolis and London: University of Minnesota Press, 1996).

Hanson, Elizabeth, 'Torture and truth in Renaissance England', *Representations* 34 (1991), 53–84.

Harvey, Elizabeth, *Ventriloquized Voices: Feminist Theory and English Renaissance Texts* (London and New York: Routledge, 1992).

Hattaway, Michael, ' "Seeing things": Amazons and cannibals', *Travel and Drama in Shakespeare's Time*, ed. Jean-Pierre Maquerlet and Michèle Willems (Cambridge: Cambridge University Press, 1996), pp. 179–92.

Hendricks, Margo, and Patricia Parker (eds), *Women, 'Race' and Writing in the Early Modern Period* (London: Routledge, 1994).

Hillman, David, and Carla Mazzio (eds), *The Body in Parts: Fantasies of Corporeality in Early Modern Europe* (New York and London: Routledge, 1997).

Huet, Marie Hélène, *Monstrous Imagination* (Cambridge, MA, and London: Harvard University Press, 1993).

Hulme, Peter, *Colonial Encounters: Europe and the Native Caribbean, 1492–1797* (London: Methuen, 1986).

Hunter, G. K., 'Othello and colour-prejudice', *Proceedings of the British Academy* 53 (London: British Academy, 1968).

Hunter, Richard (ed.), *Studies in Heliodorus*, Cambridge Philological Society Supplemental 21 (Cambridge: Cambridge Philological Society, 1998).

Irigaray, Luce, 'La Mystèrique', in *Speculum of the Other Woman*, trans. Gillian C. Gill (New York: Cornell University Press, 1985), pp. 191–202.

Jackson, Gabriele Bernhardt, 'Topical ideology: witches, Amazons, and Shakespeare's Joan of Arc', in Deborah E. Barker and Ivo Kamps (eds), *Shakespeare and Gender: A History* (London: Verso, 1995), pp. 142–67.

Jacquart, Danielle, and Claude Thomasset, *Sexuality and Medicine in the Middle Ages*, trans. Matthew Adamson (Cambridge: Polity, 1988 [1985]).

Jardine, Lisa, 'Boy actors, female roles, and Elizabethan eroticism' in D. Scott Kastan and Peter Stallybrass (eds), *Staging the Renaissance: Reinterpretations of Elizabethan and Jacobean Drama* (London: Routledge, 1991), pp. 57–67.

Johnson, Lesley, 'Return to Albion', *Arthurian Literature* 13 (1995), 19–40.

Jowitt, Claire, *Gender Politics and Voyage Drama 1589–1642: Real and Imagined Worlds* (Manchester: Manchester University Press, 2002).

——, ' "Her flesh must serve you": gender, commerce and the New World in Fletcher and Massinger's *The Sea Voyage* and Massinger's *The City Madam*', *Parergon*, ns 18 (2001).

Katz, David, *The Jews in the History of England, 1485–1850* (Oxford: Clarendon, 1994).

Kelly, Eamonn P., *Sheela-na-Gigs: Origins and Functions* (Dublin: Country House in association with the National Museum of Ireland, 1996).

Kendall, Ritchie, *The Drama of Dissent: The Radical Poetics of Nonconformity* (Chapel Hill: North Carolina University Press, 1986).

Kingsbury, Susan Myra (ed.), *The Records of the Virginia Company of London*, 4 vols (Washington, DC, 1906).

Klaits, Joseph, *Servants of Satan* (Bloomington, Indiana University Press: 1985).

Kristeva, Julia, *The Powers of Horror: An Essay on Abjection*, trans. Leon Roudiez (New York: Columbia University Press, 1982).

Laskaya, Anne, *Chaucer's Approach to Gender in* The Canterbury Tales (Cambridge: D. S. Brewer, 1995).

Lees, Clare (ed.), *Medieval Masculinities: Regarding Men in the Middle Ages* (Minneapolis and London: University of Minnesota Press, 1994).

Levy Peck, Linda, *Court Patronage and Corruption in Early Modern England* (London: Routledge, 1993).

Lomperis, Linda, and Sarah Stanbury (eds), *Feminist Approaches to the Body in Medieval Literature* (Philadelphia: University of Pennsylvania Press, 1993).

Loomba, Ania, *Gender, Race, Renaissance Drama* (Manchester: Manchester University Press, 1989).

McAvoy, Liz Herbert, ' "The moders service": motherhood as matrix in Julian of Norwich', *Mystics Quarterly* 24/4 (December 1998), 181–97.

McNally, Raymond T., and Radu Florescu, *In Search of Dracula: The History of Dracula and Vampires* (London: Robson, 1995 [1972]).

McQuade, Paula, ' "Except that they had offended the Lawe": gender and jurisprudence in *The Examinations of Anne Askew*', *Literature and History*, 3rd ser. 3 (1994), 1–14.

Mann, Jill, *Feminist Readings: Chaucer* (Hemel Hempstead: Harvester Wheatsheaf, 1991)

Maquerlet, Jean-Pierre, and Michèle Willems (eds), *Travel and Drama in Shakespeare's Time* (Cambridge: Cambridge University Press, 1996).

Martin, Priscilla, *Chaucer's Women: Nuns, Wives and Amazons* (London: Macmillan, 1990).

Matar, Nabil, *Islam in Britain, 1558–1685* (Cambridge: Cambridge University Press, 1998).

——, *Turks, Moors and Englishmen in the Age of Discovery* (New York: Columbia University Press, 1999).

Matchinske, Megan, *Writing, Gender and State in Early Modern England: Identity Formation and the Female Subject* (Cambridge: Cambridge University Press, 1998).

Mazzola, Elizabeth, 'Expert witnesses and secret subjects: Anne Askew's *Examinations* and Renaissance self-incrimination', in Carole Levin and Patricia Sullivan (eds), *Political Rhetoric, Power, and Renaissance Women* (Albany: State University of New York Press, 1995), pp. 157–71.

Metlitzki, Dorothee, *The Matter of Araby in Medieval England* (New Haven and London: Yale University Press, 1977).

Minnis, A. J. (ed.), *Gower's* Confessio Amantis: *Responses and Reassessments* (Cambridge: D. S. Brewer, 1983).

Moi, Toril, *What is a Woman? and Other Essays* (Oxford: Oxford University Press, 1999).

Mueller, Janel, 'Pain, persecution, and the construction of selfhood', in Claire McEachern and Debora Shuger (eds), *Religion and Culture in Renaissance England* (Cambridge: Cambridge University Press, 1997), pp. 161–87.

Neill, Michael, 'Unproper beds: race, adultery, and the hideous in *Othello*', *Shakespeare Quarterly* 40 (1989), 383–412.

Newman, Karen, *Fashioning Femininity* (Chicago: University of Chicago Press, 1991).

Paré Ambroise, *On Monsters and Marvels*, trans. Janis L. Pallister (Chicago: University of Chicago Press, 1982).

Patterson, Annabel, *Reading between the Lines* (London: Routledge, 1993).

Patterson, Lee, 'On the margin: postmodernism, ironic history, and medieval studies', *Speculum* 65 (1990), 87–108.

Pearson, Ann, 'Reclaiming the Sheela-na-gigs: goddess imagery in medieval sculptures of Ireland', *Canadian Woman Studies/Les Cahiers de la Femme* 17/3 (1997), 20–4.

Petzoldt, Ruth, 'Vampire', in Carl Lindahl et al. (eds), *Medieval Folklore: An Encyclopedia of Myths, Legends, Tales, Beliefs and Customs* (Santa Barbara, Denver, Oxford: ABC–Clio, 2000), pp. 1016–19.

Pippin, Tina, *Death and Desire: The Rhetoric of Gender in the Apocalypse of John* (Louisville: Westminster/John Knox Press, 1992).

Pong Linton, Joan, *The Romance of the New World: Gender and Literary Formations of English Colonialism* (Cambridge: Cambridge University Press, 1998).

Purkiss, Diane, *The Witch in History: Early Modern and Twentieth-Century Representations* (London: Routledge, 1996).

Quilligan, Maureen, 'The comedy of female authority in *The Faerie Queene*', *English Literary Renaissance* 17 (1987), 156–71.

Ransome, David R., 'Wives for Virginia, 1621', *William and Mary Quarterly*, ser. 3, 48 (1991), 3–18.

Ross, Anne, 'The divine hag of the pagan Celts', in V. Newall (ed.), *The Witch Figure* (London: Routledge & Kegan Paul, 1973), pp. 139–64.

Rubin, Gayle, 'The traffic in women: notes on the "political economy of sex"', in Rayna R. Reiter (ed.), *Toward an Anthropology of Women* (London and New York: Monthly Review Press, 1975), pp. 157–210.

Rubin, Miri, *Corpus Christi: The Eucharist in Late Medieval Culture* (Cambridge: Cambridge University Press, 1991).

Said, Edward W., *Orientalism* (New York: Routledge, 1978).

Saunders, Corinne J., 'Woman displaced: rape and romance in Chaucer's *Wife of Bath's Tale*', *Arthurian Literature* 13 (1995), 115–31.

Sawday, Jonathan, *The Body Emblazoned: Dissection and the Human Body in Renaissance Culture* (London and New York: Routledge, 1995).

Scarry, Elaine, *The Body in Pain: The Making and Unmaking of the World* (Oxford: Oxford University Press, 1985).

Schibanoff, Susan, 'Worlds apart: Orientalism, antifeminism, and heresy in Chaucer's *Man of Law's Tale*', *Exemplaria* 8/1 (Spring 1996), 56–86.

Schoenfeldt, Michael, *Bodies and Selves in Early Modern England: Physiology and Inwardness in Spenser, Shakespeare, Herbert and Milton* (Cambridge: Cambridge University Press, 1999).

Scholz, Susanne, *Body Narratives: Writing the Nation and Fashioning the Subject in Early Modern England* (London and New York: Macmillan, 2000).

Shapiro, James, *Shakespeare and the Jews* (New York and Chichester: Columbia University Press, 1996).

Sinfield, Alan, *Faultlines: Cultural Materialism and the Politics of Dissident Reading* (Berkeley: University of California Press, 1992).

Singh, Jyotsna, *Colonial Narratives/Cultural Dialogues: Discoveries of India in the Language of Colonialism* (London: Routledge, 1996).

South, Malcolm (ed.), *Mythical and Fabulous Creatures: A Source Book and Research Guide* (New York, Westport, London: Greenwood, 1987).

Spiegel, Gabrielle M., 'History, historicism, and the social logic of the text in the Middle Ages', *Speculum* 65 (1990), 59–86.

Streete, Gail Corrington, *The Strange Woman: Power and Sex in the Bible* (Louisville: Westminster John Knox Press, 1997).

Sturges, Robert S., *Chaucer's Pardoner and Gender Theory: Bodies of Discourse* (New York: St. Martin's Press, 2000).

Summers, Alinda, 'The banqueting scene in *Paradise Regained*: Milton's temptation to the anti-Puritan appetite', in William P. Shaw (ed.), *Praise Disjoined: Changing Patterns of Salvation in Seventeenth-Century English Literature* (New York: Peter Lang, 1991).

Taylor, Mark, 'Of monsters and dances: masculinity, white supremacy, ecclesial practice', in Elisabeth Schüssler Fiorenza and Mary Shawn Copeland (eds), *Violence against Women* (London and Maryknoll: SCM Press and Orbis Books, 1994), pp. 53–71.

Thomas, Keith, *Religion and the Decline of Magic* (Harmondsworth: Penguin, 1971).

Traub, Valerie, 'The psychomorphology of the clitoris', *GLQ: A Journal of Gay and Lesbian Studies* 2 (1995), 81–113.

Tricomi, Albert H., *Anti-Court Drama in England, 1603–1642* (Charlottesville: University Press of Virginia, 1989).

Tyldesley, Joyce, *Hatchepsut: The Female Pharaoh* (Harmondsworth: Penguin, 1998).

Voaden, R. (ed.), *Prophets Abroad: The Reception of Continental Holy Women in Late-Medieval England* (Cambridge: D. S. Brewer, 1996).

Warner, Marina, *Alone of All her Sex: The Myth and Cult of the Virgin Mary* (London: Picador, 1990).

——, *From the Beast to the Blonde: On Fairy Tales and their Tellers* (London: Vintage, 1990).

Warren, Ann K., *Anchorites and their Patrons in Medieval England* (Los Angeles and London: University of California Press, 1985).

Waswo, Richard, 'Our ancestors, the Trojans: inventing cultural identity in the Middle Ages', *Exemplaria* 7 (1995), 269–90.

Watt, Diane, *Amoral Gower: Language, Sex and Politics in* Confessio Amantis (Minneapolis: University of Minnesota Press, forthcoming).

Weir, Anthony, and James Jerman, *Images of Lust: Sexual Carvings on Medieval Churches* (London: Batsford, 1986).

Williams, David, *Deformed Discourse: The Function of the Monster in Mediaeval Thought and Literature* (Exeter: University of Exeter Press, 1996).

Woods, Susanne, 'Spenser and the problem of women's rule', *Huntington Language Quarterly* 4 (1985), 141–58.

Yeager, R. F. (ed.), *Re-Visioning Gower* (Asheville, NC: Pegasus, 1998).

A complete bibliography will appear on the University of Wales Press website.

Index

෯